Labor Relations in Advanced Industrial Societies Issues & Problems

Edited by Benjamin Martin and Everett M. Kassalow

Carnegie Endowment for International Peace
Washington, D.C.   New York

I.S.B.N. 0-87003-015-9

Library of Congress Catalog Card Number: 79-56777

Printed in the United States of America.

Contents

Foreword

Most of the papers that comprise this book were originally presented at a conference on international labor problems which took place during December 1977 on the Madison campus of the University of Wisconsin. This encounter represented a joint collaboration of the Industrial Relations Research Institute of the University of Wisconsin and the Carnegie Endowment for International Peace. It coincided with the celebration of the Industrial Relations Research Institute's 30th anniversary.

The conference was also prompted by the presence on the Madison campus at that time of a distinguished group of visiting foreign scholars with special interest in labor problems, including Walter Korpi, Rudolph Meidner, and Gunnar Myrdal of Sweden, Don J. Turkington of New Zealand, Russell Lansbury of Australia, and Mikio Sumiya of Japan.

In selecting topics for this conference, it was decided to seek a cross-section of issues which could shed light on some of the more vexing current labor relations problems in democratic, industrialized nations. These included the labor impact of multinational corporations, the problem of industrial conflict, the new movement of worker participation in the management of enterprises, as well as work humanization in industry.

It is not so long ago that many in positions of policy responsibility tended to view change in the world largely in terms of the comportment of political elites. Today it has become a generally accepted notion that an adequate understanding of the forces promoting change requires a grasp of underlying social and economic dynamics.

Despite this gratifying development, our knowledge of foreign industrial relations and trade union affairs remains woefully inadequate. This deficiency is particularly unfortunate because the labor relations systems of most industrially advanced nations in recent years have been an area of great dynamism and have led to significant modifications of economic and political structures.

The scope of change is greater than most of us realize. Since the late sixties, to cite but one example, the increased worker participation in managerial decision making of Western European firms promises to result in substantial alterations in the substance of labor relations. As a leading American labor journalist recently concluded, "a new industrial revolution is sweeping the most economically advanced countries, blurring the lines between capitalism and socialism and bringing to millions of workers a kind of democracy they have never before known."

These trends are by no means one-dimensional. Thus, in 1977, a proposed plan for worker sharing in the ownership of company holdings, as Rudolph Meidner observes, contributed to the defeat of the Swedish Social Democratic Party. In 1979 the breakdown of the social contract in Great Britain contributed heavily to the defeat of the labor government and the victory of conservative Margaret Thatcher.

The papers in this volume that examine the nature and problems of industrial conflict in advanced societies illuminate the complex interrelationships of economic market forces, cultural factors, social traditions, and political trends.

Growing concern over "humanization of work" has developed as still another facet of the industrial democracy movement. Both are essentially responses to the effects of the technological revolution under way since the fifties that has produced far-reaching changes in traditional work patterns. The massive simplification of job tasks resulting from this technological transformation has, in many instances, signified a "dehumanization" of work. This has stimulated the formulation of numerous schemes to enhance job satisfaction and to counteract the corresponding growth in worker boredom and job dissatisfaction. Increased concern with safety and health at the workplace is a further manifestation of this development.

Acknowledgment and thanks are due the German Marshall Fund, whose financial assistance made it possible to include as conference participants a number of leading industrial relations specialists from Western Europe.

The publication of these papers by the Carnegie Endowment implies a belief only in the importance of the subjects. The views expressed are those of the contributors.

Thomas L. Hughes
President
Carnegie Endowment for
International Peace

Editors' Introduction

It is in recent years only that specialists have begun to examine the changing physiognomy of labor relations in the advanced industrial countries in a consistent manner. Not very long ago this area was the neglected stepchild of labor studies. Occasional works of substance were produced, of course, but they were the exception in an otherwise sparse area of research. A Harvard University conference of recent memory in which European and American specialists assessed the state of industrial relations research in their respective countries gave the impression of a gathering to mourn the low estate of their discipline.

Since the late fifties the labor relations of the newly emerged nations have tended to dominate the attention of many specialists in comparative and foreign labor studies. For a time, in fact, a mini-boom developed in published work devoted to labor in Africa, Asia, and Latin America. The Ford Foundation generously funded a large-scale study of comparative labor development in the developing economies directed by Clark Kerr, John T. Dunlop, the late Frederick H. Harbison, and Charles A. Myers. Ever sensitive to ongoing trends, the International Labor Organization (ILO) also gave greatest emphasis to research and technical assistance programs for the lesser developed regions.

All this, of course was understandable and even appropriate. The transformation of many former colonial territories into independent states involved massive changes in the social and economic lives of these countries. Restructuring the systems of labor relations and nurturing emerging trade union organizations represented important aspects of these transformations. Furthermore, these new independent nations led to substantive alterations in the international political balance. The third world was converted into a major arena of East-West competition, an arena in which the trade unions of the new nations frequently found themselves. Now a redefinition of the North-South economic relationship is receiving a great deal of attention.

This preoccupation with newly developed nations to some extent has worked to the detriment of research on the advanced countries. Insufficient study and scrutiny of underlying patterns of change and of the growing malfunction of institutional arrangements left practitioners and policy makers unprepared to deal with the new situation.

During the late sixties and early seventies much of Western Europe experienced massive waves of industrial conflict and social unrest. In June 1968 a general strike of extraordinary dimensions shook the very foundations of French society and led to the eventual downfall of the government headed by President Charles DeGaulle. The Italian "Hot Autumn" of 1969 and its aftermath had an extraordinary reinvigorating effect on a weak and dispirited trade union movement and permanently altered the nature of Italy's labor-management relations. Spain's authoritarian regime of Francisco Franco was overrun by labor unrest of such magnitude that it subsequently became an important contributing element in that country's decision to restore democratic government.

Even countries that could boast stable, well-functioning industrial relations systems were not immune from the spreading discontent. Sweden and West Germany came in for their share of industrial unrest, and Great Britain's powerful labor movement acquired a new militancy amid growing industrial conflict. Australia's highly vaunted system of compulsory arbitration came under increasing stress.

Since then an effort has begun to localize the sources of discontent and disfunction. During the early seventies, numerous conferences and research projects were conducted to examine the nature of Europe's industrial relations crisis. New departures had been introduced both in the fields of collective bargaining and worker representation. But the continuing dynamism of change in the labor systems of industrial societies, the changed economic setting, and technological progress have appreciably outstripped the efforts of researchers to keep abreast. Consequently much of the industrial relations landscape of Europe, Japan, and the United States remains unexplored.

The papers contained in this volume by leading specialists are intended as a contribution to a discussion of topics that have thus far not received adequate attention. They also represent important problem areas now confronting most advanced industrial nations.

The first section deals with multinational enterprises and their impact on labor. In recent years a significant share of trade union movements' concern and activity in the international sphere has centered on the multinational corporation. To date most research on the impact of multinational enterprises on labor has taken the industrial relations system and its principal actors, unions and managements, as its point of departure. Duane Kujawa, professor of international business at Florida International University, contends that, although such research provides useful data on labor relations practices of multinationals, it does not offer a basis for judging the future of such relations. Kujawa sketches a comparative view of the labor practices of American and foreign multinationals in terms of the "product-life cycle" theory of foreign trade and investment. This theory explains, for example, why U.S. firms, more than their foreign competitors, resort to layoffs and shutdowns. While Kujawa largely bypasses the impact that the dynamic investment policies of U.S. multinational companies abroad have on domestic employment, he does observe that the professional employment sectors of such companies are likely to grow, while *manual production employment* (where unions tend to be concentrated) may decline. As would normally be expected, it is this impact that largely occupies Richard Prosten, research director of the Industrial Union Department of the AFL-CIO, and Raymond MacDonald, research director of the Allied Industrial Workers, AFL-CIO.

Prosten and MacDonald suggest that a significant part of the unemployment crisis of recent years can be attributed to American trade policy and trade performance. Again and again the promise of new jobs that were to accompany new trade legislation and related trade patterns have not materialized, while entire industries have succumbed to new trade practices. Promises of ample benefits and new jobs for those who might be displaced by trade patterns resulting from new legislation have proven disappointing. Prosten and MacDonald note that legislation has also failed to address the problem of federal tax provisions that continue to encourage investment abroad over investment at home, even in the face of growing U.S. job losses from foreign trade. Until these and some of the other problems alluded to above are faced, multinationals and U.S. trade practices which encourage them will continue to be a source of dissatisfaction to the trade union movement.

The four papers in the second section explore the theme of industrial conflict in democratic, industrialized nations. Contrary to the expectations of some social scientists a generation ago, the strike has not withered away in modern industrial conflict. It is still the dominant manifestation of industrial conflict.

Everett M. Kassalow, senior specialist in labor economics for the Library of Congress Research Service, attempts to account for the persistence of high levels of conflict in American society, compared to most other democratic industrialized nations. According to Kassalow, industrial relations practices in the United States are very different from those in Western Europe. These differences help explain the high level of conflict in the United States. This high level is somewhat paradoxical. The United States is one of the few countries in the democratic world that has a dominant labor movement with no links to a socialist philosophy or party; there is no tension between the capitalist economic system and a socialist union movement. And yet there is a high level of conflict.

Solomon B. Levine, professor of business and economics at the University of Wisconsin, and Koji Taira, professor of economics at the University of Illinois, challenge the stereotypical view of Japan as a country of remarkably harmonious industrial relations. Their examination leads them to conclude that industrial relations have been anything but harmonious in post-war Japan, and indeed, that industrial conflict is every bit as important in Japan as in other industrialized, market economies.

Don J. Turkington, senior lecturer in industrial relations at Victoria University of Wellington in New Zealand, offers an interesting description of the incidence of strike activity in two countries operating within a compulsory arbitration and conciliation framework. Ordinarily observers expect conflict to be low in such countries, but the experience of Australia and New Zealand tends not to bear this out. Australia, at least, ranks among the higher conflict countries, while New Zealand ranks in the middle in this respect. Differences between the countries can be accounted for in part by the larger number of workers in strike prone industries such as mining, quarrying and metal fabricating in Australia.

Walter Korpi, professor of social policy at the University of Stockholm, tests the academic world's dominant theory of industrial conflict. According to this theory modern industrial society tends to develop a consensus with an integrated ideology, and this renders industrial conflict innocuous. Korpi finds that the Swedish experience simply does not accord with this model. Open industrial conflict has declined to a very low level. This decline can best be explained by political change rather than by any logic of pluralistic industrialism. Looking beyond Sweden, Korpi suggests that the prevailing establishment wisdom in the field of industrial relations seems largely to have reflected U.S. experience, which, he adds, appears to be much more of a special case, strongly influenced by immigration and slavery, and much less of an explanatory model for other countries.

The last article in this section concerns labor conflict under the Franco regime. Spain's return to democracy after four decades of authoritarian rule is surely one of the most notable events of our time. A major aspect of this transformation has been the dismantling of the government-controlled corporative system of labor relations, which had served as a mainstay of the Franco regime, and the installation of a more modern and enlightened relationship. Extremely little on this subject has thus far been published outside Spain. José M. Maravall, professor of sociology at the University of Madrid, is justly regarded as Spain's leading authority on labor under Franco. His books on this subject have become standard reference works in Spain.

The essays in the final section reflect the great diversity in the evolution of what Kenneth F. Walker calls "the participatory enterprise"—a pattern of organization that has evolved during the final quarter of this century in Europe. Worker participation, industrial democracy, worker control— the various names reflect ideological and institutional particularities and bear the stamp of each country's distinctive social, political, and economic configuration.

Gerhard Leminsky, of the Institute for Economic and Social Research of the German Trade Union Federation, tells us that the origins of co-determination in West Germany are traceable to a system of worker participation introduced by the pre-Nazi Weimar regime. Today, the German system of codetermination is the most influential model of worker participation for other countries. For example, the European Economic Community's pending proposal for participation contained in the European Company Law is largely based on the German system.

In addition, the German Trade Union Confederation was the first to give serious attention to the idea of workers sharing in industrial capital— an idea discussed widely in recent years. A plan for the establishment of "social funds" to be financed from company profits and administered by the unions was formally adopted by the confederation in the early seventies. But the advent of an economic recession shortly thereafter caused the plan to be indefinitely shelved.

Nonetheless, the concept took hold in Sweden where the Swedish Labor Confederation decided actively to pursue the acceptance of its "Meidner Plan." Adopted on the eve of national elections, the plan quickly became the focus of a major electoral controversy between the Social Democrats and the opposition party. Senior Economic Advisor to the LO Rudolf Meidner, who authored the plan, comments in his essay here: "The fact that the LO (Swedish Labor Confederation) pro-posal was launched during an election campaign and without coordination between the unions and the political branch of the labor movement contributed, according to some observers, to the defeat of the Social Democratic party in the 1976 election." The writer somewhat owlishly observes, "Although this hypothesis can hardly be proved it sounds far from absurd."

Jack Barbash, John P. Bascom professor of economics and industrial relations at the University of Wisconsin, is surely correct in pointing out that the present debate on work reform "is a product of the recent full employment era." It should be added that the great waves of labor unrest that swept through most of Western Europe in the late sixties and early seventies also provided a powerful if not decisive impetus for work reform. Its greatest force was felt in France and Italy, countries with relatively weak labor movements, woefully inadequate industrial relations systems, and gross inequalities in income distribution. (Current trends in France are described here by Yves Delamotte, professor of labor law at the Conservatoire National des Arts et Métiers.) Nonetheless, the most creative and innovative advances in work reform have not taken place in these countries. Rather they have occurred in the Scandinavian countries and West Germany, countries with unified trade union movements, highly developed systems of collective bargaining, and relatively stable economic and political structures.

Barbash's essay provides a particularly illuminating insight into the basic outlooks of the two movements in his description of the highly differing approaches to industiral democracy that exist between the continental Western European and U.S. trade unions. He ascribes European labor emphasis on demands for codetermination and worker sharing in capital assets to its largely socialist orientation and greater acceptance of economic planning. The goals of industrial democracy are almost exclusively conceived by the American trade union movement as a function of collective bargaining in much the same manner as the accomplishment of improved wages, hours, and working conditions.

The divergent outlooks have led to differing priorities and emphases. West European governments, employers and, most particularly, the labor leaders, have focused either on the establishment of worker participation structures where they had not previously existed or on the further extension of already existing systems. The principal thrust of American unions, in part owing to rising public concern over the deteriorating environment, has been a successful effort to establish higher standards for industrial health and safety both at the collective bargaining table and through legislative action. The crowning achievement has been the creation of the Occupational Health and Safety Agency as an adjunct of the Department of Labor.

Concluding the volume, Harold L. Sheppard, of the American Institute for Research, argues that despite differences in the outlooks of Western industrialized societies and the nature of their institutions, a great deal of commonality exists, "more commonality than there are differences." Greater primacy should therefore be given to the common features that our societies possess, for the totality of efforts in the field of work humanization are not so "idiosyncratic" as to prevent the adaptation of some elements of these efforts by other societies.

I

Multinational Companies
and
Labor

A Union View

of the

Multinational Problem

Richard Prosten & Raymond MacDonald

THERE is no single labor view on trade. The AFL-CIO has a position, the United Auto Workers has one, and so do most other independent unions. Between groups, on occasion, there are some differences, but there is clear consensus on many issues and absolute agreement on what labor considers to be the most important point: trade and trade-related legislation should not be a vehicle for stripping American workers of their jobs and their economic well-being, while enabling certain sectors of the business community to reap unconscionable profit.

The emergence of multinational corporations has created a strange situation, not only for those who are affected by their activities, but also for the multinationals themselves. In becoming companies without a country, they eventually work themselves into the position of being companies without protection. Many U.S.-based multinationals are afraid to do what they know is right in the United States for fear that they will alienate some other country with which, or in which, they do business; by the same token, they become potentially vulnerable to reprisals in the United States.

During the debate that produced the Trade Reform Act of 1974, labor was perceived as the great stumbling block, as a collection of intransigent protectionists who just didn't understand. While rejecting the pejorative connotations of many of those perceptions, we find the characterizations at least partly correct—labor tried hard to prevent what it saw as another

1

in a series of attacks on this country's workers and jobs. What never got across to the public were the reasons that forced labor into such a position.

Labor is not opposed to trade. Labor is not flatly opposed to imports. Nor is labor so narrow-minded as to feel that the United States must, in perpetuity, be the world's sole purveyor of manufactured goods. Labor takes the view that working people throughout the world have the right to a greater degree of self-sufficiency than many of them now enjoy. We cannot, however, accept the notion that what passes for world trade should provide a framework for the exploitation of foreign labor. It is also unacceptable for a number of firms, essentially multinationals, to take advantage of U.S. citizens as taxpayers, consumers, and workers by placing short-run profits ahead of the nation's overall collective future—including the futures of workers and the business community.

Jobs Have Been Lost

For the last few years, the United States has been faced with an employment crisis of disastrous proportions. It is not reasonable to blame this dismal economic performance on trade distortions alone. However, there is a very real connection between the trade patterns fostered by the U.S. government over the last two decades and the current mess the economy is in.

Over the years, industry after industry has succumbed to a variety of pressures and has phased out most or all of its U.S. capacity. Not buggy whips or other technologically obsolete artifacts of bygone eras but everyday, commonly used American industrial products like typewriters, sewing machines, ball bearings, shoes, bicycles, and so on have been phased out. The labor movement has watched, but it has not done so silently. Time and time again labor has questioned the wisdom and purpose of legislation and regulations that, at least in its view, have encouraged the attrition of domestic industry.

Labor has not only been misled as to how many more job opportunities will be created but has also been told that in those few extreme cases where people actually lose jobs, there will be benefits galore that will tide them over and train them for new, more productive roles in the work force. It is now well known how worthless that part of the 1962 Trade Expansion Act proved to be. That section of the act was, to labor, merely another indication that it tends to get shanghaied when it rides with the traders.

Every time a piece of trade or trade-related legislation comes up—and this is true for regulations issued by agencies with discretionary rule-making authority as well—labor is told that the net effect of the new formulation will be to shore up trade and to create jobs for American workers. Obviously, a few jobs have been created. But many, many more have been lost. In short labor believes that it has been deceived.

Invariably, the result has been to pad the pockets of a few at the expense of many. The labor movement doesn't merely look at problems in abstract economic terms—it places heavy emphasis on the social consequences of events. Anguish over inequity is compounded when one notes that those who profit from much of this trade do so at once, while those who must pay the costs—workers, taxpayers, and consumers—never stop paying.

The northeast sector of this country is liberally dotted with what used to be shoe, textile, electronics, and silverplate factories. When these industries leave an area, their former employees, especially the older ones, are unlikely to find comparable employment or *any* employment, for that matter. In a period when domestic unemployment is as high as it now is in the United States, it is a poor idea indeed to go out of the way to create the conditions that will generate additional job loss.

Exporting Advanced Technology

It seems clear that we cannot forever trade American jobs for the welfare of a few. There are, of course, other aspects to the discussion. Should the practices of multinationals be allowed systematically to strip this nation of its capacity to produce a wide variety of goods? At what point does national security enter the picture?

The pattern of industry loss is clear and repeats itself with alarming frequency: first the assembly of components is exported, then the manufacture of components, then entire lines of production, followed by entire plants. Are there *any* items whose manufacture the traders think shouldn't be exported for another mill of profit?

As students, we were all taught that certain states had comparative advantages that, in no small part, were bestowed upon them by nature. If somebody wanted a Bordeaux wine there was only one place from which it could be obtained. In its formative years, the United States derived comparative advantage from its fertility and in later years added a substantial technological superiority. But recently, the United States has been rushing to export its comparative advantage—advanced technology.

A few years ago, everyone agreed that America's comparative advantage in trade was concentrated in sophisticated manufacturing industries, notably those dependent on innovations in product and process technology. Today the United States still maintains a lead in research and development, but its most significant export is now technology itself. While other countries are content to export products, Americans casually export the production process, the very means of production. This export of technology may look good in short-run balance-of-payments accounts, but tomorrow the United States will be importing the products of today's exported technology. In the process U.S. export markets will be lost to the foreign products of its own technology.

U.S. firms provide the overwhelming bulk of technology sold internationally. The United States provides between 50 and 60 percent of *all* the technology exported to *all* the countries of the Western world. But, since the United States exports ten times as much technology as it imports, its technology imports are only 5 or 6 percent of the global total.

A ten-to-one balance-of-payments "surplus" in technology transfers makes technology America's strongest export industry. It is also the fastest growing, with the value of U.S. technology exports growing from $650 million in 1960 to $3.9 *billion* in 1974. These figures account for annual licensing fees and royalty payments for transfer of (proprietary) technology and therefore represent only a tiny fraction (typically 5 percent) of the value of the items produced with that technology. As an order of magnitude figure, $80 billion represents the worth of foreign high-technology production flowing from 1974's exports of American technology.

Fully 75 percent of this exported technology goes to the controlled foreign affiliates of U.S. multinationals, the firms with a virtual monopoly on research and development and high-technology production within the United States. And, since these same multinationals also supply nearly half of the U.S. technology sold to *un*related foreign firms, they account, in total, for 88.5 percent of U.S. technology exports (based on 1966 benchmark statistics).

The prominence of multinationals in the *export* of technology parallels the technological orientation of their *direct investment* abroad. Fully two-thirds of the capital piled into their foreign manufacturing affiliates goes to high-technology industries (non-electrical machinery, electrical machinery, chemicals, and transportation equipment), while in the domestic economy these same high-technology industries receive only one-third of manufacturing capital outlays. In other words, the "overseas sector" of the American multinationalized economy is already *twice* as technology-intensive as the domestic sector of U.S. manufacturing.

The magnitude of overseas production using U.S. technology is far from inconsequential. Rising steadily since World War II (and even more rapidly since the late 1960s), overseas sales by U.S. firms had already reached $437 billion by 1974—roughly four and a half times larger than total U.S. exports in that year.

The inevitable result of exporting this comparative advantage is devastatingly clear to most members of the labor movement. It is capably summarized by Harvard economist Richard Caves, who suggests that this process:

> ... transmits an important simple message concerning the effects of technology transfers in a world of many industries and countries. The transfer of a given industry's technology tends to raise the productivity and thus the competitive clout of rival producers abroad and generally appears to reduce the real income (at least temporarily) of factors of production in the industry that has exported the technology. ... If we export "manufactures" and import "raw materials," the transfer of technology for making manufactures can indeed turn the terms of trade in favor of raw materials and leave us worse off.[1]

"Raising the competitive clout of rival producers abroad" will obviously weaken U.S. trade balances—something that has been witnessed since the early 1960s. If carried far enough, it will lead to currency devaluations for the technology-exporting countries or, under a regime of floating exchange rates, a continuing decline in the international value of national currency.

U.S. Losing Ground as an Industrial Producer

This growing export of capital, technology, production, and jobs is, of course, the result of logical, optimizing behavior for these firms, operating within existing legal, economic, and tax structures. In the short term, each of their individual decisions is prudent for the firm and may appear prudent to some observers.

Failure of the United States to regulate the export of its capital and technology has resulted in its rapidly losing ground as an industrial producer. As the United States–Japan Trade Council recently pointed out, U.S. industrial production rose only 25.6 percent between 1967 and 1973. During the same period, Japan's industrial production increased by 96.4 percent, Germany's by 51.4 percent, France's by 48 percent, and Canada's by 40.6 percent.

It's not surprising: there's a healthy tax incentive for U.S. producers to go abroad. One can't blame foreign powers for the U.S. tax laws. These tax laws have allowed companies to credit all taxes paid to foreign governments against U.S. income taxes. Taxes on foreign-derived profits may be deferred until—if ever—the profits are returned to the United States. When combined with long tax holidays, export subsidies, and other inducements provided abroad, the U.S. incentives become an irresistible lure to what might have been U.S. production. The combined tax revenue cost of the multinationals' tax credit and tax deferral was over $8 billion in 1974.

Frequently American labor is told how much cheaper or more productive foreign labor is and how unreasonable and demanding the domestic variety is. Such statements neglect one of the central issues as far as labor is concerned: the accelerating transfer abroad of U.S. technology. American workers are not competing with the dedication to their dollar-a-day jobs of some inmates of an Asian sweat shop. They are competing with, in many cases, the most modern technology that American ingenuity can create. And that's an awfully big hitch.

Told that a worker in Taiwan or some other foreign land can produce some incredible multiple of the average widget production of U.S. workers, labor is prone to answer, so what? What kind of machines are involved? When was the plant built? A number of other questions that relate to the level of technology invested in that particular location can also be asked, but, generally speaking, these are rhetorical questions. The answer is almost always that it is a new plant, using the latest available equipment from the United States.

Unfortunately, in many cases, the American taxpayer has subsidized the development and perfection of the equipment involved. The American taxpayer has also provided a variety of subsidies and inducements that encouraged the owner of the machinery or technology to ship it abroad to begin with. Now the ever-generous taxpayer must sit by and forego the tax revenues that, if this equipment were used domestically, would accrue to the U.S. Treasury and perhaps all tax revenues because, on paper at least, that poor foreign operator has no income taxable in the United States. While American workers are told that they should accept the idea of imports because in the long run imports will save the American consumer a lot of money, in many instances the production of these imported goods was effectively subsidized by U.S. taxpayers—cancelling any real savings. Labor is convinced that, until these incentives are curtailed and removed, it will be unable to deal effectively with the loss of American jobs and that U.S. taxpayers will have to continue to subsidize their own undoing.

When called upon to quantify their role in creating jobs in the United States, the firms that are involved in these international operations generally explain how big they are as domestic employers today, compared with some previous point in time. What they fail to mention is that often this increase in employment is due to the purchase of pre-existing domestic firms which, of course, had an employment complement of their own before they were bought out.

A recent study by the multinational-oriented Business International Corporation shows that U.S. multinational corporations are creating jobs in foreign countries about ten times as fast as they are creating jobs in the United States. Business International Corporation described its study as a rebuttal to those who say U.S. multinationals export jobs, on the basis that the firms studied expanded their American work force at a greater rate than the "average U.S. company" during the years 1970–73. However, the survey's figures also show that, while the 111 (self-selected) manufacturing multinationals under study were increasing their American employment at a 3.3 percent rate in the four-year period 1969–73, they were increasing their overseas employment at a rate of 31.5 percent. The reported figures show U.S.-based multinationals creating a net increase of 360,373 jobs abroad and only 90,283 jobs at home—or about four foreign jobs for every one in the United States. Clearly, this is the most important single fact revealed by the study, even though Business International chose not to highlight it. The surveyed firms expanded their overseas investment by more than 50 percent in the years 1970–73, nearly two and a half times their domestic investment expansion rate.

When labor attempts to limit the manipulation of the multinational enterprises, it is told that such limitations would invite a series of retaliatory moves on the part of other countries and bring on a trade war. In many ways, foreign governments have been "retaliating" for quite some time. Many U.S.-based multinationals merely look upon this "retaliation" as a convenient excuse for various practices that enable them to make a faster buck. Through their foreign affiliates, U.S.-based multinationals duck behind these "retaliatory moves" and compete directly with domestic companies.

Information Needed about Multinationals

The biggest problem with multinationals is how little is really known about them. The jealous care with which these firms guard the records of their activities is startling. They have successfully hampered efforts to gain data needed rationally to set public policies regarding them. Private and public researchers in and out of the United States unanimously agree that more and better information is necessary.

Jacob Clayman, president of the Industrial Union Department of the AFL-CIO, recently detailed, first to the Subcommittee on Foreign Commerce of the Senate Committee on Appropriations and then to the Subcommittee on Reports, Accounting and Management of the Senate Committee on Government Operations, the "horror story" that resulted when the government set out to collect such information in 1974.

The Bureau of Economic Analysis of the Commerce Department clearly recognized the need for a bench-mark census of U.S.-based multinational companies, Clayman noted. The information was needed for dealing with policy and analytic matters concerning multinationals. In July 1974, the bureau completed drafting its census questionnaires. The information sought was more comprehensive than is presently available, but far less so than what is obtained from domestic businesses. The proposed questionnaires were submitted to a cabinet-level interagency clearing committee, the National Advisory Committee on International Monetary and Financial Affairs. That committee approved so few of the questions that the Commerce Department decided to drop the project. It was not cost-effective to undertake what little information-gathering would have been allowed.

The National Advisory Committee hid behind the Bretton Woods agreement, which sets minimum data requirements of nations that are party to it. Bretton Woods does not set maximums.

Congress recently passed the International Investment Survey Act of 1976. While the legislation was a step in the right direction, it had some major shortcomings which are ably summed up by U.S. Representative

Jonathan Bingham, who said that he was "concerned and disappointed that the legislation fails to provide for disclosure of multinational corporate investment data on a company-by-company and country-by-country basis." He went on to say that aggregated data are not sufficient and that the United States should do something positive to enforce the disclosure principles endorsed by the Organization for Economic Cooperation and Development and its member governments on June 21, 1976.[2]

Evaluation of the 1974 Trade Act

The foregoing arguments, in addition to explaining why the U.S. labor movement worries about some aspects of transnational enterprise and often appears to be so strident in its denunciations of U.S. trade policy, have been presented to set the framework for an evaluation of the 1974 Trade Act—the most recent legislation that has been in place long enough to be scrutinized in any meaningful way.

Clearly, there were areas of the legislation that we found encouraging. The revisions of the Tariff Adjustment Assistance set-up cannot help but improve the ability of that program to deliver what it seemed to promise in the 1962 legislation. Adjustment assistance for communities is also an important breakthrough and, if it is not bogged down by a complex set of bureaucratic requirements, may prove very helpful to a jurisdiction that wakes up some morning to discover that its tax base has just moved to Hong Kong.

Paul DeLaney, former chief counsel for the Office of Foreign Direct Investment and a former consultant to the White House Council on International Economic Policy, specializes in adjustment assistance cases. He indicates that while the number of firm and worker adjustment cases successfully processed under the 1974 Trade Act has grown substantially, not a single community petition has been granted.

Given the elaborate tax favors bestowed on many of the firms that create the need for such assistance, workers and communities should not feel the least bit bad about applying for and receiving trade adjustment assistance. However, workers and their communities would surely feel much better if the jobs did not disappear in the first place. Even if it were effective, trade adjustment assistance is no substitute for what is really needed: programs to put citizens back to work, thus restoring the purchasing power and well-being of all sectors of our society.

Section 283 of the act—frequently referred to as the runaway plant section—sets up steps that should be taken by companies that are in the process of checking out of the United States. This section seems to create the potential for stopping what in the past has often been a precipitous and mindless abandonment of employees and communities by firms that decide to move to a foreign country. However, there are far too many "shoulds" and no discernible "musts" in the section, although conceptually it is a move in the right direction. In reading that section through, however, one finds that no specific sanction is mentioned. It is to be hoped that the intent of Congress will prevail and workers will not have to suffer another adjustment assistance type situation of apparent promise and no real results.

The escape clause in Title II and the various relief provisions in Title III of the act offered at least a potential source of help for workers, although it appears that lawyers familiar with international practice got the most help. For labor, the problem is that by the time injury can be proven, it may be too late to save a given plant or industry. The same problem, no doubt, hinders timely action by community groups when they attempt to preserve their local industries.

The East–West trade monitoring system, established under Section 410 of the act, is a step in the right direction. It requires a government agency to monitor the impact that imports from non-free-market economies have on the domestic industries and workers who produce like or competitive products. Unfortunately, this section does not require the collection of similar data covering trade with market economies.

Of course, there was a lot that the act did not do that U.S. labor would have liked it to do. It did not affect the job-destructive tax structure: in particular the foreign tax credit and the provisions that allow tax deferral on foreign-earned profits. It did not repeal Items 806.30 and 807 of the Tariff Code which encourage foreign production for shipment back to U.S. markets. It did not provide for the development of an orderly process of decision-making when it comes to investments—one which would attempt to promote a healthy future for this country and its workers.

Until the problems raised here are addressed from the perspective of employees and consumers, multinationals will be a continuing source of worker dissatisfaction in the United States. The problem has just started to receive attention from sources not traditionally associated with labor. For example, Betty Southard Murphy of the National Labor Relations

Board has indicated that perhaps U.S.-based multinationals should have to bargain with their domestic employees over the company's actions abroad that affect American workers. The specifics of her proposal are less important than the fact that it was made by someone from outside the immediate labor "family" who recognizes that there is a problem.

Notes

1. "Effect of the International Technology Transfers on the U.S. Economy" in *The Effects of International Technology Transfers on the U.S. Economy* (National Science Foundation, 1974), p. 61.

2. The full text of Congressman Bingham's remarks:

"While I support the provisions of S. 2839, I am concerned and disappointed that the legislation fails to provide for disclosure of multinational corporate investment data on a company-by-company and country-by-country basis. In that respect, the bill is much weaker than proposed legislation introduced by, among others, myself, Senator Frank Church, and Representative Nix (H.R. 13756 and S. 3151).

"I continue to believe that information of the kind identified by S. 2839 for collection and analysis must be available to policymakers in more than just aggregate terms. Aggregate data alone is inadquate and can even be misleading in view of the size and dominance of a few large multinational firms in particular areas of trade and investment. With respect especially to such firms some of which have budgets and resources greater than those of some of the major governments of the world, policymakers must have more detailed information identified at the level of individual firms in order fully to appreciate both the beneficial and possible undesirable effects such firms and their operations may have on the public.

"Such company-by-company data was specifically mandated by H.R. 13756 and S. 3151. This legislation was unfortunately not given sufficient consideration before the Senate passed S. 2839.

"It is especially unfortunate that the present legislation does not call for company-by-company disclosure of information on the investments and business activities of multinational firms in view of the fact that the United States has recently joined in an international declaration which clearly endorses and envisages such disclosure. I refer to the June 21, 1976, declaration of the member governments of the Organization for

Economic Cooperation and Development (OECD). That declaration commits the United States to 'recommend' to multinational enterprises operating within U.S. jurisdiction certain 'guidelines' for action, including the following:

> Enterprises should, having due regard to their nature and relative size in the economic context of their operations and to requirements of business confidentiality and to cost, publish in a form suited to improve public understanding a sufficient body of factual information on the structure, activities and policies of the enterprise as a whole, as a supplement, in so far as is necessary for this purpose, to information to be disclosed under the national law of the individual countries in which they operate. To this end, they should publish within reasonable time limits, on a regular basis, but at least annually, financial statements and other pertinent information relating to the enterprise as a whole, comprising in particular:
>
> (i) The structure of the enterprise, showing the name and location of the parent company, its main affiliates, its percentage ownership, direct and indirect, in these affiliates, including shareholdings between them;
>
> (ii) The geographical areas where operations are carried out and the principal activities carried on therein by the parent company and the main affiliates;
>
> (iii) The operating results and sales by geographical area and the sales in the major lines of business for the enterprise as a whole;
>
> (iv) Significant new capital investment by geographical area and, as far as practicable, by major lines of business for the enterprise as a whole;
>
> (v) A statement of the sources and uses of funds by the enterprise as a whole;
>
> (vi) The average number of employees in each geographical area;
>
> (vii) Research and development expenditure for the enterprise as a whole;
>
> (viii) The policies followed in respect of intragroup pricing; and
>
> (ix) The accounting policies, including those on consolidation, observed in compiling the published information.

"Government appeals to multinational firms voluntarily to disclose the kind of information described in S. 2839 and in the OECD declaration are likely to be resisted, if not totally ignored. I believe, however, that the United States, which has jurisdiction over most of the world's largest multinationals, should take the lead in requiring disclosure of such information as a model and incentive to other nations to do likewise. Legislation supplementing the current bill along the lines suggested by Senator Church and myself, combined with strong diplomatic efforts to achieve disclosure of similar information by foreign-based multinationals, would go a long way toward achieving full international sharing of essential trade and investment information on a country-by-country and company-by-company level, and should be further considered and pursued."

Labor Relations

Of U.S. Multinationals Abroad

Duane Kujawa

JUST a decade ago, John C. Shearer's "Industrial Relations of American Corporations Abroad" was published by the Industrial Relations Research Association.[1] His study, which was empirically based and quite normative in valuation, was one of the first to appear dealing with the problems and opportunities evident at the interface between organized labor and multinational enterprises. Since Shearer's classic work, several others have researched and reported on the same subject and have brought a rich variety of experiences, viewpoints, and methods to bear on it. Some have sought to promote particular partisan perspectives,[2] while others have been more concerned with the development and testing of positive models depicting the rationale for certain behavior observed and the subsequent impact on industrial relations and/or other topics of social concern.[3] Quite notably, except for appeals to sustain or improve adversary positions, few if any participants or scholars have offered prospective views embracing any significant operational inference on either labor–management relations in the multinational context or attendant public policy options.[4] The objective of this paper is to develop such a prospective model—a model based on a disaggregated analysis of enterprise, of workers and their institutions, and of accompanying social concerns and values.

Labor Relations of U.S. Multinationals Abroad

Allegations of impropriety or injustice about the labor relations of U.S. multinationals abroad generally center on either of two themes: the nature and operational characteristics of multinationals compromise the bargaining power of workers and unions;[5] and employment and other labor-relations practices of multinationals are developed and implemented with contempt for local industrial relations customs and values.

ADVERSE EFFECTS ON BARGAINING POWER

Inaccessibility of Decision Makers. Trade unionists contend that the multinationals, given their distinctive transnational tiers of managerial control and decision making, compromise the integrity of the collective bargaining process at the subsidiary level. Local management does not have ultimate authority to respond to union interests and initiatives.

Trade union representatives at the International Labour Office's (ILO) special meeting on multinationals reported

> . . . the locus of managerial decision-making . . . is not always where the confrontations between management and trade unions take place. Rather, it is contended, the relevant decisions are made at the headquarters of the multinational, beyond the reach of the union concerned. This means that trade union negotiators do not have the opportunity of personally presenting their case to those who ultimately take the decisions.[6]

An important corollary to this concern is that only the decision maker possesses the factual background and perspective on the enterprise adequate to a proper appraisal of the union's interests and proposals. Another is that cross-cultural problems and the long chain of command involved in decision making increase the probability of delays in response and errors in communication.

Considerable local autonomy in the management of overseas industrial relations by the U.S. multinationals in the automotive industry was reported in my 1969–1970 study of subsidiaries in Western Europe. Local firms had autonomy over decisions on collective bargaining structures, development of collective bargaining and strike positions, strikes and the resolution of strike issues, administration of contracts, handling of grievances, and relations with governments. Parent companies were involved with and had to approve pension plans. For pension plans, the special actuarial expertise and contingent liability of the parent were factors. The parent company might restructure its industrial relations in order to carry out a successful competitive strategy in the foreign market, such as when Chrysler–U.K. (Rootes) implemented an integrated, inter-plant production scheme.[7]

The 1975 ILO study of multinationals in Western Europe concluded that, while parent companies do at times intervene in a subsidiary's labor relations, the parent's influence varies depending on the issue, the technological or market forces in evidence, and the country.[8] It is important to note that "influences" included regarding the subsidiary's labor problems as an extension of home country operations as well as "imposing" parent country standards.

In 1975, the Conference Board's study of the locus of decision-making in 134 U.S. multinationals abroad and 34 foreign multinationals in the United States found considerable parent involvement.[9] Fully 27 percent of their respondents noted that subsidiaries had to seek parent approval of labor–management agreements on economic issues, while the remainder reported less direct but still possibly important parent involvement ranging from consultation to requiring that local agreements meet certain financial objectives. When the survey question was on the form of economic benefit (rather than the level), the percent who answered that parent approval was required dropped to 18—indicating that perhaps the budgetary impact, not labor–management relations, was the major concern. These data, however, are of limited or questionable value. Even if only one subsidiary was required to seek parent approval, the response for the entire multinational was so categorized, and subsidiaries in Canada were not treated separately. The data may characterize only the U.S.–Canadian situation, which is reportedly fairly integrated in terms of industrial relations management and practices.[10]

Management practitioners have generally been quite uniform in their acknowledgement that the important industrial relations decisions are in fact taken at the subsidiary level. Robert Copp at the Ford Motor Company has presented such a position on several occasions. Frank W. Angle at General Motors, George B. McCullough at Exxon, and John A. Belford at Massey-Ferguson have similarly gone on record.[11]

These apparent divergent views between management spokespersons and others were validated by G. B. J. Bomers in his 1976 opinion and interview survey of union and employer respondents in the Netherlands and West Germany. Bomers found general agreement from the unions, and disagreement from the employers, that multinationals (especially U.S. multinationals) tend to centralize an increasing portion of industrial relations policy making.[12] He also reported that employers could neither agree nor disagree with the statement, "Unions often do not know exactly where within multinationals . . . decision making takes place with regard to industrial relations policies." [13] Bomers's data revealed that employers felt that decision making involves the interdependent activities of many people and "complexities inherent in . . . large organizations," and that

> . . . centralization in industrial relations policy making
> tends to increase the number of people that influence the
> decision making process which, in turn, tends to obscure
> the locus of decision making.[14]

It's not clear how one can say that more people in the international organization are participating in what is purely a local decision in the non-multinational and yet deny that the process is more centralized. If the decision maker cannot be more discreetly defined, then the union allegation has not been adequately responded to. In recent years unions have used a somewhat different tactic to reveal the locus of decision making. They have looked at the types of decisions being made and asked whether or not unions can be involved in them. The objective here is the multinational's investment decision which by definition is made by management above the subsidiary level. To my knowledge, managements have uniformly denied any direct union participation in investment decisions.[15]

External Financial Resources. The ability of a multinational to maintain operations in one country if struck by a union (or unions) in a different country certainly diminishes the workers' power. Being able to generate financial inflows in environments external to a labor–management conflict truly distinguishes the multinational from the uninational company.

Bomers reports that both union members and employers in his survey agreed that "their broader financial base enables [multinationals] . . . to hold out much longer in collective bargaining with local unions than national firms." [16] Leopold Bergmann's 1973 survey similarly concluded

> At the collective bargaining table the management of a
> multinational . . . affiliate is not . . . in the same position
> as any management of a national firm. The fact that, in
> case of a strike, it can draw upon the superior (financial)
> resources of the "mother" weakens the union bargaining
> position by depriving it of a credible threat.[17]

However, transnational production integration, to the extent it exists, would give labor in any one country or at any one plant considerable financial leverage in its collective bargaining, since stalling the production of one component has the effect of stalling production of the final product. I am unaware of any systematic, empirical study of the extent of transnationally integrated production in multinational enterprises. There is some evidence, however, that production integration at any significant level does not exist.

Peggy B. Musgrave's study shows that the ratio of the value of foreign sales by U.S. multinationals to their U.S. exports grew from 2.1 in 1962–1964 to 2.8 in 1968; from that it might be inferred that production integration may even be declining.[18] Similarly, the U.S. Tariff Commission, in its comprehensive 1972 study of U.S. multinationals, concluded "most of the multinationals' . . . activity overseas consists of local production for local markets."[19] Regarding the automotive industry in 1969–1970, I found significant evidence of transnational production integration in the Ford Motor Company among its European subsidiaries.[20] Regarding other companies or other geographical areas, production integration was not significant (excluding U.S.–Canada, of course). The 1975 ILO research on European-based multinationals concluded

> Despite a good deal of interchange of components, internationally integrated production of various plants of a multinational does not appear to be a prevalent feature as regards the multinationals reviewed.[21]

The external financial resources threat to unions at an individual subsidiary of a multinational is likely to be quite realistic.

Production Switching. Clearly related to the external financial resources threat is production switching.[22] Production switching is the transfer of production among the subsidiaries of a multinational so that market commitments may still be met in the event of a strike at any particular subsidiary (or the threat of such during collective bargaining). There can also be the fear of future lost employment at any particular subsidiary because of a threat by the multinational to shift current production to other facilities or to locate new investment elsewhere as a reprisal against the union. Production switching enables the firm to maintain cash inflows during a strike and thus undermine union power. Threatening to switch production is tantamount to "whipsawing" a union. What is the evidence on production switching in U.S. multinationals abroad?

The aforementioned 1975 ILO study on multinationals in Western Europe reported several instances of production switching to offset strike losses, including examples from the food products and processing industry.[23] The expressed concerns (and claims of success) of trade unionists to coordinate internationally with other unions to prevent shifting of production support the ILO findings. For example, during the 1973 contract negotiations in the U.S. rubber industry, the International Federation of Chemical and General Workers' Unions (ICF) reportedly formed a transnational network of unions to make effective a refusal to build up inventories, to increase overtime, and to divert production to the United States or to make "exceptional transfers of output to world markets."[24]

The Conference Board's 1975 survey revealed that 10 percent of the U.S. multinational respondents had foreign subsidiaries whose union contracts included refusals to work overtime, or to handle shipments to or from struck foreign operations.[25] Bomers found substantial agreement from both union and employer respondents that multinationals undermine the bargaining position of unions during industrial disputes by temporarily shifting production within the corporation, if this is technically feasible.[26] This latest caveat—technical feasibility—is most important. My studies of the automotive industry conclude that such feasibility is quite low.[27] In addition foreign plants often do not have the capacity to pick up the large volume of lost production at a struck facility. Contrary to claims of success by trade unionists, capacity cannot be constrained by workers refusing to go on overtime, since local conditions and attitudes often do not allow for overtime work anyway, such as in the recent Ford-Belgium (Genk) situation, where workers have consistently and effectively resisted overtime work even in the absence of opportunities to support demands of workers at other Ford plants.[28]

The threat of shifting production apparently has been used by multinationals to counter union demands or to extract concessions during collective bargaining. A 1975 ILO study noted

> One of the most serious charges, which unions make . . .
> is that multinationals . . . use their internationally spread
> facilities as a threat to counter union demands and power.
> If a union will not yield, the company can . . . transfer its
> production to another country, or the company may utilize
> already existing facilities in another country to penalize
> the "demanding" union . . .[29]

To cite a case in point, the General Motors' (GM) subsidiary in Antwerp, Belgium, won a concession from the unions to expand a new afternoon production shift to forty hours from the thirty-seven and a half hour workweek whereas before only maintenance personnel had worked the shift. The local GM management was able to convince the unions of its own conviction that the workweek expansion was required to maintain a competitive alternative to losing production to a GM (Opel) plant in West Germany.[30]

Threats by U.S. multinationals to locate new direct investments in more friendly, or more productive environments have also been made with the alleged intent of undermining worker solidarity and trade union power. For example, Chrysler–United Kingdom's labor situation in 1973, which management felt to be quite onerous, was reported as "leading company planners to consider switching substantial production to its French plants and/or to a partner operation in Japan." [31] Indeed, prior to this, the company's managing director warned employees that "beyond everything else, we need a year of stable industrial relations and uninterrupted production within our plants. . . . Another year of disruption of the damaging scale of the past 12 months might well put us out of business." [32] A similar situation involved a threat by the Ford–U.S. board chairman to place new foreign investment outside the United Kingdom where he felt product quality was superior and a better return on investment was possible.[33]

Bomers's recent survey revealed unionists agreed but employers disagreed that multinationals at times threaten to shift production facilities from one country to another as a bargaining and occasionally an intimidation tactic. However, his back-up interview data showed the union respondents based their opinions "almost without exception" on the aforementioned Chrysler and Ford situations in the United Kingdom, and they reported that such a threat in the Netherlands or West Germany would be a "rare occurrence." [34]

The data appear mixed on the issue of production switching. On the one hand, the prospect of shifting production during a strike, or during labor negotiations, poses a real threat to union power. However, in some cases the potential for such production switching may be quite low, or even zero. On the other hand, the possible loss of future employment at a specific subsidiary, as new investments are located in different foreign countries, is perceived by unionists seemingly in light of publicity on the controversial industrial relations climate in the United Kingdom.

Job Losses. Declining employment opportunities for union members usually mean that workers focus more on getting and holding a job rather than on the conditions of employment, thus undermining union solidarity, worker militancy, etc. (This may be less true on the European continent than in the United States and the United Kingdom.)

The 1975 ILO study on social and labor policies reported no negative employment effects in Western Europe due to any large-scale transfers of production by non-U.S. multinationals.[35] Bergmann noted a similar conclusion for the U.S. multinationals, but thought that the structure of employment in the European Economic Community (EEC) had indeed been affected (as it relates to jobs created in the developing areas of the EEC and the practice of importing workers).[36] Bomers's survey concluded that union respondents (1) did not see the job export issue as one necessarily identifiable with multinationals, but rather felt it was related to the gradual decline of labor-intensive industries (which are characteristically not dominated by multinationals), and (2) were not against structural unemployment in principle.[37] Clearly the job loss issue, while it may be quite a topic of concern and debate in the United States, has not been an issue regarding the operations of U.S. multinationals abroad.

The evidence supports the conclusion that the nature and operational characteristics of U.S. multinationals compromise the bargaining power of workers and unions abroad. Not every allegation, however, on the details of how bargaining power is actually lost appear acceptable.

CONTEMPTUOUS INDUSTRIAL RELATIONS PRACTICES

The second of the working hypotheses presented above contended that social improprieties or injustices accompany U.S. multinationals' actions abroad because of their disregard for local industrial relations customs. Shearer's research in the early 1960s, for example, concluded

> American firms which operate in foreign countries usually premise their industrial-relation's policies on the base of values, assumptions, and habits they developed in the United States. They then may or may not modify them in response to the different circumstances abroad. There are many instances in which American companies have successfully adapted their industrial relations to fit the environments of other advanced countries and many other instances where they failed to do so, often with costly consequences for the firms and for their representation of American values abroad.[38]

Underlying this generalization, Shearer found (1) U.S. multinationals in Great Britain prefer layoffs or redundancies by seniority rather than by the local custom, where independent, parallel assessments were made by management, employees, and unions on the basis of worker qualifications; (2) U.S. multinationals will not recognize unions abroad, even when such recognition comes almost automatically, given the federated bargaining structures so prevalent in Europe; (3) U.S. multinationals resist granting improved fringe benefits abroad, even though such benefits are prevalent in the foreign environment, because of their American values; and (4) U.S. multinationals are more prone to lay off workers abroad than their locally owned counterparts.[39]

Nat Weinberg concludes from his experiences that the actions of U.S. multinationals abroad "inevitably affect the labor standards content of collective bargaining and can even result in the nullification of labor standards legislation."[40] Roger Blanpain, in a recent review of research aimed specifically at Shearer's aforementioned conclusions, found some supportive evidence but concluded that the distinguishing and influential features of the local (foreign) industrial relations system

> ... compel the multinational eventually to adjust and
> integrate within the system and to try to change it from
> within. ... Such an evolution, which seems logical, is
> illustrated by some convincing evidence in the research
> findings regarding trade union recognition, employer
> association membership, duration and nature of collective
> agreements, job security, and productivity bargaining and
> relative wages.[41]

Supporting Blanpain's conclusion of the eventual compatibility of multinationals with the host (foreign) industrial relations system, A. M. Evans observes from his own experiences as national organizer of the Transport and General Workers' Union (TGWU) in the U.K. that

> ... The TGWU has been able to bargain quite effectively
> with most of the multinationals in the United Kingdom.
> We had some problems ... in takeover situations where
> they have pressed for common pay structures and cen-
> tralized negotiating arrangements, which normally do not
> exist in Britain's metalworking industries ... [or] when
> they tried to apply home-base industrial relations
> philosophies and practices ... In time, however, most ...
> have adapted to the local environment.[42]

Bomers's survey revealed a similar finding. Union respondents were indifferent to, while employer respondents disagreed with, the statement that multinationals do not adequately take account of the rules, practices and customs existing in the local industrial relations environments.[43] Interestingly and as a final point, the ILO reports that a 1971 study by the Data Market Research Institute of thirty-three different fringe benefit practices of 158 respondent companies in Spain found "U.S. and other multinational firms provided a greater number of fringe benefits than the national firms, . . . more frequently grant reductions in hours of work per week than do national firms, . . . and are generally in line with the employment practices of what are probably the better national employers.[44]

On balance, the evidence, while not challenging the authenticity of Shearer's observations for the time period in which they were made, suggests that times have probably changed since the early 1960s and that a sense of compatibility and mutual accommodation between the industrial relations practices of U.S. multinationals abroad and the social proprieties and values of the host environments, at least as far as Western Europe is concerned. Everett M. Kassalow in his 1976 analysis reached a similar conclusion.[45]

Turning to the developing countries and the practices of U.S. multinationals, Shearer reports that they "have usually abdicated leadership in industrial relations, . . . buy peace through routine bribery of union officials and government labor inspectors, . . . [and] tend to pay only the legal minimum [wage] rates." [46] Weinberg notes too while discussing U.S. multinationals (regardless of subsidiary location) that they

> . . . will seek to bring about retrogressive changes in
> collective bargaining and in labor legislation. They will
> push constantly, everywhere they operate, toward the
> lowest attainable level of social responsibility; the
> international transfers they seek will be those that are the
> least burdensome to them and the most disadvantageous
> to their workers.[47]

In a recently concluded, but yet unpublished, 1976–1977 survey of how 228 Central American managers perceived the social effects of U.S. multinationals in comparison with similarly situated, locally owned firms, Michael Jay Jedel and I found that respondents generally agreed that local subsidiaries of U.S. multinationals, when compared to local companies, (1) paid higher wages, (2) implemented better employment practices, (3) provided better employment security, (4) provided better medical and social services, (5) enjoyed a lessened likelihood of worker unrest or discontent, and (6) followed the local labor code more exactly.[48] On only one point, the provision of training resources, more respondents were in disagreement than agreement that U.S. multinationals were outperforming local companies.

These data stand in contrast to Shearer's and Weinberg's observations, at least regarding employment practices. Also, regarding Shearer's bribery allegation, more respondents in the Central American survey disagreed than agreed with the statement, "U.S. companies 'buy' special privileges in my country."

The empirical evidence does not at present sustain the complaint that U.S. multinationals despoil the local social and cultural integrity of host environments in areas germane to industrial relations and related social policies. (More research needs to be done here, though, especially regarding the developing countries.)

Labor Relations of Foreign Multinationals in the United States

Compared to U.S. direct investment abroad, foreign direct investment in the United States is of more recent significance, and apparently of much less controversy. It has grown from $6.6 billion in 1959 to $26.5 billion in 1974,[49] and stands now at approximately 20 percent of the level of U.S. foreign direct investment.[50] Notwithstanding the acrimonious U.S. trade union response to the takeover of Copperweld Corporation by France's Inmetal in 1975,[51] the U.S. labor movement generally has been conspicuously accommodative of reverse investment. Concern has been expressed, however, by the director of the U.S. Federal Mediation and Conciliation Service who questioned

> ... whether foreign investors will insist on bringing their own management practices—forged under entirely different labor-management climates—to U.S. bargaining tables and whether American managements of foreign-owned plants will be influenced by the industrial relations policies of the owner's home country.[52]

A few others have similar apprehensions.[53] But what is the evidence?

EFFECT ON BARGAINING POWER

As noted previously, bargaining power of unions is felt to be diminished when (1) key labor relations decision makers within the firm are inaccessible and local subsidiaries lack autonomy, (2) the multinational can continue operations in one country if struck by a union in another and thus can generate financial inflows enabling it to sustain a strike longer, (3) the multinational can engage in production switching and continue to meet market commitments and generate financial inflows regardless of a strike in any one country, and (4) the multinational exports jobs and thus undermines union solidarity and effectiveness. How do these relate to foreign multinationals in the United States?

Locus of Decision Making. In our 1975 field interview study of 100 U.S. subsidiaries of foreign multinationals, Jedel and I reported on a variety of industrial relations and other practices and found that parent company involvement in labor relations at the U.S. subsidiary was minimal.[54] On union recognition, for example, affiliates of European multinationals were generally indifferent or sometimes even supportive, and those of Japanese multinationals felt a union might complicate employee relations but did not generally seek to obstruct unionization efforts. (This is not to say, however, that these firms did not oppose unionization. A few certainly did, but they tried to oppose unions through legally acceptable practices. Also, in these cases, the initiative was more likely than not taken by U.S. nationals in the subsidiary management who testified that the nationality of their parent was irrelevant to their policies.)

Regarding collective bargaining, only eight of sixty-four unionized U.S. subsidiaries reported any parent involvement. Four of these were Canadian-owned, and in two the parent company's major concern was consistency between U.S. and Canadian labor contracts (each dealt with the same union in both the United States and Canada). Two others (non-Canadian) kept the parents advised on collective bargaining developments but received neither directions nor admonitions in return. Of the two remaining, one French parent insisted on reacting to economic issues and limited its participation thusly, while a West German parent, with German nationals operating out of a North American regional office, participated in a variety of management issues and problems at its U.S. subsidiaries. On the strike issue, only in four of the sixty-four unionized subsidiaries did parent management participate—three were Canadian, the other the aforementioned West German firm. Participation in these few cases was limited to advice on strategy.[55]

The evidence (Canadian cases excepted) leads one to infer that there is considerable autonomy at the U.S. subsidiary level in the handling of labor relations. Findings on foreign parent–U.S. subsidiary organizational (control and reporting) relationships further support this conclusion. Lawrence G. Franko, for example, reported

> ... at the beginning of the 1970's the most important bonds between center and periphery in European multinational systems were still the personal relationships between presidents of parent companies and presidents of foreign ventures ... [a] mother–daughter form of organization ...[56]

and that

> ... foreign subsidiary presidents were often allowed great autonomy ... [and as] long as constraints were respected and dividend checks appeared when anticipated, the center rarely interfered with—or even asked for much information from foreign subsidiaries.[57]

In our 1975 field interview study, Jedel and I found evidence supportive of Franko's observations. Sixty-eight of the 100 participating subsidiaries indicated that the president or chief executive officer in the United States reported directly to the parent chief executive or board of directors.[58]

Managerial autonomy of foreign multinationals in the United States appears quite different from that of U.S. multinationals abroad. With the former, labor relations decisions are nearly always taken at the subsidiary level, and industrial relations, per se, are viewed as necessary for successful operations. With the latter, the parent company is often involved in these decisions and industrial relations are more likely viewed as essential to competitive strategy.

Parallel Production and Production Switching. That any multinational possesses a potential for continuously generating financial inflows in spite of a strike at the subsidiary level can hardly be denied. Foreign multinationals in the United States are no exception. In our 1975 study, Jedel and I found that U.S. subsidiaries mainly served the U.S. market and that a strike in the United States would not force operations elsewhere to shut down.[59] This confirmed our earlier findings from a 1974 mail survey of ninety-one foreign multinationals in the United States [60] and correlated well with Franko's conclusions.

Our 1975 survey reported a low potential for production switching among the U.S. subsidiaries of foreign multinationals. In only three of the sixty-four unionized subsidiaries studied

> ... the report of a strike alerted the parent to the anticipated inability of the U.S. subsidiary to meet sales commitments, with the expectation that the parent or some other subsidiary could pick up the production loss in the United States.[61]

The U.S. union's position is similarly strengthened by the fact that foreign-owned U.S. subsidiaries are more intensive exporters than U.S.-owned companies.[62] Thus, closing down U.S. operations can adversely affect the parent's performance in non-U.S. markets as well as the U.S. market. This means added leverage for the union. Similarly the 1974 findings showed that nearly half of the U.S. subsidiaries studied received supplies, components, or sub-assemblies from company operations outside the United States.[63] That also means added leverage for the union.

On balance, the evidence suggests that foreign multinationals are not unlike U.S. multinationals in their ability to diminish union bargaining power by maintaining some financial inflows to the parent during a strike at a U.S. subsidiary. For U.S. multinationals production switching was not found to be a predominant practice, nor was there much of a potential for it. For foreign multinationals in the United States production switching has never been reported, and the potential for it seems to be quite low. Interestingly, too, U.S. unions have not publicly complained of such a practice.

Job Losses. The job loss question is readily assessable. To the extent that direct investment has displaced imports into the United States, it has *created* jobs. However, if the investment has resulted in U.S.-based production expanding at the cost of driving U.S.-owned competitors out of the U.S. market, the residual effects on U.S. employment are unclear. At first imports are displaced and jobs created; then a structural employment problem may emerge. However, there appears to be nothing intrinsic in this process *necessarily* to diminish union bargaining power. Historically unions have certainly been able to cope with expansion and contraction at both firm and industry levels. To the extent that direct investment has involved the takeover of an existing U.S. firm or has represented the introduction of a new product (i.e., one previously not imported), it is not easy to conclude that jobs are being created. Nor do these factors have any effect on the bargaining power equation. As with U.S. multinationals abroad, the job loss question at the host-society level is not especially an active concern. Moreover, so far, no union has complained that foreign firms in the United States have threatened to locate new production in more friendly labor environments outside the United States.

INDUSTRIAL RELATIONS PRACTICES

Unlike U.S. multinationals abroad, foreign multinationals in the United States have never been accused of having brought onerous employment practices to the United States with them. However, if one accepts the view that the onerous practices of U.S. multinationals abroad reflect the transfer of (U.S.) home-based industrial relations philosophies and policies, then the U.S. labor relations philosophies and policies—and the social environment that spawned and nurtured them—must be deficient compared to foreign philosophies and policies. Thus, as foreign firms move into the United States, they can bring with them only superior philosophies and policies, from which superior practices evolve.

A somewhat more reasonable theory is that the relatively more autonomous position of the U.S. subsidiary implies more flexibility in adapting to and adopting local labor relations practices. Indeed, our 1975 field study reported that "management and employment practices of foreign investors in the United States were found to be more similar to traditional U.S. practices than dissimilar."[64] Where practices were dissimilar, "improved benefits" was the most commonly cited difference. These benefits were brought about because local, U.S. managers at the U.S. subsidiaries sought to upgrade employment practices and knew they had the capability and permissive corporate environments enabling them to do so.[65] Supporting this view, workers in the attitudinal survey portion of our 1975 study agreed by nearly two to one over those who disagreed that benefits (at their foreign-owned firm) were better than those at similar, non-foreign-owned companies.[66]

It is my conclusion that the labor relations of foreign multinationals in the United States are not directly comparable to those of U.S. multinationals abroad. Generally, the experiences have been quite different. This is especially true if the period of high growth in U.S. direct investment abroad (the 1960s) is compared to that of the higher growth rates of direct foreign investment in the United States (the 1970s). What gives rise to these differences? Have foreign investors in the United States been determined to learn from and not repeat the mistakes of U.S. firms abroad? Are there cultural differences which explain these behavior differences? Do U.S. multinationals have larger, more dominant affiliates that engage in monopsonistic, "price-fixing" practices, while foreign investors in the United States labor market are "price-takers?" To what extent is the nature of direct foreign investment different from U.S. investment abroad? How sensible are these differences in explaining observed behavioral differences or in predicting future behavior? These important questions are addressed in the remainder of this paper.

The Product Life Cycle and Industrial Relations

Many theories have been developed and tested to help explain foreign trade and foreign investment. The product life cycle (PLC) theory is one of the most useful theories for understanding the behavior of an enterprise in the manufacturing sector and the effects of that behavior on the location of employment, on the skills required by personnel, and on labor relations.

THE LIFE-CYCLE MODEL

The PLC is based on a disaggregated approach which looks more at individual products and individual firms rather than at impersonal markets, which, it is normally assumed, regulate product price and enterprise production behavior. The PLC has been largely developed and tested by Vernon and others at the Harvard Business School and today enjoys a high level of acceptability among academicians, government officials, and others concerned with international trade and the emergence of multinationals.[67]

According to the PLC theory, manufactured products go through three stages in their life cycle: (1) the new product—introductory or growth stage, (2) the maturity stage, and (3) the decline stage. New products, because they are significantly different from competing products, permit innovators initially to earn greater-than-average returns. Risk is thus rewarded and innovation is encouraged. Since these new products must be sold in markets in which consumers have a high level of discretionary spending power, the U.S. market, where personal income levels have traditionally been among the highest and where large numbers of high-income consumers with diversified needs and interests exist, has spawned numerous and varied new products. (Until recently, the United States was the only such market.) As the product matures, other firms begin to imitate it and drive the price down. As this happens, consumption and production expand while the profit margin declines. This, in turn, shifts the competitive strategy away from new product technology to new process technology, since competitive production costs now become crucial to success (staying power) in the market.

International trade enters the picture in the very first stage as the new product is exported to markets with income and consumption characteristics similar to the United States. Studies show that, perhaps more often than not, these initial exports are the result of a fortuitous order, that is, an order not systematically developed by the U.S. producer.[68] As exports grow, the firm becomes more organized and deliberate in serving foreign customers. Eventually, as the U.S. firm demonstrates success in the export market, foreign-based firms located in that market begin to make innovations in the product technology and adapt the product to the peculiar and changing local needs. Foreign production, unburdened with tariffs, international shipping costs, etc., begins to displace U.S. exports. The (foreign) product market expands as this competition develops, but the U.S. firm's business declines as U.S. exports are forced out of the market.

Then U.S. firms invest in foreign manufacturing facilities as a defensive response to the advent of local production by foreign competitors. The first line of defense, control over product technology, becomes ineffective over time as the demonstrated market success of U.S. exports encourages and facilitates local competition. The second line of defense, control over (superior) process or production technology, is then brought forward and made effective by the firm's very presence in the distinctive product market it seeks to serve, and by the elimination of important, non-competitive cost factors, such as tariffs, shipping, etc. A third line of defense develops as these firms, now U.S. multinationals, seek to bring new products to market on a continuous basis either by expanding existing product lines or by making innovations in other products. This ensures the firm's continuous presence in both the U.S. domestic and foreign markets. The firm is now both exporter and foreign manufacturer. Concurrently, in the United States the firm expands research and development and the technical and logistical support and managerial capabilities necessary to serve world markets. In the foreign market it seeks simultaneously to implement superior production processes and to secure the sales of mature products via advertising, control over distribution, etc. These actions, in turn, often entail, tend towards, or result in the development of large-scale, high technology, conglomerate organizations with superior financial resources.[69]

Studies show that in foreign multinationals reverse investment has occurred to a considerable extent as yet a slightly different variant on the defensive strategy theme.[70] Since the U.S. market is the largest and most sophisticated consumer-oriented market in the world, success in that market is a prerequisite for success in other markets. If U.S. firms have the U.S. market to themselves they will eventually be able to outcompete non-U.S. firms in their own home markets (the third line of defense discussed above). Thus, the strategically necessary response is that the foreign firm establish a presence in the U.S. market and generate new products in order to protect its own home territory.

LABOR RELATIONS IN A PLC MODEL

Taking the U.S. multinationals first, several important observations can be made regarding labor relations environments as U.S. firms generate new products, export them, and eventually produce them abroad.[71] In the United States, the model implies, employment in production declines as defensive direct foreign investment displaces U.S. exports. However, employment of managers, scientists, engineers, technicians, and other support personnel increases. Empirical studies by Robert B. Stobaugh and the U.S. Tariff Commission [72] support these expectations. Thus, U.S. workers who are more likely to be union members lose jobs during this process, and the more professional worker who is less likely to be a union member finds expanding employment opportunities. Also, union bargaining strength declines, and union interest in solving the problems of "job exports" increases.[73]

Turning to U.S. multinationals abroad, according to the PLC theory the U.S. parent has substantial managerial control over the foreign subsidiary. Product and process technologies are transferred to the subsidiary —technologies which are seen as essential to the success of *both* parent and subsidiary. Control over these transfers and their successful implementation are strategically important to the firm. Thus, labor relations, which involve the application of human resources to these technologies, are also heavily influenced by parent management, and parent managerial and technical personnel can be expected to be on site at the subsidiary, especially during the initial period when new technologies are being transferred. These personnel are not usually trained in the local (foreign) industrial relations environment, and mistakes in interpreting that environment can be expected. In addition, because of their cultural and experiential backgrounds, they are likely to measure subsidiary-level labor relations against the vastly different U.S. industrial relations system. Add to this a compelling, competitive foreign environment, and the potential for error escalates considerably.

Perhaps the most destabilizing element, however, resides in the very nature of the technologies exported from the United States. These technologies were developed in the United States and embody, or are responsive to, significant U.S. industrial relations practices and norms—for example, the automobile production line and the time-measured, day-rate, wage-payments system. As these technologies are implemented overseas, there is a potential for labor conflict, since key features of the foreign system often differ from those of the parent's experience in the United States. Either the environment or the technology must adapt. Also, U.S. technologies, having been developed around comparatively high-cost labor, are decidedly labor-saving. Those from Europe, in contrast, have been built around comparatively high-cost materials and energy. They are more efficient in their use of these inputs.[74] If local customs and labor relations "cultures" at a subsidiary have been developed over time and reflect technologies that are not especially labor-saving, is there not an increased potential for conflict when labor-saving technologies are suddenly implemented? (This is especially relevant in the takeover of a subsidiary.)

In contrast, the strategic elements regarding foreign multinationals in the United States imply much less control from the non-U.S. parent. Technologies are developed in the United States for eventual transfer back to the parent country.[75] The parent–subsidiary relationship is much less directive, and, in terms of labor relations, the parent's interest may well be more centered on how to adapt U.S. technologies to an existing, foreign industrial relations system. Indeed, we may even expect foreign multinationals to be more efficient in transferring technologies to their home base than U.S. multinationals are in transferring technologies abroad. Foreign multinationals may thus have a competitive advantage in their home markets.

Labor Relations Practices Analyzed in Light of the PLC Model

The local autonomy issue has not developed regarding foreign multinationals in the United States but has been a major complaint of unions facing U.S. multinationals abroad. That U.S. firms *export* technologies *to* their foreign subsidiaries while foreign firms *import* technologies *from* their U.S. subsidiary appears to be a useful observation in explaining this difference. The U.S. firms were reportedly more prone to reserve key decisions to the parent management and to be more involved in effecting changes in labor relations at the subsidiary level. The aforementioned Chrysler–United Kingdom situation in the late 1960s is an illustrative case in point. Moreover, the 1975 ILO and Conference Board studies of U.S. multinationals abroad, when contrasted to the 1975 field study of foreign multinationals, show a higher incidence of U.S. parent participation in labor relations at the foreign subsidiary than of foreign parent participation at the U.S. subsidiary. Interestingly, the ILO report even noted that U.S. multinationals tended to regard the subsidiary's labor problems as extensions of home-country operations—an observation especially relevant to the inferences of the PLC model.

The model appears to deny the contention of U.S. multinationals that important industrial relations decisions are in fact taken at the subsidiary level, while supporting this same assertion as it relates to foreign multinationals. For U.S. multinationals, the apparent discrepancy on the issue is rooted equally in semantics and substance. Key decisions which relate to technology utilization, work force requirements, and investment location are defined by management as strategic decisions with admittedly important consequences for workers, but fully within the ambit of management prerogatives. Conversely, foreign labor systems frequently try to let worker interests affect these decisions. Although one might suggest that this is yet another instance of U.S. multinationals basing their industrial relations abroad on U.S. practices, such an observation still does not address the more fundamental question of the net social utility of direct U.S. investment abroad, as a measure of the success of that investment.

Regarding external financial resources, both sets of multinationals possess the potential for generating financial inflows during a strike, thus reducing the strike's effectiveness. The PLC model suggests, however, that foreign multinationals may be more *willing* to sustain a strike than U.S. multinationals, since they are not greatly compelled to achieve financial success in the short run or near term. Countering this, however, the foreign multinational is seen as having delegated more authority across-the-board to subsidy management, which may be quite concerned with the effects of a prolonged strike on near-term profits.

Production switching in either set of multinationals would not be expected to be a predominant characteristic. The PLC model suggests that U.S. multinationals abroad invest to serve *distinctive* local markets, while foreign multinationals invest in the United States to participate in and tap *distinctive* technological developments. Regarding component parts, however, where the design may be standardized internationally, a potential for production switching may exist. According to the PLC model, U.S. multinationals operate in more competitive environments abroad than foreign multinationals in the United States; hence, production switching, at least for certain products, may be more prevalent among U.S. multinationals. Expressions of worker concern abroad on this tactic seem to support this view.

The threat of locating new investments in more congenial labor relations environments is more likely to come from U.S. multinationals— especially where more mature products are concerned and when the cost of production is high. In the foreign multinational case, location in the U.S. market is not a function of current, competitive costs but of longer-run strategic considerations. The evidence shows that U.S. multinationals abroad have voiced these threats; foreign multinationals have not.

Regarding job losses, the evidence in either case shows no aggregate, negative employment effects. Changes in employment distribution and structural employment problems are probably generated by both U.S. and foreign-owned multinationals. These are consistent with the PLC model (as it has been displayed thus far) and are expected.

The data are fairly clear on the differences between U.S. multinationals abroad and foreign multinationals in the U.S. market. In early times U.S. multinationals supposedly exported onerous practices; the others were never so characterized. The PLC model implies that, as U.S. firms were new to foreign markets and were concerned with creating viable operations capable of displacing traditional export markets with (their own) local production, significant transfers of technologies occurred. These transfers involved products, processes and productive techniques, and managerial and technical personnel and greatly increased the potential for the transfer of U.S. labor relations practices and policies to subsidiaries abroad. It's no accident, for instance, that U.S. multinationals in the United Kingdom preferred layoffs by seniority, a practice normally found in large U.S. factories or an *industrial* unionist environment, over the U.K. process of evaluating several different aspects of a worker's employment and personal situation, a practice more likely found in a *trade* unionist environment. Regarding foreign multinationals, the PLC model suggests they often invest in the United States to develop new market potential rather than to exploit existing market capabilities and thus appear less concerned with transferring practices into the U.S. market.

A Prospective View

Recent evidence suggests that the U.S. multinational is becoming increasingly less competitive in a variety of product lines.[76] Local national producers are becoming more proficient in imitating U.S. production. (Perhaps the defensive moves of the foreign multinationals are meeting with success.) The multinationals are responding in this struggle against what Raymond Vernon labels "entropy" by becoming increasingly conglomerated, and by abandoning unprofitable markets. On this latter point, Vernon notes

> ... between 1968 and 1974, 180 U.S. based multinational
> enterprises sold or liquidated 717 manufacturing sub-
> sidiaries located in foreign countries. Coming out of a total
> population of about 6,500 such subsidiaries, these with-
> drawals were not insignificant ... 449 (of these discarded)
> subsidiaries appear to have been well established in their
> networks at the time of liquidation, suggesting the
> existence of an entropic process in the multinational
> enterprise.[77]

Apparently, as existing product and process technologies become even more diffuse and further erode the competitive position of U.S. multinationals abroad, foreign subsidiary liquidations will become even more commonplace.

Accompanying these liquidations, or concurrent with the competitive pressures giving rise to them, workers at an overseas U.S. subsidiary may well face a heightened interest by local management in controlling (minimizing) labor costs. Local management may attempt to convince unions to accept less than generous employment terms and threaten that union-proposed settlements will render the operation uneconomical. Hence, the specter of loss of future employment and its intimidating inferences. Some firms analyze the costs of shutting down in one country versus those in another country. Since part of these costs are the redundancy benefits, usually legally defined, to be paid to discharged workers, a country with less onerous penalties may well enjoy more stable operations by U.S. multinationals. The social policies of one country are pitted against those of another in sort of a "beggar-thy-neighbor" environment. Policy harmonization is the only sensible response.

Liquidation tendencies may also evoke increasing political pressures for firms to maintain employment by internalizing unemployment either in terms of retraining or other manpower adjustment subsidies or in terms of some other social subsidy to keep the firm competitive. At this point it should be mentioned that several large U.S. multinationals have already voluntarily implemented policies of employment regularization, whereby manpower requirements and specific subsidiary functions are regulated so as to eliminate, or greatly reduce laying off workers. These policies involve, among other things, careful allocations of product markets among existing subsidiaries and close control over the phasing in of new products and phasing out of old.

Pressures for expanded host country control over the investment and disinvestment decisions of U.S. multinationals may likewise expand in the years ahead. As these pressures develop, the admonition by Wassily Leontief at the recent World Congress of the International Metalworkers' Federation seems particularly appropriate:

> In a complex modern society, whether capitalist or socialist, the distribution of income between groups performing different economic functions and, consequently, occupying different social positions will continue to be a major problem. So will the maintenance of sufficiently strong and steady incentives for purposeful, effective economic performance . . .[78]

Unraveling these problems as they relate to U.S. multinationals abroad and the social, cultural, and economic integrity of host societies is one of the big challenges that lies ahead.

Notes

1. John C. Shearer, "Industrial Relations of American Corporations Abroad," in *International Labor*, ed. by Solomon Barkin, *et al.* (New York: Harper and Row, Publishers, Inc., 1967), pp. 109–31. (The volume was published in the annual research series of the Industrial Relations Research Association.)

2. See, for example, on the "union side," Charles Levinson, *Capital, Inflation, and the Multinationals* (London: George Allen & Union, Ltd., 1971); Heribert Maier, "The International Free Trade Union Movement and International Corporations," in *American Labor and the Multinational Corporation,* ed. by Duane Kujawa (New York: Praeger Publishers, Inc., 1973) pp. 8–27; and Nat Weinberg, "Multinationals and Unions as Innovators and Change Agents" in *Multinationals, Unions and Labor Relations in Industrialized Countries,* ed. by Robert F. Banks and Jack Stieber (Ithaca, N.Y.: Cornell University, New York State School of Industrial and Labor Relations, Publications Division, 1977), pp. 97–119. On the "management side," see Robert Copp, "The Labor Affairs Function in a Multinational Firm," *Labor Law Journal,* August 1973, pp. 453–58; and David C. Hershfield, *The Multinational Union Faces the Multinational Company* (New York: The Conference Board, 1975).

3. See for example, Duane Kujawa, *International Labor Relations Management in the Automotive Industry: A Comparative Study of Chrysler, Ford and General Motors* (New York: Praeger Publishers, Inc., 1971); *Multinational Enterprises and Social Policy* (Geneva: International Labour Office, 1973); and G. B. J. Bomers, *Multinational Corporations and Industrial Relations: A Comparative Study of West Germany and the Netherlands* (Assen, the Netherlands: Van Gorcum & Comp. B.V., 1976).

4. Prospective views have been developed by Hans Günter and Robert W. Cox. These, however, have not dealt at the micro-level and have been concerned more with political responses to the effects of multinationals on social objectives. See Hans Günter, "Multinational Corporations and Labour: A Prospective View" (paper presented at the Third World Congress of the International Industrial Relations Association, London, September 3–7, 1973, mimeographed) and Robert W. Cox, "Labour and the Multinationals," *Foreign Affairs,* January 1976, pp. 344–65.

5. For a variation on this theme regarding the bargaining power effects of U.S. multinationals on U.S. unions, see Duane Kujawa, "Collective Bargaining and Labour Relations in Multinational Enterprise: A U.S. Public Policy Perspective," in *The Economic Effects of Multinational Corporations,* ed. by Robert G. Hawkins (Greenwich, Conn.: JAI Press, forthcoming, 1979).

6. *Multinational Enterprises and Social Policy,* p. 91.

7. Kujawa, *International Labor Relations,* pp. 181-238.

8. "Multinationals in Western Europe: The Industrial Relations Experience," (Geneva: International Labour Office, 1975, mimeo.), p. 26.

9. Hershfield, *The Multinational Union*, pp. 12–13.

10. See, for example, Kujawa, *International Labor Relations Management, passim*, and especially, pp. 212–13.

11. Robert Copp, "Labor Affairs," pp. 453–54, and Copp, "Locus of Industrial Relations Decision Making in Multinationals," in Banks and Stieber, *Multinationals*, pp. 43–48. Copp is overseas liaison manager, Labor Relations Staff, Ford Motor Company. Frank W. Angle, "The Conduct of Labor Relations in General Motors Overseas Operations," in *International Labor and the Multinational Enterprise*, ed. by Duane Kujawa (New York: Praeger Publishers, Inc., 1975), pp. 138–146. Angle is director of labor relations, General Motors Overseas Operations Division, General Motors Corporation. George B. McCullough, "Comment," in Banks and Stieber, *Multinationals*, pp. 148–152. McCullough is manager, Employee Relations, Exxon Corporation. John A. Belford, "Comment," in Banks and Stieber, *Multinationals*, pp. 135–38. Belford is vice president, Personnel and Industrial Relations, Massey–Ferguson, Ltd.

12. Bomers, *Multinational Corporations*, p. 123.

13. *Ibid.*, p. 130. (The union respondents, of course, agree quite strongly with the statement.)

14. *Ibid.*, p. 131.

15. See, for example, the experiences of the U.S. automotive multinationals in Duane Kujawa, "Transnational Industrial Relations and the Multinational Enterprise," *Journal of Business Administration*, Vol. 7, No. 1 (Fall 1975), pp. 147–53.

16. Bomers, *Multinational Corporations*, p. 120–121.

17. Leopold Bergmann, "Multinational Corporations and Labour in the EEC: A Survey of Research and Developments" (paper presented at the Research Meeting on Multinational Corporations and Labour, International Institute for Labour Studies, Geneva, December 5–7, 1973, mimeographed), p. 20.

18. Peggy B. Musgrave, *Direct Investments Abroad and the Multinationals: Effects on the United States Economy*, a report prepared for the Subcommittee on Multinational Corporations of the Committee on Foreign Relations, United States Senate (Washington, D.C.: U.S. Government Printing Office, 1975), p. 21.

19. U.S. Congress, Senate, Tariff Commission, *Implications of Multinational Firms for World Trade and Investment and for U.S. Trade and Labor: Report to the Committee on Finance of the U.S. Senate and its Subcommittee on International Trade*, 93 Cong., 1st sess., 1973, p. 291.

For a critical review of the report, see Duane Kujawa, "Book Review: Implications of Multinational Firms for World Trade and Investment and for U.S. Trade and Labor," *Law and Policy in International Business,* Vol. 6, No. 2 (1974), pp. 615–27.

20. Kujawa, *International Labor Relations Management,* pp. 79–80.

21. "Social and Labour Policies and Practices of Some European-Based Multinational Enterprises in the Metal Trades" (Geneva: International Labour Office, 1975, mimeographed), p. 8.

22. The term "production switching" is adapted from a similar concept originally presented in Bomers, *Multinational Corporations,* p. 115.

23. "Multinationals in Western Europe," pp. 24–25.

24. Hershfield, *Multinational Union,* p. 30.

25. *Ibid.,* pp. 3–4.

26. Bomers, *Multinational Corporations,* p. 117.

27. For a classic debate on this issue, see Leonard Woodcock, "Labor and Multinationals" in Banks and Stieber, *Multinationals,* pp. 21–28, and Robert Copp, "Comments," *Ibid.,* pp. 29–31. (The latter's views are felt by the present author to be more accurate than Woodcock's. Ford Motor possesses no substantive potential for production switching within Europe.)

28. Duane Kujawa, "Transnational Industrial Relations: A Collective Bargaining Prospect?" in Kujawa (ed.), *International Labor,* pp. 122–23.

29. "Multinationals in Western Europe," p. 19.

30. Kujawa, *International Labor Relations Management,* p. 228.

31. "Multinationals in Western Europe," p. 23.

32. "Chrysler U.K. Says Labor Woes Could Put Firm Out of Business," *The Wall Street Journal* (Eastern Edition), November 30, 1970, p. 8. (The warning was contained in a message from the managing director in the company's employee newspaper.)

33. "Ford Says Profit Hurt by Strikes in Britain; Blasts Industry, Again," *The Wall Street Journal* (Eastern Edition), March 16, 1971, p. 35.

34. Bomers, *Multinational Corporations,* p. 115–16.

35. "Social and Labour Policies," p. 33.

36. Bergmann, *Multinational Corporations and Labour,* p. 11.

37. Bomers, *Multinational Corporations,* p. 111.

38. Shearer, "Industrial Relations," p. 117–18.

39. *Ibid.,* pp. 116–20.

40. Weinberg, "Multinationals and Unions," p. 100. (Some participants at the conference where Weinberg presented this paper took strong

exception to this assertion. See Belford, "Comments," pp. 136–37, and McCullough, "Comments," pp. 148–49.)

41. Roger Blanpain, "Multinationals' Impact on Host Country Industrial Relations," in Banks and Stieber (eds.), *Multinationals*, p. 125.

42. A. M. Evans, "Bargaining with Multinationals: A Trade Union View," in Banks and Stieber (eds.), *Multinationals*, p. 161.

43. Bomers, *Multinational Corporations*, p. 137.

44. "Wages and Working Conditions in Multinational Enterprises," (Geneva: International Labour Office, 1975, mimeographed), pp. 40–42.

45. Everett M. Kassalow, "Multinational Corporations and Their Impact on Industrial Relations" (paper presented at the International Conference on Trends in Industrial and Labour Relations, Montreal, May 1976, mimeographed), p. 5.

46. Shearer, *Industrial Relations*, pp. 121–23.

47. Weinberg, "Multinationals and Unions," p. 104.

48. The attitudinal survey was conducted in Guatemala, Honduras, El Salvador, Nicaragua, and Costa Rica. Respondents were 59 percent from the private sector, 37 percent public sector and 4 percent "mixed." Nearly 80 percent were senior industrial relations (personnel) staff managers, *had never* worked for a U.S. multinational and *had* visited the United States at one time or another. Principal investigators were Michael Jay Jedel (Georgia State University) and Duane Kujawa (Florida International University). One might contend that U.S. firms, as profiled in the results of this survey, are viewed as superior to local companies not because of nationality, but because of size and industry differences. The survey did not seek to control respondents' perceptions along these lines. However, these latter differences, if they were a factor in the responses, could also be viewed as distinctive of U.S. multinationals (as compared to locally owned firms). The discussion of the product life cycle and industrial relations seems relevant here. Size and industry differences, therefore, are not necessarily exogenous to nationality differences.

49. U.S. Department of Commerce, *Foreign Direct Investment in the United States*, Vol. 1, *Report of the Secretary of Commerce to the Congress* (Washington, D.C.: U.S. Government Printing Office, 1976), p. 11.

50. *Ibid.*, and "U.S. Direct Investment Abroad in 1975," *Survey of Current Business*, August 1976, p. 40. Calculations done by the author.

51. The trade unions' reactions culminated in an AFL-CIO policy position opposing the "unregulated takeover of American firms." See the *AFL–CIO Platform Proposals* (Washington, D.C.: AFL–CIO, 1976), p. 31.

52. "Wary About Importing Foreign Work Rules," *Business Week,* September 29, 1973, p. 6.

53. *Ibid.,* and U.S. Congress, House of Representatives, Committee on Foreign Affairs, *Foreign Investment in the United States,* Hearings before the Subcommittee on Foreign Economic Policy, 93rd Cong., 2nd sess., 1974, *passim.*

54. Michael Jay Jedel and Duane Kujawa, "Management and Employment Practices of Foreign Direct Investors in the United States," in U.S. Department of Commerce, *Foreign Direct Investment in the United States: Report to the Congress,* Vol. 5, Appendix I (Washington, D.C.: U.S. Government Printing Office, 1976).

55. *Ibid.,* p. 37–40 and unpublished interview notes.

56. Lawrence G. Franko, *The European Multinationals* (Stanford, Conn.: Greylock Publishers, 1976), p. 187.

57. *Ibid.,* p. 192.

58. Jedel and Kujawa, "Practices," p. 61.

59. *Ibid.,* pp. 57–58.

60. Michael Jay Jedel and Duane Kujawa, "Industrial Relations Profiles of Foreign-Owned Manufacturers in the United States," in Banks and Stieber (eds.), *Multinationals,* pp. 60–61.

61. Jedel and Kujawa, "Practices," p. 39.

62. U.S. Department of Commerce, *Report of the Secretary,* p. 19.

63. Jedel and Kujawa, "Profiles," p. 59.

64. Jedel and Kujawa, "Practices," p. iii.

65. *Ibid.,* p. 30 and unpublished interview notes.

66. *Ibid.,* p. 50.

67. The purpose of this present paper is not to present the several tests and refinements attendant to the development of the PLC theory. For a more rigorous analysis, see, for example, Louis T. Wells, Jr., *The Product Life Cycle and International Trade* (Boston: Harvard Business School, Division of Research, 1972).

68. For evidence on this, see, for example, Claude L. Simpson, Jr., and Duane Kujawa, "The Export Decision Process: An Empirical Inquiry," *Journal of International Business Studies,* Vol. 5, No. 1 (Spring 1974), pp. 107–17.

69. For expansion and clarification on these latter points, see Raymond Vernon, *Storm over the Multinationals: The Real Issues* (Cambridge, Mass.: Harvard University Press, 1977). Chapter 3, "Enterprise Strategies: The Technology Factor," and Chapter 4, "Enterprise Strategies: The Drive

for Stability," are especially relevant. For data on the conglomeration tendency, see p. 65.

70. For evidence, see, for example, Franko, *European Multinationals,* pp. 162–85, and Jedel and Kujawa, "Practices", pp. 57–59.

71. For a useful framework for analyzing employment effects, see Robert G. Hawkins and Michael Jay Jedel, "U.S. Jobs and Foreign Investments," in Kujawa (ed.), *International Labor and the Multinational Enterprise,* pp. 47–93.

72. Jose de la Torre, Robert B. Stobaugh, and Piero Telesio, "U.S. Multinational Enterprises and Changes in the Skill Composition of U.S. Employment," in Kujawa (ed.), *American Labor,* pp. 127–43; Robert B. Stobaugh, *Nine Investments Abroad and Their Impact at Home* (Boston: Harvard Business School, Division of Research, 1976); and Tariff Commission, *Implications.*

73. This conclusion is developed much more fully in Kujawa, "Collective Bargaining."

74. Franko, *European Multinationals,* p. 173.

75. The reader is reminded the text here is dealing with relevant, but generalized considerations. No doubt, a variety of individual cases run counter to these considerations—and probably for a variety of reasons.

76. As reported in Vernon, *Storm,* pp. 98–101. See also, Robert B. Stobaugh, "Multinational Competition for U.S. Manufacturing Companies," *Journal of International Business Studies,* Spring/Summer 1977 (Vol. 8, No. 1), pp. 33–44.

77. *Ibid.,* p. 100.

78. Wassily Leontief, "Strategy for the 1980's: Observations on Some of the Worldwide Economic Issues of the Coming Years," (paper presented at the 24th International Metalworkers' Federation's World Congress, Munich, October 24–28, 1977, mimeographed), p. 21.

II

Industrial Conflict

Industrial Conflict

And Consensus

In the U.S. and Western Europe

Everett M. Kassalow

U NION–MANAGEMENT conflict in the United States has tended to be at a persistently higher level than in other, comparable, democratic, highly industrialized societies. This is true in spite of the apparent paradox that, whereas the American labor movement identifies itself with capitalism, labor movements in other, comparable societies tend to identify themselves as socialistic, committed in varying degrees to significant change in the class structure of their societies. One might normally expect that labor movements committed to more far-reaching social and economic change would be more conflict-prone.

It seems useful to begin by establishing that this analysis is limited to the United States and the countries of Western Europe, largely excluding the European Latin "tier" (France and Italy). For similar comparative purposes the analysis could apply to Australia and New Zealand.[1]

The discussion deals with union–management conflict in the post-World War II era. Individual worker manifestations of conflict or dissatisfaction, such as quitting, absenteeism, or sickness or injury rates are important, but the concentration here is on collective labor–management conflict, notably strikes. To the extent possible, the discussion seeks

A first version of this paper was presented to the Seminar on Comparative Labor Movements in Washington, D.C., in January 1976, and to the West European Studies Seminar of the University of Wisconsin, in March 1976.

to concentrate on industrial relations factors (rather than, for example, cultural or religious ones) in comparing U.S. strike experience to that in other countries. The principal barometer of union–management conflict in this comparison is strikes. While strikes are only one measure of conflict, in terms of union–management relations, they seem clearly to be the most significant one.

As a preliminary, it seems useful to set aside the Canadian statistics for the main line of this discussion. Industrial relations in Canada have been considerably influenced by the fact that a number of U.S. unions and many U.S.-based companies operate there and these companies and unions have often taken their direction from the United States. In some respects Canadian labor relations law is also like that in the United States, especially as regards recognition procedures that, as indicated below, have a special relation to labor conflict-producing tendencies.[2]

High Incidence of Strikes in the United States

The table on page 47 suggests that in terms of strikes, the level of industrial conflict is much higher in the United States than in the other countries under comparison here. Moreover, as indicated below, even these raw figures, in a sense, understate how much higher the incidence of strikes is in the United States than in the other countries, with the exception of Canada. As the table indicates, the rate of unionization in the United States is significantly lower than in the other countries. (Differences between countries in the measurement of union membership might account for small differences, say 2, 3, or even 4 percent; but the difference between the rate of unionization in the United States and in those other countries remains significant.) The relative time lost due to strikes in the United States would, therefore, be even higher, if one took into account the higher unionization figures in Europe. The higher the unionization figure, everything else being equal, the higher the potential time lost from strikes. Moreover, for most of continental Western Europe, collective bargaining agreements often cover entire industries and millions of workers who are not union members, with the consequence, again, that the potential for time lost from strikes is higher.

In the Federal Republic of Germany, to take one example, although total union membership, including union-style civil service associations, is in the neighborhood of 9 million, the central German Employers'

Association (BDA) estimates that collective agreements cover 18 million workers or about 90 percent of all workers. In Scandinavia, where rates of unionization are higher, the gap between union membership and agreement coverage would be much less. In many plants in Germany, the number of union members may not get much beyond 50 or 60 percent of those covered, but the *potential* time lost from strikes is much greater than the membership rate indicates because a strike call by union leaders would largely be accepted by most of the non-unionized employees. (The attempt by employers to operate in the face of an officially called strike has tended to wither in most Western European countries in the past few decades.)[3] In the United States, the wide prevalence of union

Industrial Disputes and Rates of Unionization In Selected Countries, 1967-1976

	Days Lost in Strikes (average per year)	Percentage of Unionization, 1976, of Non-agricultural Wage and Salary Earners
Australia	1,131	55
Belgium	373	70
Canada	1,906	37
Denmark	571	65
Finland	957	78
Federal Republic of Germany	56	40
Great Britain	788	51-52
Japan	244	35
Netherlands	62	39-40
Norway	67	63
Sweden	39	82-83
Switzerland	—	37
United States	1,349	28-29

Strike data are generally based on manufacturing, construction and transport industries, although local utilities are included in a few countries. Statistical collections vary from country to country; therefore, small differences may not be significant. Strikes and lockouts are included. Definitions of fully paid up membership and methods of estimating employment vary somewhat among countries; therefore, very small differences between countries should not be given too much weight. In a few countries there are agricultural workers unions with moderate size memberships, but most of these unions are quite small. (These unions are included in the membership figures.) For the United States, union membership figures include those employee associations, such as the National Education Association, that the U.S. Bureau of Labor Statistics includes in its directory of national unions and employee associations. The union membership data are generally based on 1975 and 1976 reports, as available, including some estimating by the author.
Sources: International Labour Office and *Department of Employment Gazette* (Great Britain), December 1977.

security clauses (especially the union shop), particularly in the private sector, results in a smaller number of non-union employees in an enterprise where the union is recognized, and the potential strike impact of unions is much closer to their actual size.

The table covers a period of ten years, but an additional ten years back in time would not significantly change these relativities. The differences between the United States (and Canada) and the other countries are so substantial that they cannot be seriously attributed to differences in definition of strikes or the ways in which strike statistics are collected.[4] It is also recognized that the disaggregation of strike data would be a very useful exercise and might reveal, for example, that in terms of *numbers of strikes,* as opposed to man days lost from strikes, the United States is less of a leader (because U.S. strikes have a longer duration) compared to some other countries. On the other hand, many years of observation of labor management relations in these countries, as well as conversations with labor relations practitioners, reinforces my view that the level of union–management conflict, including strikes, is significantly higher in the United States and is looked upon as a kind of norm in a way which is not generally true in these other countries.

A close examination of the statistics also seems to indicate a fairly high incidence of strikes in Australia and Great Britain. These figures, when linked with figures for Canada and the United States, suggest a kind of Anglo-American syndrome of labor conflict propensity. A number of the elements cited below that produce industrial conflict in the United States would apply in the British case (and to a lesser extent in Australia); but an examination of strike statistics for both the United States and Great Britain in the past two decades suggests a persistently higher level of conflict in the United States.

Socialism of European Unions

It is customary in comparing labor movements from country to country to characterize the European labor movements as socialist. In many European countries the labor movements are pluralistic with important Catholic and Protestant federations; but, in all the countries dealt with here, the main line of labor development has been along a socialist "axis." While it is true that this socialism seems less pronounced and traditional (certainly less revolutionary) today than before World War

II, it is a mistake to overlook this difference between American and European labor movements.

The United States is almost unique in having a labor movement which explicitly (and ideologically) accepts the capitalist system. In varying degrees almost all of the major European movements still are part of labor complexes committed to change to help bring about a socialist society. Part of this pattern of labor development [5] is the typically close association of European unions with political parties and a greater, more direct commitment to (and reliance upon) political–governmental action.[6] Practically speaking this socialism might evolve into nothing more than a more fully developed, publicly operated welfare system with a greater acceptance of economic planning than one finds in the United States; but this socialist orientation of European unions remains an essential difference and helps color and explain such domestic European union demands as codetermination and worker-sharing in capital assets, which seem so remote from U.S. union interests. The persistent anticapitalist philosophy and rhetoric of much of European labor also helps create a kind of added empathy for Third World countries, which often lean toward socialism. In a few cases, it helps explain European union attitudes toward the Soviet Union, which by this standard is regarded as a kind of degenerated and perhaps regretted socialist state. And this too is in sharp contrast with union attitudes in the United States.

Socialist labor unions of Western Europe generally operate within union–management structures that paradoxically produce fewer strikes than do the capitalism-accepting unions in the United States.[7] The very socialism of the European movements and their close relation to socialist and labor parties has led them to a greater reliance upon legislation as a means (along with union bargaining) to improve their conditions. In fact, the acceptance of the larger role of the state in regulating economic and social affairs is characteristic of all classes in European society. This reliance on legislation contrasts with the almost exclusive reliance by American unions on collective bargaining to protect and improve their wages, hours, and conditions of work. Social security legislation came after the advent of unions and is still less developed in the United States than in Europe. In recent years there has been a growing tendency for legislation to intrude on areas previously reserved for bargaining (for example, the new pension and safety laws). Legislation protecting minorities has been used to modify union–management seniority and job opportunity arrangements, often against union wishes.

Greater Reliance on Bargaining

The much greater reliance on bargaining by U.S.[8] unions makes the union–management process and the collective agreements produced by the process more complex and conflict-prone. Such critical issues as health insurance, paid vacations and paid holidays, protection against layoffs, and others are almost exclusively the province of collective bargaining in the private sector in the United States. As a consequence, the collective bargaining stakes are higher in the United States, the collective agreement is more complex, and union–management conflict is more likely.

If there were some way to measure the degree of political conflict that these same issues provoke in European parliaments, it is possible that the total level of conflict in Europe would be at least as high as it is in the United States. For example, in Sweden the enactment of a new collective bargaining law that affects managerial prerogatives over work assignments, the order of layoffs, or the introduction of new machinery— issues which would have been exclusively the subject of bargaining between particular unions and employers in the U.S.—took several years and considerable political debate and disagreement to complete. The German Federation of Trade Unions (DBG) and the German Social Democratic Party were involved for more than twenty years in a political– legislative struggle with other parties and employers to extend codetermination from the coal and steel industry to the rest of the private sector. Even the passage of new legislation on the issue in Germany in 1975 may not have ended this struggle, since the legislation is not fully satisfactory either to the DGB or to the employers. One could also cite the long debates and processes involved in legislative changes effecting paid holidays, vacations, and a standard work week in virtually every continental European country. By its nature the political–legislative process in modern, democratic societies rarely leads to open conflict and a breaking off of relations between the parties, like a union–management strike, but the conflict involved is not to be underestimated.[9]

European Union Coverage

The tendency of European unions (and correspondingly also employers) has been to build more inclusive bands of bargaining and benefit structures. Benefits, even those established through collective bargaining, are generally sought for an entire industry and have to be modest enough so that even marginal producers can afford them. This system of bargaining along a broad industry front lowers the stakes and reduces the potential resistance of many firms. By the same token it tends to elevate bargaining responsibility to the national (or regional) level, and such professional bargainers have a less immediate stake in the issues than individual employers and local union groups. In contrast, many unions in the United States tend to bargain for improved conditions in selected firms (usually the better off ones) within a given industry (at least in their leadoff efforts), and the benefits they seek cut more deeply into enterprise returns. Individual firms usually face off directly against local unions, and each concession gained by the unions is directly and almost personally felt as a loss by management negotiators. Firms react by resisting and there is a great potential for labor conflict.[10]

The very size and compass of industry- (or region-) wide bargaining, so common in Europe, may inhibit the bargaining partners from allowing negotiations to break down, since a resulting strike could embrace so many firms and workers. This is even more the case when negotiations become almost economy-wide, like the negotiating procedure for wages (and some other economic benefits) in Sweden between the Swedish Federation of Trade Unions (LO) and the Swedish Employers Confederation (SAF), which bargain simultaneously on behalf of the great mass of the privately employed manual workers.

This broad structure of bargaining tends to put much less emphasis upon union job control at the work-place level than is true of most bargaining in the United States. Job control bargaining in the United States also helps account for the higher level of employer resistance and conflict.

The upsurge in strikes in a number of European countries between 1968 and 1971 was triggered in part by a push for certain benefits and job control rights at the plant or enterprise level. To the extent that European unions concentrate more on plant and job control matters in the future, it is possible that the number of strikes may increase somewhat and come closer to the number in the United States. Employers are likely to resist such a push more than they resist industry-wide bargaining. (The rising level of strikes in Great Britain in the past two decades can be attributed, in part, to the shift of important bargaining power to the shop stewards at the plant level.) The more limited impact of plant- or enterprise-directed demands of such strikes also frees the parties, to some extent, from the central control of national unions (and employer associations). The end of full employment and the softening of labor markets during the past four years in Western Europe has, however, led to some relaxation of these union pressures at the enterprise level. In any event this tendency to concentrate upon plant and job control matters is not likely to replace the overriding importance of the wider bargaining structures prevalent in Europe.

Role of Employer Associations in Europe

Why this tendency toward wider bargaining and, related to it, the greater role of employer associations in Western Europe? To begin with, the role of collective groups (including associations of employers grouped at the national and/or industry-wide level) in economic life has traditionally been larger in Western European countries with their mercantilist backgrounds. There has traditionally been much less emphasis placed upon competition between firms, and, therefore, fewer inhibitions on cooperation between firms in particular industries, through their respective employer associations, in dealing with unions or in managing other economic and social matters. The lesser role of competition between firms may also help account for the fact that European unions seem less concerned about charges that their proposals for codetermination and other forms of worker representation on company boards would lead to a kind of union–management collusion restraining competition.

The socialist orientation of union movements has inclined them to look for wider if less favorable bands of protection and agreement structures, advancing all the workers in an industry even if this has meant only moderate bargaining gains. As an International Labour Office study of collective bargaining notes on this point, "Regarding workers and employers as the embodiment of distrust and basically conflicting forces, the unions emphasized the importance of dealing with employers through massive class action in which an industry as a whole, or a territorial subdivision of it, constituted the appropriate [bargaining] arena." [11] This contrasts with the membership only, single employer or plant-oriented bargaining thrust of most U.S. unions.

In most Western European countries, employers' associations (at least those which engage in collective bargaining) were established late in the 19th or early in the 20th century as a counterforce to the rising union movements. It is fair to say that in that era European employers were probably as resistant to unionism as their American counterparts. In several countries these associations, in an attempt to resist the unions, managed to deflect the growing union thrust from individual enterprises to an industry level.[12] This had some significant long-term effects, one of which was a lessening of the direct challenge to managerial plant prerogatives that resulted in a lowering of conflict potential.

Union Recognition

Of great importance was the subtle kind of change most of these employer associations underwent in relatively few years, as regards their attitudes toward union recognition. Indeed, associations once established to deal defensively with unions came to have a stake in seeing that comparable employers elsewhere in the country did not have the advantage of offering to workers conditions less favorable than those provided under a union–employer association contract, since this would give them a competitive edge.[13]

While it is difficult to assess, the impact of World War II, when so many West European countries were occupied by foreign powers, may have induced a greater sense of common need between employers and union leaders (often together in prison camps), leading to greater cooperation after 1945. This clearly seems to have been the case in a country like the Netherlands.

The tendency of employers' associations to accept unionism has, in most of post-World War II Europe, led to the point where, with only rare exceptions, there are no serious struggles over union recognition in middle sized or larger firms. The overwhelming majority of such firms find it expedient (in several countries just about mandatory) to join their respective employers' associations, and this usually extends union recognition automatically in their plants. Disputes over union recognition are relatively rare, and, where they have occurred, they have tended to involve the subsidiaries of U.S. multinational firms. The managers of these subsidiaries under home American influence have sometimes found it difficult to adapt to such a low key system of recognition.[14]

It is important to contrast the general European experience with the typical recognition struggle in the United States. In the United States a would-be union in a non-union plant has to win an election to gain recognition rights. To a significant extent this election has become a contest between the union and the employer. A conflict situation is the midwife of almost all new American unions.[15] It is little wonder that unions and management typically square off as adversaries from the day the union begins to organize and are subsequently fixed in adversary positions even if the union wins an election and negotiations begin.

The resistance of U.S. employers to unionizing efforts simply has no serious counterpart in Western Europe today.[16] The recent effort of the General Motors Corporation to prevent the United Automobile Workers (UAW) from gaining recognition in several of the company's new southern plants, despite the fact that the UAW already represented around 90 percent of the company's hundreds of thousands of production and maintenance workers, had a bizarre quality. I can recall conversations several years ago with some union and company officials of the Dutch Phillips electric company, where union membership was barely 25 percent of blue and white collar workers. The company never even considered not recognizing the unions at their plants.

Specialized law firms, in growing numbers, whose trademark is keeping unionism out of an employer's plant [17] (or destroying it if it comes in) are simply unknown outside of America in other democratic, industrialized countries.

This "conflictive" outlook is mirrored in the unions. I was struck by a report prepared by Sydney Roger of the University of California's Institute of Industrial Relations. He accompanied a team of San Francisco longshoremen who, with the support of the Ford Foundation, undertook a work study visit to the docks in Rotterdam, the Netherlands. In Rotterdam they found a far more cooperative work atmosphere, greater job security, and greater community respect for the Dutch longshoreman than they found in San Francisco (where automation was apparently creating considerable job insecurity). There was an outstanding contrast between the two: Dutch industrial relations were cooperative while in San Francisco an adversary relationship between workers and employers prevailed. The American unionists seemed uncomfortable with the non-adversary culture, and spoke constantly to the Dutch workers of American union members' militancy, freedom and independence, their control of the job, and above all of their fighting traditions.[18]

A group of UAW union members who visited the Saab–Scania auto-truck plant in Södertälje, Sweden, for several weeks had a similar experience. Early in their stay, the unionists raised the question of strikes and were taken aback on learning that strikes had to be approved by the Central Swedish Labor Confederation (the equivalent of the AFL–CIO) and that a labor–management disagreement would, generally, lead to a strike only when a dispute reached the national level. This troubled the UAW members who, according to the report, "see the union in a very personal way, available for discussion and action on any kind of grievance at any time." A management representative explained that a small country like Sweden could ill afford strikes, lest it strike itself "out of competition and existence." This "we-are-all-in-it-together" view contrasts, as the reporter for the trip notes, with that in the United States, "where management and unions are more often than not in an adversary relationship." This same issue "continued to arise and assumed central importance as the exchange project moved into its later stages." The resentment or irritation arising from the sense that things were over-managed with "nothing left to chance" overshadowed, in the eyes of the U.S. workers, the positive side of the favorable work environment at Saab, including the admittedly slower speed of the assembly line, the much lower noise levels, the better air, lighting, work space, etc. The American workers seemed more concerned with the role of the union vis-à-vis the employer, especially at the local level of interaction.[19]

Other Factors Limiting Union–Management Conflict

A few other factors should be listed—economic and social as against more purely industrial relations factors—which tend to limit union–management conflict in Western Europe, as compared to the United States. European economies are to a much greater degree dependent upon international trade, with as much as 20 to 30 percent (more in some cases) of the gross national product flowing through foreign trade channels, in contrast to 6 or 7 percent in the United States. An awareness of foreign competition is likely to create a sense of joint constraint on bargaining partners. It was such a sense of constraint, more than anything else, that led the steel companies and the steel union in the United States to their experimental negotiating agreement that has eliminated large-scale strikes in that industry, for the time being at least.

On the other hand, joint concern over foreign competition certainly has had no influence in reducing tension or improving cooperation between the textile unions and most of the major companies in that industry. Indeed, the U.S. textile industry may well be the only case in the modern (post-World War II) labor history of all democratic industrialized nations in which a union gained a foothold of around 25 percent of organized workers (in the late 1940s) and yet was decisively beaten back in its quest for fuller, more effective recognition in a major industry. It is a kind of special case history of conflict-prone labor relations, but as such it is also part of the now more general U.S. employer resistance to "new" unionism.[20]

Finally, the wider commitment to the welfare state and planning in Western Europe probably results in greater constraints on union–management conflict.[21] When a state is led to employ a variety of income, tax, manpower, and welfare planning policies in the pursuit of sustained full employment and economic growth, it almost inevitably is led to bring pressure upon unions and employers in pursuit of labor–management stability. The growing use in several European countries of the so-called "social-contract" device to effect income, inflation, and employment trade-offs between governments, unions, and employers is an important illustration.[22]

The fact that U.S. labor relations are conflict-prone is largely taken for granted. In a future which accords a higher priority to combating inflation or improving our competitiveness in foreign trade, or in which interest in humanizing work and improving productivity might be greater, the conflicts in U.S. labor relations might come to be viewed in a different light.

Notes

1. The substantial presence of communist controlled union movements and political parties in France and Italy made significant comparisons with those countries less useful for this discussion. For somewhat related reasons, for example, collective bargaining in France has never had the same significance as in other countries under comparison here. In Italy the influence of collective bargaining has come to the fore only in the past ten or fifteen years.

2. For an interesting critique of the conflict-prone character of the Canadian industrial relations system, see Roy J. Adams, "Conflict and the Nature of the Industrial Relations System," *The Labour Gazette* (Canada), April 1975.

3. The great furor in Great Britain over the August 1976–July 1978 strike and the occasionally rough picket line at the very modest sized Grunwick factory in North London contrasts with U.S. experience in this respect. The employer's determination to operate in the face of the strike (an extremely rare case in Britain), the rough treatment accorded would-be workers by union pickets—all this became the focus of continuing national attention in the country. (See, for example, *The Economist,* July 16, 1977, and other dates, as well as daily papers.) Similar occurrences are virtually a weekly affair in the United States.

4. For a survey of these different methods, see Malcolm Fisher, *Measurement of Labour Disputes,* (Paris: Organization for Economic Cooperation and Development, 1975). To anticipate one possible line of argument against that expressed here, on balance one would probably conclude that restrictions on strike activity in Western Europe are about equal to those in the United States. Strikes are relatively uncontrolled (by U.S. standards) in Great Britain (and to some extent in Belgium), more rigidly limited in the Netherlands, and about equally limited in Scandinavia and Germany.

5. On the reasons for the differences between U.S. and West European labor development see Everett M. Kassalow, *Trade Unions and Industrial Relations: An International Comparison* (New York: Random House, 1968) and other references cited therein. For a recent statement on why socialism did not come to the United States, see S. M. Lipset, "Socialism in America," *Dialogue,* Vol. X, No. 4, 1977.

6. Even the nonsocialist union movements usually have had a close relationship with religious types of political parties, and they have cooperated with these parties in seeking benefits via legislation.

7. British unions, with a history of lesser attachment to formal, socialist doctrine than most continental European movements, also, curiously, show a higher propensity for labor–management conflict.

8. It should be added that as regards the structure of collective bargaining—who has the right or the obligation to bargain—there are generally more detailed legislative regulations on this matter in the United States (centering on the National Labor Relations Act) than is generally the case in Western Europe.

9. For a somewhat different treatment of the political and governmental equivalents of industrial conflict, see Douglas Hibbs, Jr., "Industrial Conflict in Advanced Industrial Societies," *The American Political Science Review,* Vol. LXX, No. 4, December 1976.

10. It is admittedly hard to prove that bargaining, generally, has such different impacts in the United States and Western Europe, but this is the general perception of bargaining partners in the United States with knowledge of Western Europe.

11. International Labour Office, *Collective Bargaining in Industrialized Market Economies* (Geneva: International Labour Office, 1973), p. 94.

12. In comparing conflict in Great Britain and Scandinavia, and the greater impact of the employer associations and more centralized bargaining—and fewer strikes—in Sweden, Geoffrey K. Ingham puts great emphasis upon the higher level of industrial concentration in Sweden. See his *Strikes and Industrial Conflict: Britain and Scandinavia* (London: Macmillan, 1974). One is tempted to attribute the somewhat greater role of employer associations in countries like Sweden and Germany, and even in Belgium and the Netherlands, to the fact that they developed later than in the United States and Britain. But the case of Japan, where employer associations do not seem to have played that significant a role in industrial relations, at least not until recently, argues against too much reliance on "later development" in understanding the role of employer associations. Ingham (*Strikes and Industrial Conflict*) in the Swedish case, and Shirley Lerner, ("Factory Agreements and National Bargaining in the British Engineering Industry," *International Labour Review,* January 1964) in the British case, note the determined pre-World War I efforts of employer associations to deflect union bargaining away from the plant level.

13. Reflecting upon the lesser development of collective bargaining in France as compared to Germany, François Sellier puts great weight upon the earlier and more effective development of German employer associations. See his "Les Problemes du Travail en France: 1920–1974," paper presented to the 4th World Congress of the International Industrial Relations Association, Geneva, Switzerland, Sept. 6–10, 1975 (mimeographed).

14. See for example the experience of IBM in Sweden, Great Britain, and the Netherlands. I have dealt with this and union recognition problems of some other U.S. multinationals in a monograph prepared for the International Labour Office: *Multinationals in Western Europe: The Industrial Relations Experience* (Geneva: International Labour Organization, 1976).

15. It is curious that in the 1930s and early 1940s, the establishment of the National Labor Relations Board in the United States, and election

procedures to assist unions in gaining recognition, helped to reduce some conflict by eliminating most union recognition strikes. Changes in National Labor Relations Board policies and the basic labor law, and, of course, more effective employer resistance to union election efforts have, in the past few decades, significantly lessened the capacity of the National Labor Relations Board election process to reduce conflict.

16. From time to time the French union press contains cases of employers discharging union activists and bitter court battles over reinstatement or compensation for such employees, somewhat along American lines; but the number and extent even of these cases seems relatively low compared to the United States. In any event, as already indicated, this survey does not include France.

17. See for example, American International, Inc., Advanced Management Research, *How to Make Unions Unnecessary, Managing Without Interference,* a promotion benefit, offering a "training package" program to clients, dated February 15, 1977. An interesting description of one of these training courses is contained in the article by Dick Wilson, who attended a seminar on how to maintain non-union status, run by Executive Enterprises, Inc. (See *AFL–CIO News,* October 8, 1977.) Another organization, Management Relations, Inc., offers *Labor Unions, How to Beat Them, Out-Negotiate Them, Live with Them, Unload Them* (New York, 1975); it is offered to employers who "now have no union and want to stay union-free." (This advertisement ran in *Passages,* the magazine of Northwest Orient Airlines, January 1976.) This resistance to unionism is not limited to smaller, less known management advisory services; similar seminars are conducted by the American Management Association. See for example, "Your Employees. Are You Doing Something Wrong? Here Are Some Ways to Do it Right. The Non-union Employer Personnel Practices and Legal Obligations," brochure for meeting of American Management Association Management Center, Chicago, September 20–22, 1976. More recently the National Association of Manufacturers formed a new council to assist employers seeking a "union-free environment."

18. From Sydney Roger, "Same Cargoes, Different Cultures, The Adventures of Six San Francisco Longshoremen at Work in Rotterdam," 1976 (mimeographed).

19. *A Work Experiment, Six Americans in a Swedish Plant* (Ford Foundation, New York, 1976), esp. pp. 16–17 and 39–41. Some five weeks after their return to the United States in a post-mortem meeting

the workers were more inclined to emphasize some of the conditions which they found superior in the Saab–Scania plant.

20. The tendency for new, non-unionized, electrical and electronic plants to flourish in the South and Southwest of the United States may become a case with some parallels to the textile industry. In both instances employers have taken advantage of some shift in the location pattern of an industry. This has occurred despite the fact that there has been some cooperation between unions and employers in the electrical manufacturing industry in opposing the import of some foreign electrical goods. In contrast to textiles one might cite the men's and women's clothing industry, where unions and employers have cooperated closely in limiting foreign imports; but the structure of this industry—with many small employers—as well as the fact that the unions were very well established before the foreign import problem reached major proportions makes this a different case, and one closer to the steel industry.

21. A recent study stresses the emerging role of the Social Democratic party-controlled state in economic and social life in Sweden in the 1930s, rather than the power of the employers' association, in explaining the move to more centralized forms of bargaining and lower conflict levels. See Peter Jackson and Keith Sisson, "Employers' Confederations in Sweden and the U.S. and the Significance of Industrial Infrastructure, *British Journal of Industrial Relations,* Vol. XIV, Number 3, November 1976.

22. See Solomon Barkin, "Social Contracts in Europe," *Free Labour World,* May–June 1977.

Interpreting Industrial Conflict

The Case of Japan

Solomon B. Levine & Koji Taira

IT IS now well recognized that there are many forms of overt industrial conflict and that these forms can complement, or substitute for
each other. Work stoppage, an unqualified proxy for the *whole* of industrial conflict in many scholarly works for many years, is only one of these
forms.[1] In Japan there is little question that, since the end of the Second
World War, trends in the level and patterns of overt industrial conflict
show that considerably more such conflict has occurred than has been
popularly believed. Moreover, if one assumes, as we do, that *overt* conflict
in its diverse forms is but a small part of *latent* conflict, it becomes clear
that industrial relations in Japan have been anything but harmonious or
consensual as people have commonly believed.

Probably, the popular view has emerged from the stereotyping of
Japanese personal or social relationships as harmonious or consensual. Such
stereotyping has been a means of avoiding a serious analysis of difficult,
often intractable, problems in industrial relations. Since Japanese culture
values harmony and order, so goes the stereotype, any information on
industrial conflict in Japan, if available, should only show how orderly
and harmonious employment relationships in Japan are compared to those
in other countries where adversary confrontation and dissension are the
norms of behavior. The cause becomes the effect in the crucible of a
tautology! And no one bothers to look into the record of conflict on its

own merit. From this flows another sterotypical inference: Japanese workers and unions, well assimilated in a "harmony culture," lack militancy and aggressiveness and are easily controlled or pacified by employers and government. The causal empirical basis for such allegations is that the volume of strike activity measured, for example, by the number of man-days lost per thousand workers, has been lower in Japan than in the United States. In our view, such a simplistic conclusion is unwarranted and merely perpetuates stereotyping. Surely the stereotype should be corrected at least by comparing the volume for various forms of overt conflict over time and by taking into account the conflict experiences of industrial countries other than the United States.

Two problems must be faced, and short of overcoming them, one must admit that not too much can be said about international comparisons of industrial conflict. One is the difficulty of measuring the various forms of conflict on a national scale for all, or a majority of, countries that constitute a relevant universe for comparison; e.g., a defined type of society such as an industrialized market economy (or bourgeois capitalism). This would be a mammoth undertaking. Even the International Labour Office, which would be the most suitable agency for this kind of work, limits itself by collecting data on only a few indicators of work stoppages from member governments (as may be seen from *The Yearbook of Labour Statistics*).[2]

The paucity of efforts for measurement reflects the poverty of conceptualization about the nature of conflict, and this is the second major problem. For this, the first useful step to take is to turn to the concept of industrial relations *systems* such as that formulated by John T. Dunlop and to view conflict as an aspect or product of transactions among actors and forces that constitute a system.[3] One may criticize the Dunlopian approach, as Kenneth Walker does, for lacking dynamism and ignoring goals and motivations;[4] but in our view the framework possesses enough of the key analytical elements for evaluating industrial conflict at a national level. Dunlop puts these elements into four major groups of external and internal constraints on actors in industrial relations: markets (or budgets), technological requirements, distribution of political power in the wider society, and degree of shared ideology (or consensus) among the actors. These elements determine the output of rules that regulate or guide the behavior of actors, including manifestations of conflict among them. We begin below by evaluating the first two elements in some detail. Later we comment on aspects of the second two elements that shape the configuration of industrial conflict in Japan.

However, before we deal with the role of markets and technology, it should be pointed out that the type of society we are speaking of is one with an industrialized market economy and a constitution: first, any form of human organization is in principle an association of free and equal individuals (even the state itself is viewed as an incorporation of a certain ideal or equitable social contract among free and equal citizens); and second, the economic system is governed to a large extent by market forces, resulting in differential gains or losses for individuals.[5] The coexistence of non-economic (personal, social, and political) freedom and equality and economic inequality in such a society is a rich mine of contradictions for those analyzing the workability of this type of society. These contradictions constitute the infrastructure of latent conflict, which under certain circumstances yields overt conflict in one form or another. The common denominator of these circumstances is their unfairness.

Generally, industrial conflict is conceived of in collective or interorganizational terms, i.e., as conflict between employer or management and groups of workers informally or formally organized. It then falls in the domain of labor law. Conflict in an employment relationship can take either an individual or a collective form. The individual worker desirous of correcting an injustice has the choice either to go it alone or to work for common goals through association with other workers. If the latter is chosen, collective bargaining takes the place of individual bargaining and collective disputes may accompany collective bargaining in resolving the issues. In addition to the exchange aspects of the employment relationship, collective bargaining may also deal with its non-exchange aspects; namely, the inter-relatedness of various jobs within an enterprise. The joint product of coordinated jobs within an organization cannot always be fully imputed to the productivity of each separate job. The joint product is obviously a variable which can increase or decrease depending upon the quality of management, the type of technology, and the morale of the work force.[6] How the joint product should be shared by workers and management, and among workers, requires labor–management consultation and bargaining. Most important in the process is that the organizations, unlike the individual, develop strategies and amass resources to compel concessions from one another. Disagreements on the sharing of the joint product may give rise to overt conflict. To all this, one may finally add conflict arising from the human side of organization; i.e., how the management affects the sensibilities of workers who are jealous of safeguarding their human dignity. For example, an authoritarian management may be associated with more

Selected Dispute Statistics for Five Countries, 1974

	(1)	(2)	(3)	(4)
	Disputes Involving Work Stoppages	Workers Involved (in thousands)	Man-days Lost (in thousands)	Wage and Salary Earners (in thousands)
Japan	5,211*	3,621*	9,663*	36,100
United States	6,074	2,778	47,991	84,223
United Kingdom	2,922	1,626	14,750	21,890
France	3,381**	1,564**	3,380**	17,675
West Germany	890	250	1,051	23,375

* Excludes work stoppages lasting less than four hours.
** Excludes agriculture and public administration. However column (4) includes all wage and salary earners.

conflict than a democratic one. In this area of human conflict, workers find collective action especially useful.

We should always assume the existence of, and try to understand the nature of, *latent* conflict in employment relationships. For this, expanding the Dunlopian insights into the role of markets and technology in industrial relations systems, we offer five specific areas for observation that constitute a minimum framework for the analysis of industrial conflict. The first four of these are: (1) how efficient labor markets are in general, (2) how well firms manage their internal labor markets, (3) how satisfactory relative shares in the firm's gains are to labor and management, and (4) how enriching (or diminishing) work life in the firm is to workers compared with their aspirations for decency and dignity. In an ideal state of equilibrium under perfect competition, problems associated with these areas are optimally solved and conflict of any kind disappears except for whatever is implied by a possible disruption of the equilibrium. One may suppose that conflicts in employment relationships arise more or less in proportion to the deviation of the real economy and society from that state of equilibrium under perfect competition. From this follows our fifth, and last, area for observation with respect to industrial conflict: (5) how effective arrangements, procedures, or machineries are that are designed to identify problems arising from disequilibrium and to solve them through negotiations. Collective bargaining is a central feature of this last area for observation.

(5) Man-days Lost per 1,000 Workers [(3) ÷ (4)]	(6) Workers Involved per Dispute [(2) ÷ (1)]	(7) Workers Involved as % of All Wage and Salary Earners [(2) ÷ (4)]	(8) Man-days Lost per Worker Involved [(3) ÷ (2)]
268	695	10.0	2.7
570	456	3.3	17.6
675	554	7.4	9.1
191	461	9.0	2.2
45	282	1.1	4.2

Sources: International Labour Office, *Year Book of Labour Statistics 1975 and 1976;* and Japan, Ministry of Labor, *Year Book of Labour Statistics 1974.*

International Comparison

Work stoppage is the most popularly used indicator for the comparison of industrial conflict among various countries. To lead off the discussion of industrial conflict in Japan, one may ask how Japan stands among industrial market economies by this measure of conflict. Graphs by Douglas A. Hibbs showing man-days lost per 1,000 workers (which Hibbs calls "strike volume") give one the impression that Japan occupies a mid-point in the rank order among selected countries; i.e., Italy (highest), the United States, Canada, the United Kingdom, France, *Japan,* Norway, Sweden, and the Netherlands (lowest).[7] (We will later return in our discussion of political power distribution to how Hibbs himself explains international differences in the strike volume.)

It may be noted that among the countries selected, those well known for industrial democracy are associated with lower strike volumes than other private enterprise countries. If Japan is left out, the extent of industrial democracy may even be considered an effective explanatory variable for international differences in the strike volume. One might conclude, for example, that, since industrial democracy is less extensive in the United States than in Sweden, the strike volume is higher in the United States than in Sweden. But since Japan is also in the sample, any general explanation must also apply to it; i.e., by that token one may have to admit that industrial democracy is stronger in Japan than in the United States. Many, no doubt, would find their intuition at odds with this kind of comparison, for, whenever Japan is compared with the United States, one is regarded as representative of the hierarchical authoritarian East and the other of the egalitarian West—a rather facile "cultural" explanation for any differences between the two countries. However, on the graph Japan is not a representative of the East against the West, but is a unit of observation which can claim its weight only as much as allowed for any one of the other units. If Japan cannot represent the East in this setup, none of the rest, not even the United States, can represent the West.

The table on pages 64–65 illustrates the failure of culture to explain Japan's strike record. This table presents data on different aspects of work stoppages for five countries: the United States and Great Britain reputed to be countries of "adversary" culture, France well-known for its individualistic and well-nigh "ungovernable" citizens, Japan characterized as a country of "consensus" culture, and Germany, despite a long history of *Sozialpolitik* and the invention of *Mitbestimmung,* allegedly authoritarian in outlook and temper. Japan aside, the other countries show a predictable ranking in terms of strike volume. That Japan resembles France closely in important strike characteristics belies Japan's reputation as a country of "consensus" culture. If there is any truth in the French reputation for ungovernable individualism, the strike record suggests that the Japanese workers must be just as individualistic and ungovernable. Alternatively, the French should be just as consensual as the Japanese. Because of their preconceived stereotypical ideas about Japan, many would find the strike record of Japan difficult to accept, let alone to try to explain.

A recent Organisation for Economic Co-operation and Development (OECD) publication has a firm and correct grasp of the Japanese pattern of overt industrial conflict but advances a muted form of "cultural" explanation for it applicable only to Japan. First of all, the publication accurately notes: "Man-days lost are proportionally considerably higher than in, for instance, West Germany or Sweden but much lower than in Italy or in the U.S.A. Many of the strikes occur in connection with the Spring Labour Offensive. The duration of strikes is usually short. Lockouts are very rare." [8] This accurate description of the situation is followed by a statement which appears to reject the possibility that the nature and characteristics of Japanese industrial conflict could be attributed to factors common to industrialized societies: "But the important differences between

Japanese disputes and disputes in other countries are in kind rather than in quantity." Then, three "unusual characteristics" of Japanese disputes are mentioned.

The first characteristic is "the societal pressure towards consensus, which places a heavy responsibility on the parties to resolve a dispute by themselves and without resort to overt conflict." By itself, this statement makes almost no sense, for the publication has just pointed out that overt conflict is considerably higher in Japan than in West Germany or Sweden, from which one can only infer that "the societal pressure towards consensus" should be stronger in Germany or Sweden than in Japan and that such pressure cannot be considered an unusual characteristic of Japan.

The second "unusual characteristic" of industrial conflict in Japan is "the tendency for industrial action to be taken in a demonstrative form— as it were, to make the public aware that the workers feel that the employer has failed to do what he should to meet their needs." Examples offered of "mild forms of such action," include "taking vacations en masse, banning overtime, pasting posters or wearing head or armbands bearing their unsatisfied demands." [9] None of these is unusual in any country, perhaps with the exception of the head or armbands, in lieu of which American workers in a similar situation carry pickets or distribute leaflets. The Japanese use of demonstrative forms thus *does not differ in kind* from practices in other countries. The difference, already indicated, is in relative quantity.

The third, and final, "unusual characteristic" of Japanese industrial conflict pointed out in the OECD publication is that "the union, being mindful of the extent to which its members' interests are bound up with the enterprise, is likely to refrain from any action likely to prejudice its long-term future: thus, harassment rather than damage is what is aimed at." [10] The interdependence of the union and the firm for the common purpose of greater worker well-being is not unusual anywhere; nor is it always the case that in industrial disputes, unions in other industrialized market economies aim at damaging their employers. A high degree of overlapping loyalty to the firm and the union is also well known with respect to workers in other countries.[11]

Analysis of industrial conflict is far more complex than reliance upon a single variable such as "culture." The strike is, of course, one of many collective forms of industrial conflict. One may maintain that Japan has a rather high incidence of strikes because it has concentrated all industrial conflict in this one form, while other countries have allowed other kinds of collective conflict. One is in for a disappointment, however, because collective forms of conflict other than strikes are just as richly developed in Japan as elsewhere.[12] In official statistics, industrial disputes are first classified into two categories: (1) those not accompanied by dispute tactics but settled with the interventions of third parties and (2) those accompanied by dispute tactics. The dispute tactics in the second category are then enumerated under several headings including strikes and lock-outs. Man-days lost through work stoppages are calculated on the basis of work stoppages lasting more than half a workshift (at least four hours). In addition there are strikes lasting for a shorter time, slow-downs, sick-outs, leave-taking, and diverse demonstrative forms of conflict such as rallies, picketing, billboards, flyers, armbands, headbands, etc. The strike volume alone therefore underestimates production losses due to industrial disputes and underrates the intensity of conflict.

At this point a comment may be added on how workers choose forms of industrial dispute action. This leads us into the decision-making process within the Japanese labor union. A notable characteristic of this process in most circumstances is its intensely democratic nature—full and active involvement of an overwhelming majority of the membership, facilitated no doubt by the union's being an enterprise union. [13] In order to safeguard against the possibility of dictatorial leadership, the Japanese union stipulates that a quorum is needed before any official decision is made; however, this requirement is unimportant in most cases because actual attendance is greater than the stipulated quorum. There is active participation by the entire membership; extreme views can be shouted or voted down by more numerous voices of moderation. Japanese workers probably have a pretty good idea of the cost-effectiveness of various dispute tactics and decide on a strategy that uses the least-cost combination of tactics. For example, if an x-percent increase in pay is the target and if this can be won by announcing the demand and demonstrating worker solidarity, there is no need to resort to a long strike. Since the financial base for a typical Japanese union is largely limited to the dues of its membership, which consists of the entire work force of a firm, the union is constrained from entertaining a costly adventure in the contest of power with the firm. Management also has a pretty good idea of how the union strategy evolves. A rational calculation is possible as to whether the firm should comply with the union demand at the armband stage or at the strike stage. The interaction of the union's vector of costs and the firm's vector of damages produces great variations in the form, style, and intensity of union–management negotiation and industrial action. Since competition in the product market of unionized firms tends to be relatively oligopolistic, Japanese management probably fears the work stoppage more than management in other countries and settles readily rather than facing enormous losses.

A Rationalized Labor Market

What distinguishes Japanese practices then is not especially qualitative or cultural, but quantitative on the common spectrum of labor market types ranging from the unstructured, individualistic, and open type to the highly structured and internal type with highly unionized workers in large-scale firms. The organized sector of Japan perhaps shows a higher degree of elaboration and rationalization of the internal labor markets than the equivalent sector in other countries. This has been far more the product of labor market and skill development in rapid industrialization than of cultural preference.[14] In Japanese firms, workers can probably anticipate with a high degree of certainty and accuracy how they will advance in jobs, wages, and other amenities as a function of time spent with the firms. Thus, the restraint that the union imposes on the development of an open contest of power reflects an astute calculation based on the realities of labor market conditions. What is striking about the Japanese industrial scene is the degree of synchronization of the type and strategy of unionism with the objective conditions of the labor markets which evolve with changes in technological requirements. Once the rules of the internal labor market are so firmly established as to offer the near certainty of career prospects and to remove the question of employment security, the one remaining major bargaining issue that gives rise to occasional overt conflict is the pricing of jobs in the internal labor market. Indeed, only when the issue has been employment security for unionized workers, as in coal mining, shipping, and rail transportation, have strikes tended to be of long duration. Otherwise, until the recession precipitated by the 1973 Middle Eastern oil crisis, the rate of pay increase was for a long while the principal conflict area between labor and management. Throughout the era of rapid economic growth the division of a growing pie was not a zero-sum game; therefore conflicts over wages were always resolved in ways that made both parties better off.

This discussion of collective forms of industrial conflict must be supplemented by an observation on how individual workers cope with occasional disappointments and frustrations in particular work places. Such individual conflict finds its expression mainly in low morale, absenteeism, and turnover. The Japanese appear to be more at peace with their working conditions than workers in some other countries. But the individual expression of conflict may be substituted by the collective expression. For example, Sweden has a lower strike volume than Japan, but its absenteeism is much higher than Japan's. One could say that Swedish workers, instead of collectively expressing their dissatisfactions through strikes, individually "strike" by not showing up for work. By contrast, Japanese workers do not individually "strike" but collectively do so more frequently than Swedish workers. Although Swedish firms are well known for their innovations for the enrichment of work life, a recent study finds that many of the job enrichment schemes, thought to be Swedish specialties, have been in practice in Japan for a long time.[15] This is not surprising in view of the elaboration and rationalization of internal labor markets in Japanese firms. In addition the Allied occupation imposed fair labor standards for most working conditions (including job security) by law under the administrative supervision of the then new Ministry of Labor, labor relations commissions, and other government agencies. Wage agreements, it should be noted, are separated from general labor–management contracts.

With the passing of the economic miracle of Japan in recent years, labor–management relations in Japan have acquired new complexities fraught with greater potential conflict. Much depends upon how the aggregate demand and the conditions of specific product markets affect various firms and how the internal labor markets are adjusted. In many firms, the work force may have to be reduced further and jobs more drastically restructured than what has been effected so far. The crucial question is how these disruptions in the internal labor markets can be minimized through labor–management negotiations.

Trends of Industrial Conflict in Japan

The graph on page 71 presents some statistics used widely in discussing industrial conflict. The curve at the top shows how the denominator of strike volume (the ratio of man-days lost through work stoppages

Labor Disputes and Related Information

Japan, 1946-1976

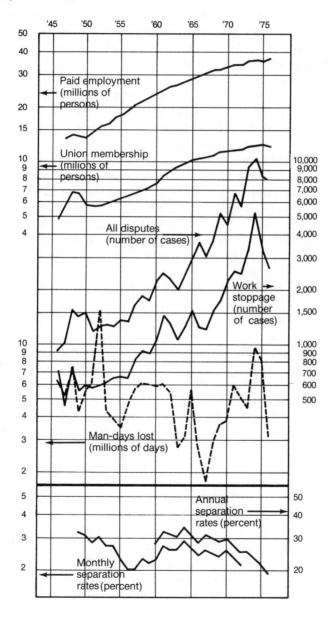

to the number of wage and salary earners) has changed over time in Japan. The numerator is shown by a widely fluctuating series farther down. Wage and salary earners increased substantially from rather fewer than 14 million persons in the late 1940s to about 37 million in the mid-1970s. The second curve from the top of the graph shows the movement of labor union membership over time. This time series roughly keeps pace with that of wage and salary earners. The ten years or so around 1950 were the most eventful period of the postwar Japanese labor movement. The sharp rise from 1945 to 1948 and a sharp fall thence to 1951 statistically summarizes the dramatic story of the resurgence and setback of the labor movement during the Allied Occupation of Japan.[16] The Japanese labor movement did not quite regain its earlier numerical strength until 1957, by which time a new style of collective bargaining had begun; i.e., *Shuntō* ("Spring Offensive")—a sort of whipsawing tactic in which initial gains made by a strong union federation in a promising industry were followed up by a schedule of demands for higher wages in other industries culminating in a wide pattern of similar settlements. The Spring Offensive is still alive and well, but its concentration on wage increases seems to be giving way to a broader-front bargaining over working conditions and economic policy at the enterprise, industry, and national levels. The labor leader who invented the Spring Offensive in the 1950s now considers its exclusively wage-oriented era to be over.[17]

The next three saw-tooth time series in the graph have to do respectively with all industrial disputes, disputes accompanied by work stoppages, and man-days lost through work stoppages. The number of disputes has clearly increased more sharply than paid employment or union membership. The ratio of the number of disputes to the number of wage and salary earners, which may be called "frequency of disputes," has therefore increased markedly over time. From this point of view, one may say that Japan has increasingly become a country of industrial conflict. In contrast, the man-days lost through disputes do not show a steady upward trend at all. Japan thus appears also to be a country of steady industrial peace. The Japanese tend to attach more weight to the increasing frequency of disputes, while foreigners watching Japan tend to pay more attention to the apparent stability of man-days lost. Both, of course, are right.

INDIVIDUAL MOBILITY AND COLLECTIVE CONFLICT

The two curves at the bottom of the graph show average monthly and average annual separation rates as indicators of labor turnover. There are apparent cycles in labor turnover, one full cycle being from the trough of 1957 to the peak of 1964 and a subsequent decrease. The behavior of labor turnover rates over time can be explained, in part, by the changing conditions of the demand for and supply of labor in the labor market.[18] But some part of labor turnover may also represent the individual expression of latent industrial conflict. It has been pointed out that a collective form of conflict may take the place of individual conflict. Interestingly, man-days lost through disputes and labor turnover rates in the graph appear to be inversely correlated with a lag of three or four years led by labor turnover. Labor turnover troughed in 1956–57, while man-days lost peaked in 1961. Labor turnover then peaked in 1964, followed by the trough of man-days lost in 1967. The relationship between labor turnover and man-days lost through disputes as revealed in the graph requires an interpretation. One possible line of interpretation is that greater commitment to the firm by workers as indicated by decreasing labor turnover may generate a greater desire on the part of workers to seek improvements within the firm without leaving it for elsewhere. In other words, committed workers do not exit, but voice dissatisfaction in search for improvements, to mimic Albert O. Hirschman's theory of loyalty.[19] To say that a stronger attachment to the firm brings with it a higher possibility of conflict sounds paradoxical at first, but becomes entirely plausible when we think of it this way: if workers can pick up the stakes and leave for better opportunities elsewhere, why should they organize themselves with a view to winning improvements from the present employer? Because Japanese workers are really so attached or loyal to their employers as to have a relationship of lifetime commitment, they must also have a high likelihood of conflict with their employers! The intensive investment by management in personnel administration in Japan is a reflection of this fundamental paradox. This interpretation renders untenable the conventional association of loyalty with peace and order in industrial relations that many foreign observers of Japan have entertained among themselves.

The formulation of the theory of lifetime commitment by James Abegglen occurred against the backdrop of sharply falling labor turnover rates during the 1950s.[20] The stabilization of employment relationships obviously was the trend of the times. But it was also during this period that the Spring Offensive was invented. It now appears to have been unfortunate that the theory of employment stabilization was not accompanied by a theory of industrial conflict. During the 1960s, a widespread

Selected Dispute Statistics and Job Separation Rates By Sector and Size of Establishment

Japan, 1974

	(1) Workers Involved in Work Stoppages (in thousands)	(2) Man-days Lost (in thousands)	(3) Paid Non- agricultural (in thousands)
Private Sector			
500 and over	2,227	6,404	9,281
300-499	149	461	1,537
100-299	201	627	3,747
30-99	68	247	5,356
1-29	8	40	11,244
unspecified	26	115	NA
total	2,679	7,894	31,165
Public Sector	942	1,769	4,350

* Manufacturing only.
** Establishments employing 5 to 29 workers.

impression of peaceful industrial relations evidently arose against the backdrop of fewer man-days lost through industrial conflict. This impression then found theoretical support in the concept of lifetime commitment of ten years earlier. This was an error in light of Hirschman's theory. Indeed, one should have looked at the increasing labor mobility during the same period as a concurrent, and intimately related, phenomenon, making a set with the industrial peace of the period. When individual mobility was a feasible exit from unsatisfactory conditions of employment, workers had a reduced need for organized conflict with their employers, who, reading the signs of the times, were also disposed toward readier concessions to worker demands. The spread of *Shuntō* indicated that the unions could mobilize worker dissatisfaction within these enterprises.

Another illustration of the relationship between individual mobility and collective conflict is the inverse correlation between job separation rates and man-days lost per 1,000 workers through industrial disputes, as presented in the table above. Generally, the separation rates are higher and man-days lost fewer in smaller establishments than in large, even though

(4) Man-days Lost per 1,000 Workers [(2) ÷ (3)]	(5) Workers Involved as % of All Workers [(1) ÷ (3)]	(6) Man-days Lost per Worker Involved [(2) ÷ (1)]	(7) Annual Job Separation Rate* (percentage)	(8) Union Members as % of All Workers
690	24.0	2.9	17.9	63.6
300	9.6	3.1	} 23.8	31.5
167	5.4	3.1		
46	1.3	3.6	25.9	9.0
4	0.1	5.0	23.2**	3.4
NA	NA	NA	NA	NA
253	8.6	2.9	22.2	28.0
407	21.7	1.9	unavailable	76.8

Sources: Japan, Ministry of Labor: *Year Book of Labour Statistics, 1974* and *Rōdō hakusho* ("White Paper on Labour"), 1976.

on the average strikes are longer in duration in the small compared to the large. At the same time, it can be seen from the table that workers in larger private establishments and in the public sector are far more extensively organized than those in small. More than 500 man-days lost per 1,000 workers in larger establishments as shown in the table exceeds the record of most years of the United States since 1950. Furthermore, unlike the experience in the United States, the rate of participation in strike activities (as measured by the ratio of strikers to all workers) is rather high: 10 percent (see pages 64–65). This table certainly shows that strikes were astonishingly widespread in larger establishments in 1974. And yet, these are the workers with whom many associate the label lifetime commitment. These workers, who supposedly enjoy greater job security, higher wages and benefits, and better working conditions than workers in smaller enterprises, are strongly attached to their firms *and therefore* always ready to pick quarrels with management regarding how the working conditions can be improved. This is even more so in the public sector where the *right* to strike has been denied since the late 1940s.

PUBLIC SENSITIVITY

In addition, if we take into account disputes not accompanied by strikes or lockouts, the participation rate among the workers of larger establishments rises significantly above 25 percent and may be as high as 50 percent. That more than a quarter or possibly one-half of the workers in a well established sector of the economy were engaged in one form or another of industrial conflict in a year would not fail to catch the attention of the press and surprise the public. One would also notice that a typical strike is short. Presumably, the number of workers on strike rather than the length of the strike is a sufficient demonstration of organized strength. Again, which aspect of the conflict situation should be emphasized is a problem, but the Japanese public itself would emphasize the frequency and spread of strikes and tend to see behind all this the specter of a general strike, semblances of which have been threatened off and on seriously enough to worry the government, employers, and general public.

How sensitive the public is to industrial conflict is difficult to measure, but must influence the evolution of public policy. Economists would perhaps ask whether industrial conflict costs society anything at all. Industrial conflict may often create public inconveniences (even the overworked National Railroad workers' "work to the rule" campaign, which occurs almost every year, angers at least some people enough so that they smash trains and railroad stations), but the hard core of respectable measurability must be the cost of man-days lost through strikes. That a thousand workers lost 300 man-days of work among them per year only means the equivalent of one worker out of work for the full year, one-tenth of one percent of all workers. This appears to be too small an addition to the rate of unemployment to bother about, especially compared to absenteeism due to illness or accidents. Nevertheless, the public still may be sensitive to these work stoppages.

At the risk of over-elaboration, what is involved is the relative quantity; i.e., the number of man-days lost through disputes *relative to* the rate of unemployment a society is used to. These figures are readily available in internationally comparable statistical sources such as the *Yearbook of Labor Statistics* of the International Labour Office. For 1973 (the year preceding the full impact of the oil crisis that descended on the world in October), the ratio of man-days lost per 1,000 workers to the rate of unemployment for a few countries is as follows: Japan, 10.0; the

United States, 8.1; the United Kingdom, 11.4; France 10.1; Germany, 2.5. The numbers refer to man-days lost through industrial disputes per unemployed worker. If these numbers indicate the impact of strikes on public awareness of the problem, one would say that the Japanese should be more aware of the cost of industrial disputes than the Americans. In other words, the Japanese should be thinking that whatever losses of work they are suffering as a consequence of industrial disputes are disastrous, while the Americans with twice as many man-days lost for a similar cause as the Japanese would not mind the problem as much.

One might also argue that the accustomed level of employment security is the basis for the greater sensitivity on the part of the Japanese. The United Kingdom comes out the worst in this calculation because its rate of unemployment is lower and its man-days lost through disputes higher than in the United States. The unusually bad image of the state of industrial relations in the United Kingdom may be based on this ratio. As might have been expected, France is just as good or bad as Japan. West Germany has very little to worry about regarding industrial peace or conflict. This smooth sailing in industrial relations is another reason the Japanese are so sensitive about the amount of industrial conflict in their country. Aside from the United States, the Japanese compare themselves more consciously with Germany than with any other country. Indeed, the Japanese feel that until they attain the German level of stability and order, they can hardly call their actual state of industrial relations harmonious or orderly.

However, there is one small consolation in the Japanese pattern of industrial conflict, especially in the relationship between all disputes and those accompanying work stoppages, as illustrated in the graph on page 71. The considerable, and widening, gap between all disputes and those only accompanied by work stoppages implies that the Japanese unions, managements, and public authorities have devised dispute tactics to contain conflict without letting it develop into a strike or lockout. As may be seen from the graph, the disputes accompanying work stoppages decreased between 1946 and 1967, from 77 percent to 40 percent of all disputes, the latter being an all-time low before 1976. During the 1950s, disputes were generally fewer than before or after, and more than half of all disputes were kept from developing into strikes or lockouts. This was due in part to the then newly imposed legal restrictions on union activity, especially in the public sector. There was an upsurge of work stoppages in the early 1960s (a high of 57 percent of all disputes recorded for 1962), after which, especially following 1965, there were substantial relative decreases in disputes involving work stoppages, or relative increases in disputes resolved without the resort to work stoppages. There was another upsurge in work stoppages in 1974, but this was apparently short-lived. An all-time low for work stoppages as a percentage of all disputes since 1949 was the 34 percent of 1976. These ups and downs, of course, in part reflect major structural shifts in the Japanese economy, such as the decline in the strike-prone coal mining industry in the 1960s and the expansion of transportation and communication systems largely in the public sector after the mid-1960s.

These figures show that, although industrial conflict has become extensive and frequent lately, it has been increasingly expressed through forms other than those leading to work stoppages. They further imply that dispute tactics have multiplied in kind and that unions and managements have become sophisticated in maneuvers and counter-maneuvers to steer the "game" away from a deadlock as much as possible.[21] In this sense, industrial conflict in Japan seems to have become somewhat more "civilized" lately (to borrow a word from a work on industrial relations in the U.S. automobile industry).[22] The *Shuntō* strategy is a prime example of this trend.

Another source of consolation, though not shown in the graph, is that there has not been much change in the indicators of individual conflict, e.g., low worker morale, high absenteeism, featherbedding, informal worker control over the pace of work, etc. Data are sparse on these aspects of industrial relations and do not come in the form of handy time series. The average rate of absence from work (measured by days not attended for reasons of sickness, accident, annual leave, and other often legitimate reasons, as a percentage of regular working days) was about 2 percent in 1973.[23] According to a study of four factories, the rate of absence not accounted for by vacations and leaves is but 1 or 2 percent.[24] Even so, there is a general feeling among the observers of Japan that the Japanese work ethic has eroded considerably in recent years.[25] The hours worked have also declined. The average, at least among large enterprises, is an eight-hour work day and a five-day work week supplemented by annual leave and seasonal vacations. The regular hours worked per worker per month in Japanese manufacturing decreased from 182 hours in 1950 to 165 hours in 1973. These indicators should be interpreted with caution. One must first allow for the effect that rising real income has on the meaning of work to the worker before one starts crediting the apparent increase in a preference for leisure to job dissatisfaction or industrial conflict.

Macro-Forces: Political Power and Social Consensus

However one evaluates the state of industrial conflict in Japan, one must at least recognize that the present state is a consequence of great efforts often involving painful decisions and adaptations on all sides— employers, workers, unions, government, and the general public. The Japanese system has not been entirely free of test cases so bitterly fought that they came close to barbarous violence. These test cases more or less determined the perimeters of industrial conflict. The general public, for example, would not tolerate the lawlessness that violent industrial disputes might create. The government, and presumably the public, would not tolerate a nationwide general strike (an example set by General Mac-Arthur in 1947). The perimeter on this flank was further tightened by legally banning strikes by civil servants and public enterprise workers beginning in 1947. Employers and the courts would not tolerate worker takeovers of the work place, having learned a bitter lesson from earlier "production control" by workers, although the sit-in remains a common dispute tactic. Unions naturally would not tolerate anything that even remotely intimated "unfair labor practices." All of these limits to tolerance are, of course, under constant pressure from many sources in Japan, and infringements and retaliations on the perimeter are daily shaping the evolution of the industrial relations system.

The source of these pressures on the industrial relations system are mainly government policy, on the one hand, and, on the other hand, the degree of consensus among the industrial relations actors themselves as they react to the wider social context. It is to these two macro-forces which we now turn in concluding our analysis of industrial conflict in postwar Japan. Admittedly, these forces deserve fuller analysis than we give here, but their importance is probably equal to, if not greater than, the influence of markets and technology.

Hibbs's study of the relationship between strike volume and political structure and policy has been one of the few serious systematic attempts in this direction in recent years.[26] According to his analysis, the huge percentage rise in Japan's average strike volume (more than 400 percent from the interwar period to the postwar period) can be attributed to the almost complete dominance of conservative political parties and to their failure to develop labor-oriented welfare programs in the allocation of national income. In our view, while we would not quarrel with this general observation, it says too little about the actual political process over the past thirty years in Japan. Given the repression of organized labor throughout the 1920s and 1930s, one would expect that with the far-reaching, near revolutionary labor and other reforms under the Allied Occupation—including representatives of the left in the legislature—there should have been even a larger than actual increase in the volume of strikes. In absolute volume by standardized measures, strikes have reached only the mid-position among the industrialized market economies. Some further explanation of the political process in the postwar period is needed.

In examining how political systems work, there is the conventional choice of applying either the notion of "democratic pluralism" or of a "ruling class." In the former, groups in both public and private spheres are likely to be in conflict, but the conflict is mediated and resolved by a "neutral" government, to which each interest group has equal access and which fashions a policy outcome that reflects the relative voting strengths of the interests actively seeking favor. In the "ruling class" approach, a relatively small elite commands all the resources and ignores or represses any challenge to its power and authority. With regard to industrial conflict, these competing concepts have very different outcomes. In the "democratic pluralism" model, one would expect the government to make and enforce rules about relations between labor and management that would channel their behavior into mutually acceptable, largely peaceful, patterns. In the early stages before these rules are adopted and institutionalized, one could expect a high degree of overt conflict among the industrial actors; but once the rules are established, the frequency and intensity of overt industrial conflict would taper down and level off—the "maturing" process and "the withering away of the strike." [27] In the "ruling class" model, overt conflict would be suppressed, if necessary by military force, giving rise in all likelihood to class struggle on the part of workers and other alienated groups. Industrial conflict, in this scenario, would at first remain low and then would rise to a crescendo ending with the complete defeat of one class or the other.

Postwar Japan does not appear to fit either of these political models. Japanese industrial conflict in the postwar period, with and without strike activity, has followed neither pattern, but has exhibited ups and downs and the substitution of one form of conflict for another in rough alternating sequence. This suggests that the Japanese political system lies somewhere between the "democratic pluralism" and "ruling class" types (and, in this sense, may be similar to most other political systems with industrialized market economies). Some analysts have labeled this model as "establishment orchestration of econopolitical life." [28] In this depiction, pluralism holds only in minor matters (of which government policy toward less critical industrial relations issues may be a part), but, in major issues (such as basic economic and political arrangements), power holders write the score and call the tune and lead the public by engaging in a wide variety of reassuring symbolic actions to gain wide support or acquiescence for the status quo. In this conceptualization, admittedly too briefly stated here, the general public for the most part is quiescent toward political policy over long periods of time, receiving constant psychological assurances that what is done is in their best interest. Outbursts of protest are likely to occur only as various groups see and experience sharp deprivations in their expectations either absolutely or in relation to other groups. Industrial conflict, then, becomes part and parcel of social conflict in general, and will rise and fall as social conflict itself rises and falls.

It is of interest to note in this connection that the recent climb in industrial conflict in Japan since the late 1960s has occurred within the context of a rapid growth of formal and informal protest movements led by citizen or resident groups against rapidly growing pollution, inflation, urban congestion, and the like. In the drive to achieve "production first" goals, conservative government policies had neglected, by the standards of other industrialized market economies, a wide range of social welfare improvements (housing, social security, urban safety, education, recreational facilities, etc.).[29] These problems had been long in the making, from the time Japan's "miraculous" industrial growth began, but were disguised, as material living standards and personal incomes for almost everyone steadily rose from an extremely low level. It took almost two decades for the social costs of the production first policy to be widely perceived and expressed overtly. With conservative government promises (and some legal enactments) to achieve a better quality of life, it now appears that the Japanese, reassured once again, will slip back into a more quiescent state, at least for a while. This is illustrated in the drop of man-days lost from work stoppage in 1975 and 1976 when the government promised and successfully delivered a cut in the inflation rate, an income tax rebate, and wage subsidies for firms to maintain employment.

Until recently there have been few serious checks on the political dominance of the conservatives in Japan.[30] Propped up initially by Allied Occupation approval, they have remained in power for thirty years. At the same time, the opposition—socialists, communists, and other left-of-center parties with which the national labor confederations have been affiliated—has remained highly divided and unable to challenge even the malapportioned representation in the national Diet that heavily favors maintenance in power of the well financed and efficiently organized factions of Liberal Democrats despite a steady slippage in their popular support at the polls. The sharp split among the opposition parties provides no realistic alternative to conservative government policy even for those who have been sorely disenchanted with production first. Opposition parties appear to be content to play only the role of opposition without bidding seriously for dominance. Even if the Liberal Democrats lose their majority in the Diet—and they are now perilously close to that point—they are likely to continue as the leading minority in a coalition government for the indefinite future.[31] Of course, should there be a sharp deterioration in Japanese economic conditions, occasioned, for example, by rapid changes in international relationships unfavorable to Japan, there could be dramatic political and social upheavals with a considerable upturn in overt industrial conflict.

In spite of the fact that the political system has by and large induced a state of quiescence that constrains the industrial relations actors, conflict among them has been legitimized as part of a general revolution in social values throughout Japan in the postwar period. The reforms installed by the Allied Occupation set the stage for this legitimization of conflict in Japanese industrial relations with the enactment of the Trade Union Law, the Labor Relations Adjustment Law, the Labor Standards Law, and the new constitution between December 1945 and April 1947—a period perhaps even more revolutionary than the New Deal was in the United States.[32] Organized labor, which rose so rapidly from zero to six million members, was eager to test out its new rights and to discover what limits there were to exercising the strike and other overt forms of dispute. The decade up to 1955 was just such a test.[33] While neither the Allied Occupation nor the government was to tolerate an unbridled use of the strike or other disruptive action for long (especially after occupation policy shifted from democratizing and pacifying to industrializing Japan so it could become a major ally in the East–West cold war), nonetheless the reforms left a strong acceptance of conflict as a legitimate form of behavior in industry. When the government in rapid succession prohibited general strikes; put legal curbs on labor's right to organize, to bargain, and to strike in the public sector; tightened legal requirements for bona fide union qualifications; enacted a cooling-off period in "national emergency" disputes; purged radical labor leaders; curtailed disputes in coal mining and electric power; and put administrative limitations on picketing and other dispute actions—its so-called "reverse course" ran against the widely held demand for equity that had been generated throughout Japanese society. While the conservative government justified its "reverse course" as in the interests of public welfare, those affected by the restrictions have smarted from them and continued to turn to protest. The legal right to engage in disputes was heavily protected in the private sector; as a result, there was a deep sense of inequity in the public sector. The most dramatic instance of this was seen in the imbroglio over ratification of the International Labour Organization Convention 87 on the right to organize, which aroused public attention for several years.[34] Denial of the right to strike of public employees in government-owned enterprises, especially the National Railways, the postal system, and the telephone and telegraph corporation, has continued to be a major reason for unions in the public sector to call strikes to win the right to strike. Some would argue that restoring the right to strike to public sector workers, at least in a limited form, would actually reduce work stoppages in that sector.

Legitimization of conflict in postwar Japan has been reinforced by continuous resort to overt actions, often symbolic. Short walkouts and other demonstrations serve in part as constant reminders to management, government, and the general public that organized labor possesses the right, gained after decades of repression, to make demands for the redress of widely felt grievances. Even if there were no specific issues to negotiate, one would suspect that the Japanese unions would still engage in such demonstrations for the purpose of maintaining morale and solidarity. No doubt, this is an important ritualistic aspect of *Shuntō* itself in serving as a highly visible gesture to the entire population all at once of the right of protest possessed by labor. In this function, the waves of scheduled walkouts in the spring struggle are in a sense final steps in the year-long maneuvering and negotiations between management and unions (as well as annual budget making by the government), rather than mere signals of breakdowns in collective bargaining. The labor leadership thus utilizes its own set of symbols to reassure its members of organized labor's role.

As we noted earlier, conflict (and hence a demand for fairness) as a major strand of Japanese social values runs counter to the popular image of Japan as an ordered and peaceful society. It has perhaps been to the political and economic advantage of the establishment to stress almost exclusively the popular image, especially to convey abroad an impression of how smoothly and harmoniously Japan has been able to recover from wartime devastation, rising to build the second largest economy of the world and to become a dependable ally of the West. However, we would argue that industrial conflict has become as much a part of the Japanese ethos as it has in other industrialized market economies. The idea that Japan stands apart as a unique case of harmony and consensus compared to other nations was simply dreamed up. If an objective of the political establishment is to achieve a low level of overt conflict in industrialized Japan, it must increasingly cater to a demand for equity. Otherwise, we can expect to see new peaks (as well as valleys) in the indices of industrial conflict in Japan.

One conceivable development helpful to a peaceful management of change may be the full formal participation of labor in it. The long practiced labor–management consultation at the company level on managerial aspects of working conditions involving technological change, work rules and worker grievances, work-force training and deployment, welfare facilities, utilization of leisure, and so on may be a prelude to formal industrial democracy at the industry or national level. The fusion of union leadership with management through promotions within a firm is a sort of participation, though delayed, of labor in management. Furthermore, the Japanese style of decision making, which encourages lower-level initiative and the participation of all parties likely to be affected, has made work life in the Japanese firm highly egalitarian. The formalization of industrial democracy and work group autonomy that already exists may have the effect of raising the status of labor to full-fledged partnership with management and may prevent potential conflict from becoming overt because of suspicion or misunderstanding.

Notes

1. Clark Kerr said it all way back in 1954. Speaking of "variety" of industrial conflict, he notes: "Industrial conflict has more than one aspect, for the manifestation of hostility is confined to no single outlet. Its means of expression are as unlimited as the ingenuity of man. The strike is the most common and most visible expression. But conflict with the employer may also take the form of peaceful bargaining and grievance handling, of boycotts, of political action, of restriction of output, of sabotage, of absenteeism, or of personnel turnover. Several of these forms . . . may take place on an individual as well as on an organized basis and constitute alternatives to collective action. Even the strike itself is of many varieties. . . ." He then illustrates these varieties and, in the next paragraph, cites specific instances which show that "various kinds of actions are alternatives to one another." He also indicates that the political framework he has in mind for the discussion of industrial conflict is "a democratic nation, where the coercive power of the state against individuals and groups is limited." These two paragraphs under the heading of "variety" adequately formulate the theme of the present paper. See "Industrial Conflict and Its Mediation," reprinted in Clark Kerr, *Labor and Management in Industrial Society* (New York: Doubleday, 1964), pp. 170–171. For a more recent discussion, see Don J. Turkington, *The Forms of Industrial Conflict* (Occasional Papers in Industrial Relations No. 18) (Wellington, New Zealand: Victoria University of Wellington, 1976).

2. For example, see Malcolm Fisher, *Measurement of Labour Disputes and Their Economic Effects* (Paris: Organisation for Economic Co-operation and Development, 1973).

3. John T. Dunlop, *Industrial Relations Systems* (New York: Holt, 1958).

4. Kenneth Walker, "Toward a Useful General and Comparative Theory of Industrial Relations," paper presented at IV World Congress of the International Industrial Relations Association, Geneva, Switzerland, September 1976.

5. The relationships between personal, social, and political freedom and equality of individuals on the one hand and economic inequalities among them on the other give rise to the question of justice as fairness. See John Rawls, *A Theory of Justice* (Cambridge, Massachusetts: Belknap Press of Harvard University Press, 1971).

6. Solomon B. Levine and Koji Taira, "Labor Markets, Trade Unions and Social Justice: Japanese Failures?" *Japanese Economic Studies* 5 (Spring, 1977): 66–95.

7. Douglas A. Hibbs, Jr., "Industrial Conflict in Advanced Industrial Societies," *American Political Science Review* 70 (December 1976): 1033–1058.

8. *The Development of Industrial Relations Systems: Some Implications of Japanese Experience* (Paris: Organisation for Economic Cooperation and Development, 1977), p. 25.

9. *Ibid.*, pp. 25–26.

10. *Ibid.*, p. 26.

11. Kunio Odaka, *Toward Industrial Democracy* (Cambridge, Massachusetts: Harvard University Press, 1975), especially Chapter 4.

12. This may be seen by comparing the inventory of conflict tactics made by Turkington, "The Forms of Industrial Conflict," and a similar enumeration for Japan by Tadashi Hanami in his *Rōdō sōgi: rōshi kankei ni miru Nihonteki fūdo* ("Labor Disputes: Industrial Relations in the Japanese Climate") (Tokyo: Nihon Keizai Shimbunsha, 1972). An English language version of the latter is *Labor Relations in Japan Today* (Tokyo: Kodansha International, Ltd., 1979).

13. Taishiro Shirai, "Decision-Making in Japanese Labor Unions," in Ezra F. Vogel, ed., *Modern Japanese Organization and Decision-Making* (Berkeley and Los Angeles, California: University of California Press, 1975), pp. 167–184. Some observers have reported somewhat less democratic procedures in the case of Japanese unions. See Robert E. Cole, *Japanese Blue Collar: The Changing Tradition* (Berkeley, California: University of California Press, 1971) and R. C. Clarke, "Union–Management Conflict in a Japanese Company," in W. G. Beasley, ed., *Modern Japan: Aspects of History, Literature, and Society* (London: George Allen & Unwin, Ltd., 1975), pp. 209–226.

14. Levine and Taira ("Labor Markets, Trade Unions, and Social Justice"). See also Koji Taira, "Labor Markets, Unions, and Employers in Inter-War Japan," in Adolf Sturmthal and James G. Scoville, eds., *The International Labor Movement in Transition: Essays on Africa, Asia, Europe and South America* (Urbana, Illinois: University of Illinois Press, 1973), pp. 149–177.

15. Kazutoshi Koshiro, "Humane Organization of Work in the Plants: Production Techniques and the Organization of Work in Japanese Factories," paper presented at the Sixth Japanese–German Cultural Exchange

Seminar, October 3–6, 1977, Dusseldorf, Germany. See also Kazuo Koike, "Who Regulates On-The-Job Problems," in *Industrialization and Manpower Policy in Asian Countries* (Tokyo: The Japan Institute of Labour, 1973), pp. 243–256.

16. Solomon B. Levine, *Industrial Relations in Postwar Japan* (Urbana, Illinois: University of Illinois Press, 1958) and Wakao Fujita, "Labor Disputes," in K. Okochi, B. Karsh, and S. B. Levine, eds., *Workers and Employers in Japan* (Princeton, New Jersey and Tokyo: Princeton University Press and University of Tokyo Press, 1973), Chapter 9. Fujita's time series stop at 1964.

17. Kaoru Ota, *Shuntō no shūen* ("The End of the Spring Offensive") (Tokyo: Chūō Keizaisha, 1975).

18. Koji Taira, *Economic Development and the Labor Market in Japan* (New York: Columbia University Press, 1970), Chapter 7.

19. Albert O. Hirschman, *Exit, Voice, and Loyalty* (Cambridge, Massachusetts: Harvard University Press, 1970).

20. James G. Abegglen, *The Japanese Factory* (New York: Free Press, 1958).

21. Hanami, *Rōdō sōgi*. A trend away from the strike after 1955 is also discussed by Fujita ("Labor Disputes").

22. William Serrin, *The Company and the Union: The "Civilized Relationship" of the General Motors Corporation and the United Automobile Workers* (New York: Knopf, 1973). Akira Takanashi, on the basis of the relationship between all disputes and those accompanying work stoppages, also argues for an increasing stabilization of Japanese industrial relations. Takanashi, "Rōdō sōgi ni miru roshi kankei no anteido" ("The Degree of Stabilization of Labor–Management Relations From the Perspective of Labor Disputes"), *Tōyō Keizai Shinpō*, 3851 (January 1975): 112–119. In this article, all the time series used stop at 1973. However, as the graph on page 71 indicates, there was a flare-up of labor disputes in 1974 to an all-time high.

23. *Katsuyō Rōdō Tōkei* ("Practical Labor Statistics") (Tokyo: Nihon Seisansei Hombu, 1975), p. 125.

24. Koshiro, "Humane Organization of Work in the Plants."

25. Odaka, *Toward Industrial Democracy*, pp. 128–154. For further discussion of this point, see John W. Bennett and Solomon B. Levine, "Industrialization and Social Deprivation: Welfare, Environment, and the Postindustrial Society in Japan," in Hugh Patrick, ed., with the assistance of Larry Meissner, *Japanese Industrialization and Its Social Consequences*

(Berkeley, California: University of California Press, 1976), pp. 439–492.

26. Hibbs, "Industrial Conflict in Advanced Industrial Countries," and "Long-run Trends in Strike Activity in Comparative Perspective," Center for International Studies, Massachusetts Institute of Technology, Cambridge, Massachusetts, August 1976, mimeo.

27. See Arthur M. Ross and Paul T. Hartman, *Changing Patterns of Industrial Conflict* (New York: Wiley, 1960).

28. Kenneth M. Dolbeare and Murray I. Edelman, *American Politics: Policies, Power and Change,* 3rd. ed., (Lexington, Massachusetts: D. C. Heath and Co., 1977), pp. 437–454.

29. Bennett and Levine, "Industrialization and Social Deprivation." The rise in industrial disputes and work stoppages is also notable at the time of a general protest against the U.S.–Japan Security Treaty in 1960–61, and during an outbreak of student riots from 1968 to 1970.

30. Our view of the Japanese political process diverges from that of other close observers who hold that pluralism characterizes government economic decision making in postwar Japan. For a recent example of the pluralist interpretation, see Hugh Patrick and Henry Rosovsky, eds., *Asia's New Giant: How the Japanese Economy Works* (Washington, D.C.: The Brookings Institution, 1976), especially the editors' chapter, "Japan's Economic Performance: An Overview," pp. 51–52, and the chapter by Philip H. Trezise, with the collaboration of Yukio Suzuki, "Politics, Government, and Economic Growth in Japan," pp. 753–812.

31. Nathaniel B. Thayer, "Elections, Coalition, Prime Ministers in Japan, 1976–1985," in Lewis Austin, ed., with the assistance of Adrianne Suddard and Nancy Remington, *Japan: The Paradox of Progress* (New Haven: Yale University Press, 1976), pp. 11–30.

32. Toru Ariizumi, "The Legal Framework: Past and Present," in Okochi, Karsh, and Levine, *Workers and Employers in Japan,* p. 131.

33. *Ibid.,* p. 90.

34. For a full discussion of this episode, see Ehud Harari, *The Politics of Labor Legislation in Japan: National-Inter-national Interaction* (Berkeley, California: University of California Press, 1973). It should be noted that most stoppages in Japan coordinated by national labor organizations, especially Sōhyō, usually are aimed at political as well as industrial issues.

Industrial Relations

And Industrial Conflict

The Case of Sweden

Walter Korpi

I N industrial relations, the study of industrial conflict has been a central topic; some have even described it as an obsession. But the discipline of industrial relations has been largely non-theoretical, focussing on various aspects of the practical workings of industrial relations in different countries. A scanning of the journals of industrial relations from the past decade in the United States and Britain, for instance, yields few theoretical articles. An empirically oriented, fact-gathering approach has much to commend for itself and is, in my judgement, more fruitful than the opposite position—the theorist in his armchair. But for an applied discipline, it is, however, worthwhile to remember Max Weber's dictum that there is nothing as practical as a good theory. It is also necessary to remember that applied research, which may appear devoid of theories, is never value-free nor unbiased and is also generally guided by implicit theoretical notions and assumptions. Since these theoretical starting points and guidelines are not made explicit, however, the cross-fertilization between facts and theory is rendered difficult.

The purpose of this essay is to contribute to the interplay between facts and theory in the study of industrial conflict. It will do so by the case-study approach, focussing on Sweden as a test case. I will begin by delineating the theoretical themes in post-war social science that have played an important role in the analysis of industrial conflict, analyze to what extent these theoretical themes can explain the long-run variation in industrial conflict in Sweden, and conclude with a discussion of alternative approaches to the study of industrial conflict.

Industrial Relations Theory and Industrial Conflict

In the post-war period, academic thinking on industrial conflict has been clearly set within a school of thought that has dominated the social sciences in this period and that can be loosely referred to as "pluralistic industrialism." This body of thought has been developed by writers coming from different backgrounds, such as Raymond Aron, Daniel Bell, Robert A. Dahl, John Kenneth Galbraith, Ralf Dahrendorf, John T. Dunlop, Clark Kerr, Robert Dubin, and Wilbert E. Moore. (See the list of references at the conclusion of this essay.) In spite of individual overtones, these writers have shared many basic perspectives and assumptions.

Central to this body of thought is the view that industrial technology is the prime mover of societal development. The pattern of economic organization of production is only accorded a secondary role in this context. The key importance of technology is derived from the assumption that industrialism requires a specific type of labor force, characterized, for instance, by relatively high levels of education and technical skills. Thereby, a "logic of industrialization" is imposed on industrializing societies. With the development of industrialism, the pattern of social stratification in a society is assumed to change, primarily through an expansion of the middle strata. Geographical and social mobility is assumed to increase and to help to blur class lines. This body of thought has a markedly evolutionary cast. With the development of industrialism, societies in the east as well as in the west are seen as moving along converging paths. The United States, being the technologically most advanced society, is often seen as showing the path for other nations.

In this body of thought, the increasingly complex occupational structure of industrial society is seen as forming the bases for a multiplicity of specific and competing interest groups, among which power is widely diffused and shared with the state. Within this pluralistic power structure of countervailing groups, conflicts of interest are recognized as inevitable but are seen as based on a fundamental consensus on the economic organization of society. The often violent clashes characteristic of the early period of industrialization, when the economic organization of production also was questioned, will gradually vanish. Conflicts will be narrowed down to questions concerning the distribution of the results of production. Industrial society is thus assumed to develop a "distinctive consensus which relates individuals and groups to each other and provides an integrated body of ideas, beliefs, and value judgements." [1] Thus, while conflict remains in industrial society, it is gradually rendered innocuous to society's basic organization. Instrumental in changing the role of conflict is the development of new institutions for the resolution of conflicts. Once new and functional institutions are developed in place of those which broke down under the onslaught of industrialism, the expressions of conflicts will decrease. Most important among these new institutions are political democracy and collective bargaining. The orderly and regulated expression of conflict through these institutions is seen as contributing to the stability of the basic structure of society.

The increasingly complex occupational structure in industrial society is also assumed to be reflected in interest-group organization. Unions are thus assumed to become based on profession or occupation rather than on class and therefore to form sectional rather than class-based interest groups. Furthermore, unions are assumed already to have reached their "prime age" and to be on the beginning of a decline. "The union belongs to a particular stage in the development of the industrial system. When that stage passes so does the union in anything like its original position." [2]

Academic writing on industrial relations has by and large taken place within the framework of the "pluralistic industrialism" body of thought. In discussions of industrial conflict, the institutionalization of such conflict through collective bargaining plays a crucial role. "Collective bargaining is the great social invention that has institutionalized industrial conflict. In much the same way that the electoral process and majority rule has institutionalized political conflict in a democracy, collective bargaining has created a stable means for resolving industrial conflict." [3] The development of a "web of rules" and institutions of industrial relations, together with the evolution and "maturation" of the unions, involving for instance an increasing centralization of their decision-making procedures, is seen as a key factor for the "withering away of the strike." [4]

An important complement to institutions that dampen industrial conflict is the institutional separation of industrial and political conflict. Dahrendorf maintains, for instance, that "in contemporary societies, industrial conflict and political conflict are no longer identical. The protagonists, issues, and patterns of industrial conflict make for a discrete set of social relations. Industrial conflict has been severed from the antagonisms that divide political society; it is carried out in relative isolation." [5]

The disappearance of the "superimposition" of industrial and political conflict, which characterized the early days of industrialism, is not a phenomenon limited to the institutional sphere. Rather, it is seen as based on changes in the class structure of society, where the mechanisms that allocate citizens to positions in industry tend to become independent from those that allocate them to positions in the political sphere. Therefore "membership in an industrial class leaves open to which political class an individual belongs" and "the participants in industry, upon leaving the factory gate, leave behind them with their occupational role their industrial class interests also." [6]

Like much of post-war research on conflict, research on industrial conflict has paid little attention to the distribution of power resources between the contending parties on the labor market.[7] In accordance with the general assumption that power is widely diffused among a plurality of interest groups in industrial society, the sellers and buyers of labor power have often been seen as having roughly equal power. Big labor has been assumed to counterbalance big business.

Many of the ideas above were summarized in the theoretical scheme of "the industrial relations system" developed by John T. Dunlop in *Industrial Relations Systems* (New York: Holt, 1958). The industrial relations system is seen as a subsystem of society, and its central function is to develop and to administer rules for the workplace and the work community. It is composed of three groups of actors: managers and their organizations, workers and their organizations, and specialized government agencies. It operates in the context of production technology, market constraints, and the distribution of power in the larger society. An important element of the industrial relations system is an ideology that binds the system to an entity and recognizes an acceptable role for others.

This body of thought thus has its main emphasis on the rules and institutions of industrial relations. It sees the parties in the labor market as sharing a basic consensus on the economic organization of society. Production technology is accorded an important place in shaping industrial relations at the workplace, something that has also been strongly underlined in the so-called "technological implications" approach to industrial sociology.[8] Although the role of the locus and distribution of power in the larger society is recognized, it does not appear to be a major element in the analysis of industrial relations in western democratic countries.

The ideas basic to this body of thought have not been limited to the United States. They are, for instance, also clearly evident in industrial relations writing and policy in Britain. The so-called "liberal pluralist" or "Oxford school" of industrial relations shares the assumptions of a roughly equal distribution of power in industrial society and in industrial organizations, of a basic consensus on the economic organization of society among the parties in the labor market, and of the key impact that industrial relations institutions have on the pattern and level of industrial conflict. Thus, for instance, one of the leading writers in this school, Hugh A. Clegg, makes the institutions of collective bargaining the hub around which most of the relations between sellers and buyers of labor power turn.

This stress on the importance of the institutions of industrial relations has also permeated political efforts to find ways of improving industrial relations in Britain. As is well known, the Royal Commission on Trade Unions and Employers' Associations argued that the root of the British strike problem was a conflict between two systems of industrial relations that were operating in Britain, one industrywide and formal, the other informal and limited to the workplace.[9] The informal system, largely outside the control of the union hierarchy, had a wide scope and relied on tacit understanding and informal agreements rather than on written agreements. It was therefore seen as undermining the formal, industry-wide system. The commission's central proposal was that companies and unions together should develop a comprehensive and authoritative collective bargaining machinery at the workplace level, which would increase the control of the union hierarchy over workplace bargaining and increase its level of formalization.

Industrial Conflict and Institutional Development in Sweden

As is well known, Sweden has highly developed institutions of industrial relations. The level of industrial conflict in Sweden has shown dramatic changes over the years. In the beginning of this century, Sweden together with Norway had the highest relative levels of industrial conflict among western nations. In the post-World War II period, however, Sweden has been renowned for its industrial peace. Therefore, an analysis of the contribution of institutional development to the reduction of industrial conflict in Sweden should be a test case in evaluating one of the central tenets in mainstream industrial relations thinking.

To test this tenet, we must examine the relationship between the timing of changes in institutions and the timing of changes in the level of industrial conflict. The institutional developments that appear to be most important in this context are the recognition of the legitimacy of the unions, the growth of union membership and centralization, the development of authoritative and formalized collective bargaining procedures, and the establishment of institutions for arbitration and mediation in industrial conflict. Let us now briefly sketch Swedish developments in these areas.

Industrialization in Sweden started relatively late, in the 1870s, and the first union organizations date back to this period. While unions were not illegal, employers often tried to crush them. They also used legislation to hinder the growth of the unions and the Social Democratic Workers' party, founded in 1889. Union growth, however, continued with industrial expansion. In the 1880s, a number of nationwide union organizations were formed. In 1898, they combined into the Swedish Confederation of Trade Unions, the LO. At that time, the unions were already socialistic and cooperated fully with the Social Democratic party. In 1902, a general strike was staged to support the demands for universal suffrage. This show of coordinated strength, as well as the relatively successful strategy of the national unions to split the unorganized employers, was important in initiating the formation of the Swedish Employers' Confederation (the SAF) and of employers' associations in different branches of industry later the same year. The formation of employers' associations was significant in moving the conflict with the unions to the organizational field. The employers' associations started a strategy of large-scale and often successful lockouts. This strategy implied, however, that they had accepted the legitimacy of unions. The battle for union recognition was formally won in 1906 when the LO and the SAF entered into the "December Compromise." The SAF recognized the right of unionization and the LO accepted the managerial prerogatives at the workplace.

The unions expanded rapidly in the economic boom period around the turn of the century. By 1906, about one-third of male workers in the secondary and the tertiary sector of the economy were unionized. Since the national union organizations had expanded by building up local union branches, the unions from the beginning had relatively centralized decision-making procedures. Thus, for instance, the right to call a strike generally was in the hands of the union executives.

Collective bargaining at the workplace level was well developed even before the turn of the century. Since the union branches had their suborganizations at the workplace level, workplace unionism was from the beginning integrated with the activity of the national union. When the employers' associations were formed, industry-wide agreements became common. The first major industry-wide contract was signed in the engineering industry in 1905. Since several unions were involved in these negotiations and the threat of a lockout was ever present, the LO took an active part in the negotiation of these early industry-wide contracts. Already in the second decade of this century, two-thirds of all LO members were working under industry-wide contracts or their derivatives.

Through intervention from the state, the development of institutions for the handling of industrial conflict was enhanced. Mediation in industrial disputes was provided through legislation enacted in 1906 and amended in 1920. The law concerning arbitration in industrial disputes dates back to 1920. According to a ruling by the Supreme Court in 1915, collective agreements were considered legally binding. In 1928, new laws made the legal force of collective agreements explicit and created a labor court to adjudicate in disputes in the area of industrial relations. The LO opposed these laws by calling for nationwide protest strikes.

As early as in the first decade of this century, Sweden thus had highly developed institutions for the regulation and containment of industrial conflict. This, however, did not decrease the level of industrial disputes. On the contrary, industrial conflict soared in the beginning of the century and turned into a prolonged test of endurance between well organized parties (see the table on page 97). A decline came after 1909, when the LO-led general strike was lost, a disaster which halved the membership of the LO. Toward the end of the First World War, however, unions had regained their strength. Industrial conflict reached new records in the years following the war. In the post-World War I depression, these disputes were often lockouts to enforce demands for wage decreases. A high level of industrial conflict continued through the 1920s, and an increase came in the first years of the 1930s.

Thus, we can find no indication that the rich institutional development in the area of industrial relations led to a gradual decline in the level of industrial conflict. The decisive breaking point in the level and pattern of industrial conflict that transformed Sweden to the country of industrial peace in the post-World War II years came instead around 1934–35. It is thus apparent that the ideas central to mainstream industrial relations thinking cannot explain the changes in the level and pattern of industrial conflict in Sweden. Although the institutions of industrial relations, by providing an alternative to open conflict in affecting the views of the other party, are of unquestionable significance, the source of the drastic change in the industrial conflict in the mid-1930s in Sweden must be sought outside the realm of industrial relations institutions.

The Separation of Political and Economic Power in the 1930s

In retrospect, it is evident that the drastic change in the level and pattern of industrial conflict in the mid-1930s had its background in the political changes in the country in connection with the coming to power of the Social Democratic government in 1932. The change was, however, not a result merely of a formal accession to the government of the Social Democrats. In fact, the Social Democrats had already participated in a coalition government with the Liberals during the First World War. This coalition broke up when it had achieved its primary goal, the introduction of universal suffrage in 1918. In the following decade, the Social Democrats formed three minority governments, based on socialist support from about 40 percent of the electorate. These governments, however, were short-lived and had neither the power nor a policy to attack the central political question of the 1920s, the persistingly high level of unemployment.

The Social Democratic government formed in 1932, however, started from quite different conditions. It had a clear conception of what should be done to decrease unemployment in the Great Depression. With 50 percent of the electorate voting for the socialist parties, it had a much stronger political background than the previous Social Democratic governments. However, since the first chamber of the *Riksdag* reflected an older electoral opinion, the Social Democrats did not have a majority there. Therefore, the Social Democrats entered into a deal with the Agrarian party, where agrarian support for the expansive economic policies of the Social Democrats was traded for Social Democratic support for restrictive policies favoring the Swedish farmers. The Social Democratic government was successful in combating unemployment, and the party increased its electoral support. In the elections of 1936 and 1938, the socialist parties received well over 50 percent of the vote.

After this massive political breakthrough there was a widespread feeling in the country in the latter part of the 1930s that the Social Democrats had come to stay as the dominant force in the government. This implied a dramatic shift in the distribution of power resources in society. Political

Work Stoppages, Industrial Disputes, and Unionization

Sweden, 1863-1976

	Average Yearly Number			Approximate Percentage of Unionization
	work stoppages	workers involved (in thousands)	man-days idle (in millions)	(male workers in manufacturing, mining and building)
1863-1864	1			
1865-1869	2			
1870-1874	7			
1875-1879	3			
1880-1884	6			
1885-1889	27			2
1890-1894	58	2.1	0.1	4
1895-1899	110	7.8	0.1	10
1900-1904	150	12.6	0.4	20
1905-1909	246	83.4	3.4	35
1910-1914	105	11.6	0.4	25
1915-1919	386	43.0	1.1	37
1920-1924	338	78.3	4.5	48
1925-1929	203	58.5	2.0	57
1930-1934	176	31.5	2.2	67
1935-1939	71	16.5	0.7	75
1940-1944	118	4.2	0.1	83
1945-1949	92	39.7	2.3	87
1950-1954	30	10.7	0.3	92
1955-1959	15	1.7	0.1	95
1960-1964	18	2.0	0.0	95
1965-1969	18	7.8	0.1	95
1970-1974	105	25.8	0.2	95
1975-1976	186	24.0	0.2	95

power was now separated from economic power. The employers and their allies could no longer count on having a legislature and a government which was friendly to their point of view. Instead, they had to confront a situation where governmental power was in the hands of their traditional opponents. The LO unions and the Social Democratic party, on the other hand, had cemented their traditionally close alliance in the fight against unemployment in these years. For the unions, the Social Democratic hold on the government opened up new alternatives for improving the welfare of their members. They were no longer forced to fight costly battles over the distribution of the results of production in the industrial sphere, where the coordinated lockout strategy of the employers often had proven overwhelmingly strong. Now, also, political means were available for affecting the distribution of the results of production. The shift in the distribution of power resources in society implied in the separation of political from economic power was to have important consequences for the conflict strategies of the labor movement as well as of the employers.

New Strategies of Conflict

Up to the mid-1930s, unions and employers in Sweden had been involved in a "zero-sum" or "fixed-sum" type of conflict over the distribution of the results of production. The shift in the power structure of society, which gave the labor movement access to legislative and political power, opened up new avenues of action for the unions. Of central importance was that the level of employment, which is crucial for the welfare of workers, now could be affected by political means, through the economic reform program of the Social Democratic government. In addition, fiscal, social, labor market, and educational policies could be used to affect the distribution of welfare in society. For the employers, however, the alternative courses of action had narrowed. Their ultimate weapon, the large lockout, had become much more difficult to use since the positive neutrality of the state no longer could be guaranteed. They also had to fear government controls and policies which could increase costs and wages.

This change in the power structure formed the background against which the parties had to reassess their conflict strategies. The initiative was now with the Social Democratic government, which through its policy could show what its goals were.

In a speech to a businessmen's organization in 1938, Ernest Wigforss, minister of finance and an important theoretician in the party, summarized the background to the political situation and made a formal invitation for cooperation with the private business sector. He made it clear that within the foreseeable future, neither the representatives of private industry nor the representatives of the labor movement could hope to resolve the conflicts of interest between them through the surrender of the other party. He continued, "Expressed without euphemisms this means, on the one hand, that those who have power over larger or smaller sectors of the private economy must not base their actions on the assumption . . . that a political change will take place within a future near enough that a discussion based on the possibility of concessions, accommodations, compromises, becomes unnecessary. On the other hand it also means that the representatives for political power admit the necessity of maintaining favorable conditions for private enterprises in all those areas where they are not prepared without further ado to replace the private enterprises with some form of public operations." [10]

In the new situation with a Social Democratic government in power, opinions differed strongly among the representatives of industry and the employers on which strategy they should choose. A recent study[11] shows that in 1933, the directors of the five largest Swedish multinational export firms formed a half-anonymous, informal organization, known as TBF or "The Big Five," which advocated a militant course of action against the new Social Democratic government, involving cooperation with the bourgeois parties in an effort to unseat the Social Democrats. Within the SAF, however, where the home-market industries dominated, a different strategy was to win acceptance. The leaders of the SAF were of the opinion that the Social Democratic hold over the government was to be long lasting. The best course of industry, then, was to maintain formal political neutrality, to seek an accommodation with the LO and the government and to act as a pressure group in influencing the political process.

The compromise between the Swedish labor movement and the representatives of the economic power holders that was gradually worked out in the latter half of the 1930s was based on the formula of cooperation between labor and capital in order to achieve economic growth. It thus implied a shift to a "positive sum" type of conflict between the parties. From the point of view of the labor movement, this formula would allow for a decrease in unemployment and provide the necessary bases for welfare policies as well. These policies would make it possible to increase political support for the long-term strategy of the Social Democratic party and also hasten the "maturation" of capitalist society. The representatives of industry, on the other hand, were granted favorable conditions for expansion and growth. An important part of the compromise was that the state, which previously had often intervened in favor of the employers, now was to remain neutral, leaving the regulation of relations between the parties on the labor market to their own organization.

The acceptance of these new strategies was facilitated by generational shifts in the leadership both in the LO and the SAF. Within the SAF, the more moderate course of action was accepted. In 1936, for the first time since the general strike in 1909, the LO and the SAF started direct negotiations with each other, negotiations which two years later were to lead to the symbol of the new relationship between the parties on the Swedish labor market, the Main Agreement. In terms of bargaining procedures, etc., this agreement essentially only put in writing what was already widespread in practice. Its main importance was that it was a symbol for the new relationship and strategies of the parties.

In these new strategies of conflict, industrial disputes no longer played any important role. Already in 1933–34, the LO had intervened to hinder strikes that were considered detrimental to the efforts of the Social Democratic government to get the economy going. The LO came to play a major role in guiding its member unions into the new strategy of action. Since the disastrous defeat of the LO-led general strike in 1909, it has relinquished its previously active role in the negotiations of its member unions. In 1937, however, the LO again intervened in wage negotiations by calling a conference of its member unions with the intention of hindering the termination of contracts and strikes during the sensitive stages of negotiations with the SAF concerning the Main Agreement.

Since the late 1930s, the LO and the unions have generally come to take the orderly progress of the national economy into account in its wage policy. They therefore have generally limited wage demands to what has been permitted by increases in production. Strikes became regarded as something unnecessary. In the latter part of the 1930s, strikes decreased markedly. The big strike among the metalworkers in 1945 was clearly against the wishes of the leaders of the unions and the LO. In the post-World War II period, the LO and the union leadership came to view strikes even more negatively. Neither could the employers use the lockout weapon with good chances of success.

Workplace Industrial Relations and Unofficial Strikes

According to the "liberal-pluralist" school of industrial relations, the nature of workplace bargaining plays a key role for industrial disputes and is seen as a major factor behind the high level of unofficial disputes in Britain. The approach of this school would thus lead us to expect that the very low level of unofficial strikes in Swedish industry in the post-World War II period has been based on workplace bargaining procedures different from those prevailing in Britain. One would expect to find workplace bargaining procedures narrow in scope, tightly controlled by the central union officers, and strongly reliant on formalized procedures. A closer look at the Swedish scene, however, indicates that there is no basis for such an interpretation.

A study that I have done in the metalworking industry indicates, for instance, that workplace bargaining procedures are largely informal with little reliance on predetermined agendas or written agreements. The organization of workplace bargaining also varies from firm to firm and reflects specific conditions in the firm. Workplace bargaining in the Swedish metalworking industry has been largely limited to wage issues. Rather than lowering the number of unofficial strikes, however, this limitation has tended to generate strikes in areas related to control at the workplace, issues which have been very difficult to take up in the negotiations between the works club and the management. While the works club is a suborganization of the union, it acts quite independently from the union branch as well as from the union headquarters. The elected members of the board of the works club, that is laymen, represent the workers of the firm in negotiations with management. The works club has the authority to sign all agreements with management. The representatives from the branch have not even had the right to enter the premises of the firm without permission from management.

In the post-World War II period Swedish industry has relied extensively on the piece-work system of payment, with roughly two-thirds of all work-time being paid on a piece-work basis. Since the collective agreements generally specify minimum rather than normal wages and in many of the large firms several thousands of new piece-work rates are set each week, piece-work rate negotiations have been one of the main activities of the work clubs. The "wage drift" resulting from these negotiations has contributed about as much to wage increases for workers in Swedish industry as have the increases negotiated between the national union headquarters and the employers' associations. This has been a major concern for the unions as well as for the employers.

The central role of production technology in the quality of industrial relations in firms has been an important part of mainstream industrial relations thinking in the post-World War II period. The pattern of unofficial strikes in the Swedish metalworking industry indicates, however, that the role of technology is considerably more limited than what is often assumed.

The Conditions of the Postwar "Industrial Peace"

An analysis of the drastic decline of industrial conflict in Sweden in the mid-1930s thus indicates that its main cause was a shift in the societal power structure involving a separation of political and economic power that changed the action alternatives available for the parties in the labor market and led to a change in their strategies for dealing with conflict. Although of significance because they offered an alternative to work stoppages, the development of institutions of industrial relations were in themselves not able to generate a decline in the level of conflict. Rather than being the result of institutional development, the change in strategies for dealing with conflict came to generate institutional changes. The Main Agreement was thus a symbol of these changing strategies. The new course of action also resulted in a centralization of decision-making procedures within the LO, with significant changes introduced by its new constitution in 1941. In the 1950s, the decision-making procedures in collective bargaining were further centralized when the use of advisory referendums on contract proposals fell into disuse and membership consultations came to take place through indirect, representative channels only. The new pattern of centralized collective bargaining involving "frame agreements" between the LO and the SAF, which were introduced in the mid-1950s, were a consequence of the new strategies. They also came to be important in the so-called solidaristic wage policy of the LO, aiming, in principle, toward equal wages for similar jobs, irrespective of the profitability of the firm, and especially toward improving the wage-levels of low paid workers.

This analysis also brings us to the conclusion that the forms of workplace bargaining and the types of production technologies in Swedish industry have not been major factors behind its low levels of unofficial strikes in the post-war period. A condition of major importance for the successful carrying out of the new strategies for dealing with conflict of the parties in the Swedish labor market, however, has been the very favorable economic development of the country. The stable growth of the Swedish economy has made it possible to increase the real living standards of the workers without major changes in the distribution of income. The shortage of labor has also provided workers with efficient leverage in negotiations with employers in both industrywide negotiations, where the unions generally could get what was possible in terms of productivity increases without recourse to strikes, and on the workplace level, where the workers were backed in piece-work rate negotiations by the labor shortage. When international "stagflation" hit Sweden in the late 1960s, the level of unofficial strikes increased markedly. That the well developed institutions for industrial relations could not hinder this increase is again an indication of their relative limitations.

The Limitations of the Pluralistic Industrialism Theory

The body of ideas incorporated in the "logic of industrialism" or "pluralistic industrialism" school of thought has not proved itself fruitful in attempts to explain the changing pattern of industrial conflict in our test country, Sweden. Apparently the basic reasons for this failure are that this school of thought overemphasizes the role of industrial technology in changing the social structure of society and neglects the importance that the distribution of power resources in society has on the pattern of exchange and conflict between its major collectivities.

The Swedish case clearly contradicts the prediction of the "pluralistic industrialism" school of thought that organizations for collective action among the wage earners would decline in importance. Swedish unions have shown no tendency to decline. Instead, the LO unions have continued to grow in the post-World War II period, reaching a level of organization above 90 percent in the 1970s (see page 97). And union growth has not been limited to the blue-collar sector. The unions of the salaried employees —the TCO (Swedish Central Organization of Salaried Employees) and the SACO/SR (Swedish Confederation of Professional Associations)— which were established in the 1930s and 1940s, have experienced a very rapid growth since the mid-1960s, which has more than doubled their membership and increased the level of organization to about 75 percent in the late 1970s. Contrary to the predictions of the "pluralistic industrialism" school of thought, the principle of industrial unionism has come to dominate. In the late 1970s, only 5 percent of the LO members belonged to craft unions, and the principle of industrial or "vertical" unionism also strongly dominated among the salaried employees. In the 1970s, the LO and the TCO came to cooperate relatively closely.

The pluralistic industrialism school of thought assumes that power in industrial society is widely and relatively evenly distributed. The decline in industrial conflict is not related to changes in the distribution of power but to the growth of institutions for conflict resolution and the separation of political from economic conflicts. Our analysis indicates instead that institutions of industrial relations should be seen as variables intervening between the power structure of society and the processes of exchange and conflict. These institutions can be seen as residues of conflict; they reflect attempts by the parties to stabilize and routinize exchange relationships. Since exchange relations and patterns of conflict depend intimately on the structure of power between the parties to exchange, the forms and functions of the institutions will reflect changes in the underlying power structure.

Our analysis also indicates that there is an intimate relationship between, on the one hand, political and economic conflict and, on the other, the changes in the power structure of society. The power resources of the wage earners lie primarily in their numbers and depend on organization for their successful mobilization. In Sweden the unions and the Social Democratic Party have cooperated closely as the two wings of the labor movement. As long as the labor movement was weak, political issues were brought into the industrial arena, as witnessed by the political strikes. When the labor movement won political power, however, conflicts over the distribution of profits and social welfare could be shifted from the industrial arena to the political arena. Thus the intimate connection between political and economic conflict, rather than their separation, was conducive to the decline of industrial conflict in Sweden in the mid-1930s.

According to the "pluralistic industrialism" school of thought, consensus on the economic organization of production is a natural development resulting from the evolution of industrial society. It thus fails to recognize the extent to which the levels of aspiration and the social consciousness of the wage earners are dependent on the distribution of power resources in society and are likely to change with the changes in their organizational and political strength. The precarious nature of such a consensus is indicated by recent proposals put forth in Sweden and in Britain that, if realized, would lead to important changes in the pattern of control over the means of production. The evolutionary cast of this school of thought must further be questioned.[12] Rather than leading the way in the evolution of industrial society, the United States can be seen as a special case, strongly affected by its history of immigration and slavery that distinguishes it from the countries in Western Europe.

To what extent do the experiences in other countries support the interpretation suggested here that the decline in industrial conflict in Sweden was the result of changes in the societal power structure? An answer to this question would require longitudinal analyses of changes in societal power structures and industrial conflict in various countries. This can obviously not be done here, but a brief discussion will be attempted.

Sweden in an International Perspective

One can begin by looking for parallels to the Swedish case, that is, countries where social democrats have come to stable governmental power before or after the Second World War and where the level of industrial conflict has declined. Austria and Norway appear to come closest as parallels to Sweden. Especially Norway follows a course quite similar to that of Sweden. In both countries the unions are closely allied with the Social Democratic party. In Norway, the Social Democrats came to power in 1935. Also in Norway there was a dramatic change in the level of industrial conflict, with a decrease from one of the very highest levels of conflict before 1930 to one of the very lowest levels in the post-World War II period. The very high level of industrial conflicts in Austria in the period between the wars was followed by "industrial peace" after World War II in connection with a Social Democratic presence and a relatively close relationship between the union movement and the Social Democratic party. In Denmark, Britain and Belgium, however, the social democratic position in government has been weaker and much more unstable. In these countries the relationships between the unions and social democratic parties have often been highly problematic and strained. The level of industrial conflict in these countries has remained relatively similar to that between the wars.

On the opposite end of the spectrum we find countries like Italy, France, Finland, Ireland, Australia, Japan, the United States, and Canada, where the level of industrial conflict has remained high or increased during the post-World War II period. In these countries socialist parties either have been excluded from any major role in the government or have been very weak. In addition, in Italy, Finland and France the labor movements have been seriously split between communists and social democrats.

West Germany, the Netherlands and Switzerland, the three religiously split European countries, appear to contradict the interpretations suggested here. In West Germany, the level of industrial conflict has been very low, much lower than the level of conflict in the pre-Nazi period. The Social Democrats, however, remained outside the government up to the mid-1960s. The specific economic and political situation in post-World War II

Germany, with the need to build up a country devastated by war, would appear to be important in explaining its low level of conflict. Switzerland, on the other hand, has had a very low level of industrial conflict since World War I and it also has a relatively weak labor movement. The Netherlands is in some respects relatively similar to Switzerland.

The ideas based on the pluralistic industrialism school of thought, which continues to permeate most of the social sciences, cannot explain the changes in industrial conflict in Sweden, which is an important test case in this respect. The point of departure for an alternative theory suggested here is that the distribution and changes in power resources between the major contending collectivities or classes in the capitalist democracies is of key importance for the action alternatives open to these contenders and thus for their conflict strategies. Where political parties based on the working class receive a strong and stable control over the executive branch of government, labor can move manifestations of the conflicts of interest with capital from the industrial to the political arena. Where this occurs industrial conflict will tend to wither away. Where, however, labor has only a weak or unstable control over the government, industrial conflict will remain at relatively high levels. Although there undoubtedly are exceptional cases which do not fit this hypothesis, it appears to be a fruitful one in attempts to understand the dramatic, complicated and often puzzling changes in the patterns of industrial conflict in the Western countries during this century.

Notes

1. Clark Kerr et al., *Industrialism and Industrial Man* (London: Penguin Books, 1973), p. 53.

2. John Kenneth Galbraith, *The New Industrial State* (New York: Signet Books, 1967), p. 274.

3. Robert Dubin, "Constructive Aspects of Industrial Conflict" in Arthur Kornhauser, Robert Dubin and Arthur M. Ross, *Industrial Conflict* (New York: McGraw-Hill, 1954), p. 44.

4. Arthur M. Ross and Paul T. Hartman, *Changing Patterns of Industrial Conflict* (New York: Wiley, John, & Sons, 1960).

5. Ralf Dahrendorf, *Class and Conflict in Industrial Society* (Stanford: Stanford University Press), 1959, p. 277.

6. *Ibid.*, pp. 271–74.

7. One of the few exceptions is Robert Dubin's article, "A Theory of Conflict and Power in Union–Management Relations," *Industrial and Labor Relations Review* 13 (July 1960): 501–18.

8. See for example, Joan Woodward, *Industrial Organization: Theory and Practice* (London: Oxford University Press, 1965); Fred E. Emery and Eric L. Trist, "Socio-Technical Systems" in C. W. Churchman and M. Verhulst, *Management Sciences: Models and Techniques* Vol. 2 (Elmsford, N.Y.: Pergamon Press, 1960), pp. 83-97; James Kuhn, *Bargaining in Grievance Settlement* (New York: Columbia University Press, 1961); and Leonard Sayles, *Behavior of Industrial Work Groups* (New York: Wiley, John, & Sons, 1958).

9. *Minutes of Evidence/The Royal Commission on Trade Unions and Employers' Associations* (London: H.M.S.O., 1966-68).

10. Ernst Wigforss, *Minnen 1932–1949 (Memories 1932–1949)* (Stockholm: Tiden, 1954), p. 111.

11. Sven Anders Söderpalm, *Direktörsklubben-Storindustrin i svensk politik under 1930- och 1940-talen (The Manger's Club—Big Business in Swedish Politics in the 1930s and 1940s)* (Stockholm: Zenit Raben och Sjögren, 1976).

12. For a critique, see John H. Goldthorpe, "Theories of Industrial Society: Reflections on the Recrudescence of Historicism and the Future of Futurology," *Archives Européennes de Sociologie* XII (1971): 263-88.

Other References

Aron, Raymond. *Eighteen Lectures on Industrial Society.* London: Weidenfeld & Nicholson, 1967.

Bell, Daniel. *The End of Ideology.* New York: Free Press, 1965.

————. *The Coming of Post-Industrial Society.* New York: Basic Books, 1973.

Bullock, Alan Louis Charles. *Report of the Committee of Inquiry on Industrial Democracy.* London: H. M. S. O., 1977.

Clegg, Hugh A. *Trade Unionism Under Collective Bargaining.* Oxford: Basil Blackwell, 1976.

Converse, Elisabeth. "The War of All Against All: A Review of the Journal of Conflict Resolution, 1957–1968." *Journal of Conflict Resolution* 12 (December 1968): 471–532.

Dahl, Robert A. *Who Governs? Democracy and Power in an American City.* New Haven, Connecticut: Yale University Press, 1961.

Dunlop, John T. *Industrial Relations Systems.* New York: Holt, 1958.

Fox, Alan. "Industrial Relations: A Social Critique of Pluralist Ideology" in John Child, ed. *Man and Organization.* London: Allen & Unwin, 1973, pp. 185–233.

_____. *Beyond Contract: Work, Power and Trust Relations.* London: Faber & Faber, 1974.

Kerr, Clark, John T. Dunlop, Frederic H. Harbinson and Charles A. Myers. *Industrialism and Industrial Man.* Cambridge: Harvard University Press, 1960.

Korpi, Walter. "Conflict, Power and Relative Deprivation." *American Political Science Review* 68 (December 1974): 1569–78.

_____. *Strikes, Industrial Relations and Class Conflict—Sweden in an International Perspective.* Swedish Institute for Social Research, 1975.

_____. *The Working Class in Welfare Capitalism—Work, Union and Politics in Sweden.* London: Routledge & Kegan Paul, 1978.

Landsorganisationen (LO). *Kollektiv Kapitalbildning Genom Lontagarfonder (Collective Capital Formation Through Wage-Earners Funds).* Stockholm: Prisma, 1976.

Lester, Richard A. *As Unions Mature.* Princeton: Princeton University Press, 1958

Moore, Wilbert E. *Industrialization and Labor.* Ithaca, N.Y.: Cornell University Press, 1951.

Industrial Conflict
In New Zealand and Australia

Don J. Turkington

THE 1970s have been years of high, and in some ways record, strike activity in Australia and New Zealand. Governments in both of these countries and elsewhere have become more involved in industrial conflict, attempting to control both the strike itself and its perceived consequences (such as inflation). But the systems for dealing with strikes —conciliation and arbitration—differ in each country, reflecting the centralized government in New Zealand and the federal structure of the Australian government. The significance of some of the similarities and differences are apparent when recent patterns of strike activity in the two countries are examined.

Compulsory conciliation and arbitration are usually associated with limitations on the legal use of the strike and lockout. Governments of both Australia and New Zealand have taken the view that the provision of such dispute settlement machinery makes recourse to strike or other action unnecessary and undesirable. This view is by no means universal. Unions in particular see the right to strike as fundamental and have long expressed a preference for keeping this option. Unlike their American counterparts, unions in Australia and New Zealand have no commitment to a grievance procedure that uses arbitration instead of a strike. For them any dispute will be handled according to the tactical dictates of the situation, irrespective of whether it involves rights or interests.

Partly because they can occur over any issue, strikes in the two countries are brief relative to those in other places.

The table on page 111 shows variations in man-days lost per worker (a frequently used method to measure a strike's economic impact) both over time and among countries. It is clear that Australia loses many more man-days per worker due to strikes than does New Zealand. Australia also tends to be significantly more strike prone than New Zealand in terms of frequency and worker involvement. Both countries experienced significant increases in average man-days lost per worker from the latter sixties to the early seventies, but the increase for Australia was relatively greater than that for New Zealand. Such increases were obviously widespread with only three countries in the table (Ireland, Italy and the United States) experiencing a reduction in man-days lost per worker in the early seventies. Several others, by contrast, had massive increases (e.g., Denmark and Germany).

Any explanation of the difference in the strike levels of Australia and New Zealand must be speculative because there is no detailed comparative research. The differences in the industrial distribution of the labor force are important. The proportion of the Australian labor force in the typically strike prone mining and quarrying sector is over twice that of New Zealand. Another sector that tends to be strike prone—metal products, machinery and equipment—is also relatively much larger in Australia. Both these sectors are important contributions to total strike activity in that country.

In explaining the recent high level of strikes in both countries, research has indicated a close relationship between aggregate strike incidence and economic conditions. Higher prices appear to have a strong upward effect on strike frequency and possibly on other dimensions of the strike, partly because rising prices produce higher wage demands. Inflation has been unusually rapid in the seventies, averaging over 10 percent a year for both countries. (The seventies have also seen rapid wage increases, but I have found that, at least for New Zealand, past wage increases have an insignificant effect on current strike frequency.) In the sixties, by contrast, inflation was less than half as rapid.

A frequent consequence of such inflation is an attempt by government to intervene in the setting of wages and prices through income policy or wage–price controls. An income policy can exacerbate conflict by restricting the extent to which worker expectations can be met and causing disenchantment with conventional wage fixing machinery and procedures. In New Zealand an income policy has been in force for most of the seventies and has undoubtedly produced conflict. (Not all this conflict has been recorded. Until recently only "industrial strikes," which are those involving a demand on the employer [or on the employees in the case of the lockout], have been included in the official statistics. Other strikes, such as protesting a measure taken by the government, were excluded. In both New Zealand and Australia it appears that strike activity over nonindustrial matters has been high, and possibly increasing, during the seventies.) The Australian federal government has limited power to intervene in wage determination. The power to make general adjustments to all existing wage rates lies with a statutory body, the Australian Conciliation and Arbitration Commission. The parties, including the federal government, present evidence before this commission. The government has argued for restraint, contending that any wage indexation (a system adopted by the commission in 1975) should not

Man-Days Lost per 1,000 People Employed

Country (in rank order)	Average 1966-1970	Country (in rank order)	Average 1971-1975
Canada	1,836	Canada	1,862
Italy	1,822	Italy	1,730
United States	1,500	India	1,553 **
India	1,204	Australia	1,464
Ireland	1,102	Finland	1,410
Australia	608	United States	1,173 **
United Kingdom	404	United Kingdom	1,146
New Zealand	326	Denmark	1,006
Belgium	314	Ireland	752
France	263 *	Belgium	422
Finland	256	New Zealand	384
Japan	166	France	342
Denmark	64	Japan	328
Sweden	36	Norway	104
Netherlands	34	West Germany	92
Norway	18	Netherlands	90
West Germany	12	Sweden	62
Switzerland	(fewer than five)	Switzerland	2

In most cases the industries covered are mining, manufacturing, construction, and transport.
 * 1968 figure unavailable and not included in averages.
** 1975 figure unavailable and not included in averages.
Source: Derived from *Department of Employment Gazette* (Great Britain), December 1976.

be applied in full because it would prolong high rates of inflation. Possibly in response, less than full indexation has been granted in some cases. Recently the Australian prime minister persuaded the state premiers to attempt a voluntary freeze on wages and prices. This policy was unsuccessful and was soon dropped. Both attempts at intervention were opposed by the unions.

The distribution of income between profits and wages is another important influence on strikes. When profits are relatively high, it is more likely that employers will accede to union demands and obviate the need for a strike. When profits are low, employers may resist and so face a strike. The latter tendency has operated in the seventies, years of relatively low profits. In New Zealand the average ratio of company income to wage and salary payments during 1971–75 was 20 percent as compared to 24 percent in 1966–70. In Australia, the fall in the share of profits has been particularly marked since 1973. During the early part of that year the ratio of gross operating surplus of companies to gross nonfarm product was over 17 percent. Since then this ratio has been as low as 12 percent and never higher than 15 percent.

Labor market conditions also influence strike activity. The cost of strikes to workers may be less inhibiting when such conditions are tight. For New Zealand it is difficult to generalize about the state of the labor market during the period 1970–76, the first and middle years of which were characterized by a tight labor market and the rest by a slack one. This market pattern is not reflected by strike activity: 1975 and 1976 were slack labor market years, but high in strike activity. The effects of labor market conditions seem to have been more than counteracted by other influences such as an exceptionally high inflation rate and a very low ratio of profits to wages during those years. This tendency may have been even stronger for Australia where the unemployment rate increased fairly consistently throughout the seventies.

A number of institutional changes may also have influenced strike activity. Both countries changed from a Conservative to a Labor government in late 1972 and then reversed the change in late 1975. The effect of a Labor government on strike activity is complex. On the one hand, the official links between unions and the Labor party and the ideological sympathies that cause trade union members to support the Labor party might be expected to restrain workers from embarrassing a Labor government through strikes. On the other hand, a Labor government might raise worker expectations that, if unfulfilled, could lead to higher strike levels. While it is difficult to isolate any independent effect of a particular government on the level of industrial strikes, it should be noted that strike activity during 1973–75 was at least as high as during the preceding Conservative administration.

In New Zealand new industrial legislation, the Industrial Relations Act, was introduced in 1973 and amended in 1976. The new act firmly emphasizes the use of conciliation and arbitration and seeks to make these and other devices more efficient and attractive to all parties. Many people held high expectations that this act would reduce industrial conflict, especially the strike. That it has not done so reflects not only the limited nature of the changes but also the fact that industrial conflict is shaped by more influences than legislation. The 1976 amendments, opposed by the unions, re-introduced many of the penalties for strikes and lockouts removed from the law by the 1973 act and introduced some new ones as well. The illegality of the strike and associated penalties are long standing features of New Zealand industrial relations. That strikes have occurred despite them indicates the ineffectiveness of these penalties. Certainly, their re-introduction has not depressed the level of strikes. The Australian government, again in the face of union opposition, has been considering new industrial legislation to impose penalties *inter alia*.

While inflation, wage controls, relatively low profits, tight labor markets, high worker expectations, and some legislative and institutional changes create a general atmosphere conducive to conflict, they may vary in their impact on particular industries. Moreover, the situation within industries means that some have many more strikes than others. In New Zealand and Australia, as in many countries, a few industries account for a disproportionate amount of strike activity. Prime among these industries in New Zealand are meat slaughtering and preserving, waterfront (or longshore), construction, and shipping. (While these industries account for only one-tenth of all wage and salary earners, they contributed 51 percent of the strikes, 68 percent of man-days lost, and 75 percent of workers involved between 1971 and 1975.) Construction and waterfront are also prominent in Australia and together with mining and metal products, machinery and equipment accounted for 66 percent of the number of strikes and man-days lost and 65 percent of workers involved over the same period.

Many of the reasons why the meat, construction, and waterfront industries in New Zealand are conflict prone undoubtedly also apply to Australia. (I have analyzed the situation in New Zealand in detail in

Industrial Conflict: A Study of Three New Zealand Industries.) The emergence of shipping as a "strike center" in New Zealand is of recent origin and any explanation of it is speculative. But features of the industry seem to predispose it toward strikes; employment is casual, the availability of work may fluctuate and bargaining power vary, the ship's crew is an isolated group with few outside social contacts, authority relationships are strictly hierarchical, and top management is remote and often located overseas. The recent higher level of strikes may reflect more rapid technological change, a decline of demand for some important trades (coastal and trans-Tasman) and merger activity among shipping companies. Seamen have resisted these and other changes that reduce employment opportunities, often with strikes the result.

The factors that influence strikes in the Australian coal mining industry have been much studied and include: the economic uncertainty arising from the wide fluctuations in the demand for coal; variations in mining conditions, payment systems and the way earnings are calculated; the nature of the work (particularly its danger); and the isolated social environment. Strike levels in the Australian metal industries are influenced by regional characteristics, the nature and multiplicity of bargaining relationships, and the structure and policies of metal trade unions and employer associations.

An industry may be strike prone yet have variations in strike proneness within it. In the three major New Zealand strike centers (meat, construction, and waterfront industries), some employment units have many strikes while others have few or none. In the meat industry, for example, the average number of strikes per plant between 1967 and 1973 ranged from a low of 0.3 a year to a high of 10. Moreover, in the case of the meat and construction industries, strike proneness varies even within the works or projects themselves. Intra-industry variations also exist within some Australian strike centers. There are regional differences, and both inter- and intra-plant, mine, or enterprise variations. Again taking the meat industry in New Zealand as an example, small, rural, New Zealand-owned plants tend to have relatively less strike activity than large, urban, overseas-owned ones. Within the plant, slaughtermen tend to be more strike prone than workers in other departments due to their strategic position at the start of the production process, and the particularly monotonous, unpleasant and dangerous nature of their work.

The predominance of a few industries in total strike activity masks the increasing number of industries that experience strikes in both countries.

In New Zealand an average of 44 industries a year experienced strikes during 1971–75 as compared to only 29 industries a year in the period 1966–70. Among traditionally strike free industries having strikes in recent years are banking and wholesale–retail trade. A few industries in New Zealand and Australia account for a disproportionate amount of strike activity but an increasing number of other industries also are experiencing strikes. The strike experience of both countries in the 1970s parallels that of many other industrialized nations. This is due partly to widespread inflation, relatively low profits, and high worker expectations. The full effects of high unemployment and concurrent inflation and relatively low profits on strike activity are not yet known. Thus, the continued importance of studying strikes must be underscored.

References

Bentley, Philip and Barry Hughes. "Cyclical Influences on Strike Activity: The Australian Record 1952–68," *Australian Economic Papers* 9 (December 1970): 149–170.

Carr, Bob. "Australian Trade Unionism in 1976," *Journal of Industrial Relations* 19 (March 1977): 80–86.

Dufty, Norman F. *Industrial Relations in the Australian Metal Industries.* Sydney, Australia: West Publishing, 1972.

Gordon, B. J. "A Classification of Regional and Sectoral Dispute Patterns in Australian Industry, 1945–64," *Journal of Industrial Relations* 10 (November 1968): 233–242.

Hibbs, Douglas A., Jr. "Industrial Conflict in Advanced Industrial Societies," *American Political Science Review* 70 (December 1976): 1033–1058.

Kerr, Clark and Abraham Siegel. "The Interindustry Propensity to Strike —An International Comparison" in Arthur Kornhauser, Robert Dubin, and Arthur M. Ross, eds. *Industrial Conflict.* New York: McGraw-Hill, 1954.

Organisation for Economic Cooperation and Development (OECD). *OECD Economic Surveys: Australia.* Paris: OECD, 1976.

Pencavel, John H. "An Investigation into Industrial Strike Activity in Britain," *Economica* 37 (August 1970): 239–256.

Seidman, Joel. "New Zealand's Industrial Relations Act, 1973," *International Labour Review* 110 (December 1974): 515–538.

Spicer, Ian. "Employer Matters in 1976," *Journal of Industrial Relations* 19 (March 1977): 87–92.

Turkington, Don J. *The Forms of Industrial Conflict.* (Occasional Paper in Industrial Relations No. 18.) Wellington, New Zealand: Victoria University of Wellington, 1976.

_____. *Industrial Conflict: A Study of Three New Zealand Industries.* Wellington, New Zealand: Methuen, 1976.

_____. "Strike Incidence and Economic Activity in New Zealand," *New Zealand Economic Papers* 9 (1975): 87–106.

_____. "The Trend of Strikes in New Zealand 1971–75," *Journal of Industrial Relations* 19 (September 1977): 286–295.

Walker, Kenneth F. *Australian Industrial Relations Systems.* Cambridge, Massachusetts: Harvard University Press, 1970.

_____. *Industrial Relations in Australia.* Cambridge, Massachusetts: Harvard University Press, 1956.

Woods, Noel S. *The Industrial Relations Act 1973: A Study of the Legislation.* (Occasional Paper in Industrial Relations No. 11.) Wellington, New Zealand: Victoria University of Wellington, 1974.

The Evolution

Of Industrial Conflict in Spain

1939-1975

José M. Maravall

A T THE END of the Spanish Civil War, the new government of Generalissimo Francisco Franco reorganized the underdeveloped capitalist economy along autarchic lines. Its purpose was the transformation of the country into a self-sufficient economic entity including the protection of noncompetitive and costly private industries. The autarchic structure not only received the support of "protectionist" elements, but was also generally accepted by most Spanish enterprises because of the Second World War, which immediately followed the conclusion of the Spanish Civil War, and the subsequent economic and political isolation of Spain that took place following the Allied victory in 1945.

Government policies sought to replace imports with domestic products by utilizing protectionist tariff barriers and quantitative restrictions on imports through import quotas, strict licensing of import goods, and exchange controls. Rapid industrialization was sought through economic protectionism, labor-repressive policies, and a government-directed mobilization of resources. The Second World War created various problems for the accomplishment of these policies, especially because of the difficulties in importing basic capital goods and machinery that would provide the foundation for industrialization and make possible the gradual substitution of imported manufactured goods.

Autarchy and Isolation

The conclusion of the war, however, and the ensuing political–economic isolation of the Spanish regime (1946–1950) reinforced the autarchical economic orientation. It also became a means of defense; aside from serving as the basis for industrialization and strengthening the capitalist elite, it appeared as the sole alternative available for the economic survival of the regime.

During the period of autarchy which lasted approximately from 1939 to 1955, the Franco regime sought to stimulate industrialization by means of a money flow from the Bank of Spain. The infusion of paper money, however, failed to produce the desired level of investment in manufacturing. The money was often employed for short-term speculative investments only, while productive investment was hindered by the low level of internal aggregate demand, by limited markets, and also by incongruences in the tax system (e.g., the fact that capital allocated to sinking funds was considered as profit). Private capital failed to take advantage of the internal political context and Spanish capitalism therefore remained weak and stagnant for more than fifteen years. In the 1950s, for example, the average number of workers per industrial enterprise was only eleven, and productivity did not increase. A typical strategy resorted to during the period of autarchy was, first, to achieve adequate tariff protection from foreign competition, then to obtain licenses to import raw materials and, finally, to achieve national market predominance with the assistance of the government. Business activity was not so much cost-oriented as demand-oriented; competition was almost nonexistent; and the government controlled imports, production, distribution, and prices by means of a rickety economic structure.

To a large extent, state intervention was carried out through the National Institute for Industry (INI—*Instituto Nacional de Industria*), which was created in 1941 to perform an economic function similar to that of the Italian IRI (Institute for Industrial Reconstruction). Its primary purpose was to intervene in areas that did not offer lucrative prospects to private capital or that required large investments. This was justified by "a principle of subsidiarity" (*principio de subsidiaredad*) in which public funds are subsidiary to private capital so that whenever a given economic activity becomes profitable it is reverted back to private control. The activities of the INI extended to steel and metallurgy, chemicals, shipbuilding, electric power, mining, petrochemicals, oil refining, synthetic fibers and cellulose, manure, foodstuffs, and transport. These were mostly financed by credits from the Bank of Spain and budget consignments, both of which became important sources of inflation. From 1941 to 1949, the INI was deficient in economic planning, poorly managed, and made a series of disastrous economic decisions. During this time, there was no public control of INI activities and its use of huge amounts of public funds which subordinated national resources to private profit through the "subsidiarity principle."

The Labor Structure of the Franco Regime

Private capital accumulation was largely based on profit making through labor-intensive production and inflationary pricing in an economy with a weak manufacturing structure and consumer goods scarcities. As previously noted, capital accumulation was supported by government intervention through the INI and the constant infusion of paper money by the Bank of Spain. Another factor was the corporative organization of the working class, which was largely inspired by the model of fascist Italy. The *sindicatos verticales* bore strong similarities to the Italian *corporazioni* and were a key element in the political system of Francoism and a congruent development of the philosophy of the "organic state." Workers were compulsorily affiliated into organizations together with management for each branch of production. Representatives were not elected but named by the government. These *sindicatos* were part of the government and strongly represented in the *Cortés* (the non-democratic parliament) and by a minister in the cabinet. The program of the Falange, which served as the regime's sole political organization, states that "we shall assure the corporatist organization of Spanish society through a system of vertical unions in the different branches of production at the service of national economic integration" (point 9), and that "our regime will make class struggle radically impossible through the integration of every participant within an organic totality" (point 11).

The corporatist concept is elaborated in various constitutional statutes. The 1938 Labor Charter (*Fuero del Trabajo*), which bears similiarities to the Italian *Carta del Lavoro* of 1927 and the Portuguese *Estatuto do Trabalho Nacional* of 1933, stated that "vertical unions are a corporation . . . hierachically ordered under the direction of the state . . . whose posts of command will necessarily be given to militants of the Falange . . . [and they are] an instrument in the service of the state." The Labor Charter also declared that "national production constitutes an economic unity at the service of the country" and "any individual or collective activity that in any manner disturbs or undermines production will be considered a crime against the state." Three additional laws, passed in August 1939 and in January and December 1940, further subordinated the vertical unions to the single party and the government.

In addition to the regimentation of the working class, the government assumed control over the regulation of industrial relations. Collective bargaining was not permitted. By a 1942 law, the Ministry of Labor set wages and working conditions by means of labor regulations. The right to strike and the existence of autonomous, democratic trade unions were suppressed along with political parties, political expressions of dissent, and democratic political representation.

The 1950s—The Beginnings of Change

The fearful consequences of the civil war, military defeat, exile, and repression explain the lowered resistance after 1939 of the working class and the traditional left wing unions and parties to the corporatist labor-repressive structure. The two big labor organizations, the anarchist CNT (*Confederacion Nacional del Trabajo*) and the socialist UGT (*Union General de Trabajadores*), were outlawed after the civil war and their supporters persecuted, as was the case with all working class political parties. Attempts to organize underground military resistance were deprived of any chance of success once the Franco regime was able to survive the end of the Second World War. In October 1948, the socialist guerrilla effort was ended. Both socialist and anarchist organizations found it difficult to adapt to the new situation. The socialists, operating mainly in exile, had committed errors while awaiting the expected collapse of the Franco regime in a post-fascist Europe. Anarchists had resorted to short-term terrorist tactics following the end of the civil war, and their structure of organization was little suited to clandestine struggle. This led to the gradual elimination of anarchist groups within Spain and their increasing confinement to organizations in exile. The Communist party, however, more readily adapted itself because it was much smaller, better protected, with a rigidly centralized leadership and ample financial support. Starting in the early fifties, the Communist party gradually rebuilt its organization in the interior of Spain by developing a strategic and tactical approach that was based on the concept of struggle from within.

During the 1950s, the Spanish political scene changed. New tensions in the international arena—the cold war, Berlin, Czechoslovakia, and Korea—brought an end to Spain's isolation. In August 1950, the U.S. Congress voted financial assistance to the Franco regime, and by 1951 the diplomatic and economic boycott was ended. The 1953 agreement between the United States and Spain was an important landmark in the gradual shift within the Spanish regime from autarchical industrialization to a liberalization of economic policies.

From Stagnation to Expansion

An expansion of economic activity followed in which credit facilities were enlarged and foreign trade normalized. The growth of per capita income, which had been nonexistent between 1941 and 1950 (in fact, there had been a slightly negative rate of .02 percent), attained an annual rate of 3.3 percent between 1951 and 1960 (reaching a high of 6.9 percent between 1955 and 1956). Between 1951 and 1958, the gross national product (GNP) per capita grew at an annual rate of 4.45 percent, higher than any other European country except West Germany and Italy. The percentage of the population involved in agriculture fell from 49 to 42 between 1950 and 1960. External migrations of workers also began to make important contributions to the growth of Spanish capitalism. On the one hand, they provided essential hard currency which aided the balance of payments (second only to tourism, which also started to grow in the 1950s); on the other, they provided a safety valve for the full employment policy that was part of the populist rhetoric of the regime. Nonetheless, the shortage of skilled manpower pushed wages up, particularly after 1962. During the 1960s, economic development in Spain was no longer based on wage squeezing.

The reactivation of the economy had a crucial impact on industrial relations as the labor market began to operate with increasing independence from government controls. Managerial policies linking productivity to wage increases led to a growing disparity between real and official wages as productivity and competition again became a prime concern for much of management. Wage drift became especially serious in Spain during the mid-1950s and contributed to the inflationary spiral. Anti-inflationary policies called for instruments to determine wages, working conditions, and stimulate productivity. In 1956, two decrees introduced changes, which permitted employers to effect informal agreements with workers. The changes were intended to favor more competitive firms and encourage productivity.

The new economic outlook was reinforced by the cabinet changes of February 1957. The reshuffle reflected a shift in the balance of economic hegemony within the heterogeneous social and political coalition of the dictatorship. The new government introduced reforms in the tax system and public administration and unified foreign currency exchanges. It also sought to stimulate productivity and control incomes and prices. To this end, it set up a system of collective bargaining, which was regarded as an important component of economic policies. The participation of Spain in the international scene was also expanded; Spain successively joined the International Monetary Fund, the World Bank, and the Organisation for Economic Co-operation and Development (OECD). Negotiations were also inaugurated with the European Economic Community. Finally, the new government initiated a policy of indicative planning, which resulted in the stabilization plan of 1959. It included a devaluation of the peseta, restrictions on imports, financial aid to exports, reductions in public expenditures, a squeeze on credits, and a freeze on wages and salaries.

The Early Phase of Labor Dissent

The second half of the 1950s brought not only a period of economic change, but also heralded the first overt manifestations of working class struggle and student dissent. A few scattered strikes had taken place before 1956 (particularly in 1947 and 1951), but none had been on a scale such as they were in the late fifties. Initial industrial conflicts were isolated, often violent, and obviously illegal. Political repression combined with difficult economic conditions and control by the corporative bureaucracy produced a sort of fatalistic radicalism in these early struggles that were led by the miners of Asturias and the metal workers of the Basque area and Barcelona. No effective underground trade union organization was in existence as yet. The UGT and CNT were severely persecuted between 1940 and 1947; seventeen national executive committees of the CNT were apprehended and seven of the UGT between 1939 and 1954. To cite some examples of the repression: twenty-two UGT miners in Asturias were executed with dynamite and petrol in the *Pozo Funeres* mine in 1948; Tomas Centeno, the general secretary, died in the headquarters of the General Directorate of Security in Madrid. Worker mobilization was extremely difficult and the effect of the stabilization plan (wage freeze, unemployment, etc.) added to the difficulties.

Worker Militance Grows

The stabilization plan ended in 1962 and the economy once more began to expand. The annual GNP growth rate between 1960 and 1965 rose to 9.2 percent, while the rates of two other growing European economies, Italy and Portugal, were respectively 5.1 and 5.8 percent. The annual growth rate for per capita income in Spain between 1950 and 1966 also rose to 7.5 percent. Industrial expansion produced far-reaching alterations in the social structure. The proportion of the active population in the agricultural sector fell from 42 percent in 1960 to 30 percent in 1966 and 25 percent in 1971. Between 1960 and 1968, more than 1 million people out of a population slightly over 30 million abandoned agriculture. The population redistribution was dramatic; internal migrations between 1961 and 1968 totalled almost 3 million men and women. The urbanization process was intense; in 1960, 19.1 percent of the population lived in cities of over 100,000 inhabitants. By 1965, this percentage had risen to 32.7, higher than Italy, Sweden, or the USSR. Moreover, between 1960 and 1967, almost 2 million Spanish workers emigrated to different European countries.

In 1964, the government, seeking to stimulate and direct economic growth by following the French model of indicative planning, introduced its first development plan. Over the ensuing decade, annual growth was high, averaging approximately 7 percent of the GNP, while unemployment, aided by the large emigration to other European countries, never rose above 2 percent. However, development was uneven, agricultural reform was excluded, and the public sector continued to be managed by the "subsidiarity principle" and the interests of private capital. Moreover, the tax system remained inequitable and non-redistributive, and the imbalance between the supply of manufactured goods and aggregate demand (an imbalance due to rapidly expanding private consumption and public expenditure) produced a growing balance of payments deficit that continued unresolved. As a consequence, inflation remained very high and the regime was obliged to employ stop–go policies, including monetary restrictions and wage controls, especially during 1967 and 1971.

It is in this new context of economic expansion and occupational *bouleversement* that the resurgence of organized, working-class dissent must be viewed, for these changes opened up new possibilities for workers to organize and struggle. It also led to increased activity by clandestine political groups. During the early 1960s, the socialist UGT and the anarchist CNT formed a coalition together with the STV (*Solidaridad de Trabajadores Vascos*) known as the Trade Union Alliance *(Alianza Sindical)*. In 1962, dissident elements from the UGT and the CNT established another coalition with a small workers group in Catalonia (*Solidaridad de Obreros Cristianos de Cataluna*), which took the name of the Worker Trade Union Alliance (*Alianza Sindical Obrera*—ASO). The ASO succeeded in gaining the support of a faction of the STV and received assistance from the International Metalworkers Federation (IMF). At the same time, the Communist party sought to establish a new labor organization, the Workers Trade Union Opposition (*Oposicion Sindical Obrera*—OSO). The proliferation of groups with highly varying degrees of influence was perhaps the most salient characteristic of the period. It was, moreover, a manifestation of weakness. But the changing nature of Spanish society in the 1960s soon provided a firmer basis for the development of the trade union opposition movement, one that took place beginning with shop-level struggle and the intensive utilization of collective bargaining.

In 1962, the working class movement truly began to emerge. Contributing heavily to the growing working class assertiveness was the conclusion of economic stabilization, the growth of collective bargaining promoted by employers to increase productivity and by workers seeking to advance wage demands, and the expansion of shop-floor organization. In the first months of 1962, a wave of strikes hit Valencia, Barcelona, Madrid, Cartagena, and the Basque area. In April, May and June, a second wave involved the coal mining districts of Asturias; the metallurgy, chemicals, electrical, and shipbuilding industries in the Basque region; and the metal sector in Barcelona. These strikes also affected the mining zone of Linares, Puertollano, and Riotinto as well as the metal industries in Madrid. The most dramatic conflicts occurred in the mining areas, where long and desperate confrontations took place. An industry crisis had led to a drastic reorganization of the Asturian coal mines, where production had been reduced. In 1962, coal output was 7,904,427 metric tons; by 1963, output was reduced to 7,140,056 tons. Layoffs and discharges were high between 1959 and

1962, involving 11.2 percent of the employed labor force. A general strike in the Asturian mines lasted from July 16 to September 20, 1962. Nationwide, there were 425 industrial conflicts in 1962. Although most were of local origin, they signified an extremely important change in industrial relations dynamics and political life in Spain. The growing number of industrial conflicts made it untenable for the government to continue to define strikes as acts of sedition, and Article 222 of the Penal Code was eventually modified in 1965. The conflicts also led to a new decree, which legalized "economic" strikes, and established complicated, compulsory mediation and arbitration procedures.

Differing Concepts of Labor Organization

The year 1962 was also important in a movement to develop factory committees in plants, mines, building sites, and offices that were independent of the government-controlled trade unions. The movement began in the Asturian mines—the first reported instance was a lengthy strike in the La Camocha mine, where miners elected a democratic committee to negotiate with management—and spread throughout the country, especially to metallurgy in the Basque region. These shop-floor committees represented a major innovation in Spanish industrial relations. In industries such as steel, metal, and mining, they assumed a leading role in collective bargaining and industrial disputes. The UGT and USO joined the movement; they supported the factory committees against the official unions and sought to convert the committees into a full-scale challenge to the government-led *sindicatos*.

Soon the factory committees were viewed as the basis for a totally new type of trade union movement, one that would go beyond the traditional forms of labor organization represented by the UGT and CNT. Based on factory assemblies and committees, the movement would eventually evolve into a single unified trade union. This view was particularly advocated by the Communist party, which in 1963–64 abandoned support of the OSO for the factory committees which subsequently became known as the workers commissions (*comisiones obreras*—CCOO).

During its initial phase, the movement, which consisted of autonomous shop committees elected by workers, was compatible with existing democratic trade unions. In its second phase, it became more like an organized union (although the difference between "movement" and "organization" was rather ambiguous). At that point, the existing unions abandoned it—the UGT immediately, the USO not until 1967. Thenceforward, the CCOOs fell under the domination of the Communist party, but left-wing Catholic organizations retained considerable influence. These Catholic groups later merged into the Marxist Revolutionary Workers Organization (*Organización Revolucionaria de Trabajadores*—ORT). The turning point in the conversion of the CCOOs from a movement into an organization was the formation in 1964 of a CCOO for the metal industry of Madrid. This served as the principal catalyst for the development of a national network of CCOOs on an industry basis coordinated by provincial inter-industry commissions and a national secretariat. Nonetheless, the "organized" CCOOs did not absorb all the elected workers committees, although considerable overlapping existed.

A basic difference between the organized CCOOs and the movement of workers committees was that the former followed a strategy of infiltration and takeovers of the official employee representation committees, which since the mid-1950s had functioned as the lower echelon of the government-controlled unions. The Communists had tried to infiltrate the official unions since their formation, and the CCOOs successfully accomplished this goal. They were particularly successful in the metal industries of Madrid, mostly in the large plants south and southwest of the capital, and in the metal plants of Barcelona, mainly in the areas of Baix Llobregat and the Valles. They were less influential in the Asturias and the Basque provinces, where the UGT was relatively stronger and where a strategy of open boycott of the official unions received wide support.

The boycott strategy, supported by the UGT, and the CCOO tactic of infiltration represented a major difference between the two. The CCOO was the product of an attempt, particularly by the Communist party, to unite into a new organization both the autonomous workers committees which had spread since the late 1950s, and the groups of officially elected workers delegates, who were regarded as truly representative and often infiltrated by Communist activists. Thus the CCOO was based on both legal and illegal workers groups. Although the UGT had taken part in the CCOO movement, it abandoned the movement when it became controlled by the Communists, who intended to relegate the UGT to historical oblivion.

It is therefore not surprising that in the initial stages the CCOO was permitted a semi-legal existence. The commissions were seen as an extralegal, but not necessarily subversive movement, by official shop-floor representatives. Some "liberalizing" members of the Franco regime considered them as a potentially promising development for the official trade unions. The CCOOs, however, viewed activity in the legal shop floor committees merely as a means of conducting the struggle against the corporatist system and of strengthening their clandestine movement. They intended to undermine the official trade unions from within and acquire greater influence among workers through such activities. This objective was clearly articulated in March 1975, by Julian Ariza, one of the leaders of the CCOO.

> When wide sectors of the working-class movement
> participate in the union elections and defend the idea of
> using the premises and material means of the official
> union, we do so not because we accept its structure, its
> principles or its hierarchies. We do so to facilitate the
> exercise of workers' democracy. . . . The use of legality in
> this terrain forces in fact the exercise of trade-union rights
> and simultaneously negates the validity of the official scheme.

The elections for official shop-floor representatives in September 1966 were a great success for the CCOOs, and as a consequence, efforts from within and without the official corporative organization were intensified. This achievement, together with the greater possibilities for working-

Evolution of Disputes in Spain between 1966 and 1976

	Number of Disputes	Number of Hours Lost on Strikes
1966	179	1,478,080
1967	567	1,887,693
1968	351	1,925,278
1969	491	4,476,727
1970	1,595	8,738,916
1971	616	6,877,500
1972	853	4,692,925
1973	931	8,649,265
1974	2,290	13,989,557
1975	3,156	14,521,901
1976 (first three months)	—	15,000,000 (estimate)

class mobilization that resulted from the new system of collective bargaining and the strategic exploitation of grievances and negotiations by all the clandestine unions, is the source of increased working-class activity and widespread industrial conflict since 1966.

The Workers Commissions

The Spanish working-class militancy that began in the late 1960s can be gauged by a comparison with France in the 1970s. In France, where working-class organizations and militants were not persecuted and strikes were legal, about 3 million man-hours were lost because of strikes. (Compare these figures with the figures for Spain in the table on page 127.) The Spanish workers' growing strength was met with repression in 1967; states of emergency were declared in the Basque provinces during 1968 and for the entire country in 1969 and 1970. The Supreme Court in 1968 declared the CCOO to be an illegal and subversive organization. Repression took place on three levels: job dismissals, dismissals from posts held in official shop floor representation, and direct political sanctions.

Increased repression by the government led to a severe internal crisis within the CCOO. It has been previously observed that the organization had not followed a strategy of clandestine long-term operations but operated on a quasi-public basis. This made it highly vulnerable. In 1968 provincial and national committees were repeatedly dismantled by the police. The most spectacular arrests were those of the nine leading members of the national committee in 1972, which led to what was known as "trial 1,001" resulting in prison sentences ranging from six to twenty years. As a result, some within the commissions demanded that operations shift underground to make the organization more secure, and that the emphasis be broadened from plant activities to the wider political arena. This policy was advocated by two Maoist organizations, the Workers Party of Spain (PTE) and the Revolutionary Workers Organization (ORT) in opposition to the Communist party line.

Repression and internal divisions appreciably weakened the CCOO between 1968 and 1973. Eventually, however, the Communist party was able to impose its strategy of making full use of legal means, organizing on a quasi-public basis, and mobilizing workers openly. More attention also was given to improving protective measures against repression by wider involvement of activists in representational functions and by increasing workers support within the factories. The crisis of the CCOO in this period was particularly acute in the metal industry of Madrid, which had served as the core of working-class militancy ever since 1966. It should be noted, however, that the internal problems of the CCOO did not result in a decrease of labor unrest and militancy. Solidarity actions against repression actually increased and other labor groups, the UGT and USO in particular, were not affected by the difficulties of the CCOO.

The Growth of Labor Conflict

Labor conflict was particularly centered in industrial areas with high worker concentrations. The Basque region, Barcelona, Madrid, and Asturias accounted for 70 percent of all conflicts between 1963 and 1974. Conflict was especially high in steel and metallurgy, mining and building construction.

Increased worker militancy was particularly notable among steel and metal workers; between 1967 and 1975 they were responsible for 47 percent of industrial conflicts. Labor disputes were concentrated in medium-sized and large firms; between 1968 and 1974, 67.4 percent of strikes took place in plants employing more than 100 workers (although the proportion of these plants in Spanish industry is only 1.3 percent).

After 1967, industrial disputes assumed a more militant tone. Strikes and work shutdowns accounted for a larger portion of labor disputes, amounting to 30.3 percent (507 out of 1,676 actions) between 1963 and 1966. The percentage increased to 86.6 percent (6,663 out of 7,694 disputes) in the eight years between 1967 and 1974.

Under a dictatorship the costs of striking were, of course, high since such actions were legally defined as subversive. The success of general strikes required good organization, competent leadership, and security from repressive measures. Strikes were called mostly in strong worker enclaves such as the Asturias, the Basque country, and Barcelona. They proved more difficult to organize in Madrid, where the objective of the illegal unions was to strengthen the movement and gradually mobilize workers through careful displays of action. In-plant work stoppages had the advantage of surprise; they enabled workers to get control of the plant from within and presented fewer opportunities for repressive action. They were a useful means for organizing coordinated action and testing the strength of the movement.

Distribution of Industrial Conflict in Spain

By Branch of Industry between 1963 and 1974

	Active Labor Force	Number of Disputes	Percent of Total Disputes	Ratio: Active Labor Force to Average Disputes per Year
Steel and Metallurgy	991,700	4,172	44.5	2,850
Mining	177,900	1,224	13.1	1,744
Building	925,000	899	9.6	12,333
Textile	713,400	553	5.9	15,509
Chemicals	196,200	448	4.8	5,303

From 1963 to 1974, strikes were the most frequent type of action (45.8 percent), followed by in-plant stoppages (29.2 percent). There appears to be a relationship between these two types of activities. From 1967 to 1973, an increase in one led to a decrease in the other. During the same period, a strike often represented a confrontation that, in turn, produced work stoppages in sympathy with the strikers. Moreover, since 1967, cooperation increased between labor actions in different factories and geographical areas. Thus, as workers resorted more frequently to the strike weapon, labor conflict assumed a more aggressive character and became more unified through coordinated efforts in various locations. Within the factories, labor conflict became more endemic and in the large steel and metal plants of the Basque area, Barcelona, and Madrid, as well as the mines of Asturias, a climate of ever present underlying conflict developed. Periodic open outbreaks occurred, which clandestine labor groups sought to utilize to foster their organizations and to develop working-class solidarity.

During the last years of the Franco regime, a new form of action appeared, the "area general strikes" (*huelgas generales locales*). These involved the workers of all sectors in a given area and were organized to press for economic and political demands including free and democratic labor organizations. Several important area general strikes occurred in 1973, in Pamplona (Basque area) and Sandanyola and Ripolles (Catalonia). By the end of the year, general strikes became the most spectacular form of labor conflict. In December alone there were five: in the Basque provinces, Baix Llobregat (Catalonia), and Madrid involving 1,719 plants and over 300,000 workers. A year later, in December 1974, 80 percent of the working population of the Basque region joined a general strike in solidarity with 140 political prisoners who had gone on a hunger strike. These strikes represented the broadest and best organized form of working-class action under Francoism. It was a major step forward in the long and difficult struggle in the reorganization of the working-class movement, and it was widely employed towards the end of the dictatorship and in the first months of the monarchy, particularly in January and February 1976, when 20,000 workers were sanctioned and dismissed due to their involvement in strikes.

As industrial conflict grew more intensive after 1976, it also became more politicized. From 1963 to 1967, economic demands predominated (44.2 percent of 1,676 cases), followed by demands related to collective bargaining (15.2 percent), while solidarity claims were relatively rare (4.0 percent). After 1967 the situation changed; solidarity claims reached 45.4 percent (of 7,694 cases), demands related to collective bargaining increased to 20.1 percent and economic demands dropped to 25.6 percent. Solidarity was not limited to the individual firm; it was extended to the inter-industrial and later to the inter-provincial levels in support of workers who were engaged in labor disputes or who had suffered sanctions. Politically oriented demands generally consisted of demands for free and democratic unions and the right to strike.

The change in the nature of demands reflects the growing strength of the movement compared with the earlier period of fear and inhibition. This difference was expressed in the following comment by a democratic union leader:

> You see, workers were even frightened to sign letters . . .
> for purely economic demands, you see . . . with nothing
> political. Even in the early 1960s to sign a letter was seen as
> dangerous. It was a totally different situation from today!
> In 1955 there was a letter in my firm, in Isodel, which
> ended with something like "please do forgive us if our
> demand is too inconsiderate," and they were only claiming
> something about a bloody bus, that it should stop here
> instead of there.

Collective bargaining was used by the clandestine organization to stimulate demands of an increasingly political character, which focused the struggle on the labor-repressive system. It was generally accepted that despite limitations placed upon bargaining, it could be useful in

Distribution of Industrial Conflict in Spain

By Size of Plant between 1968 and 1974

Number of Employees	Number of Plants	Number of Conflicts	Percent of Conflicts	Ratio: Number of Plants to Average Disputes per Year
1- 24	619,056	638	9.0	6,803
25- 49	22,626	829	11.6	192
50- 99	10,266	853	12.0	84
100-500	7,579	2,924	41.0	18
Over 500	1,267	1,883	26.4	5
Total	660,794	7,127	100.0	649

building the cohesion and organization of the working class. That is the reason why the movement used plant bargaining so frequently and sought to avoid bargaining on the national level where it would have been conducted by the *sindicatos'* corporatist bureaucracy. In the steel and metal industries of Barcelona, Madrid, and Vizcaya, plant bargaining was most frequent. The Ministry of Labor intervened through compulsory arbitration whenever there was a deadlock in bargaining, a role which exemplified government intervention in industrial relations. A look at forty-one arbitration cases in 1971, representing 30 percent of the total for that year and 32 percent of the workers affected by compulsory arbitration, reveals that while collective agreements on the average had increased wages between 12.6 percent (for one-year agreements) and 16.6 percent (for two-year agreements), the arbitration panels raised wages by only 10 percent. Government intervention through compulsory arbitration reflected the degree of conflict in industrial relations. It is possible to interpret the increase in the ratio of compulsory arbitration to collective agreements as a manifestation of the growing strength of the working class movement, a ratio that increased from 2.6 percent in 1960 to 20 percent at the end of the decade. In the 1970s, however, because of the detrimental effect of government intervention, the democratic unions sought to avoid imposition of arbitration panels and deadlocks in bargaining, while at the same time continuing to employ collective bargaining as a mobilization instrument. The CCOOs envisioned two possibilities, which had to be simultaneously employed in collective bargaining: the struggle for specific, immediate demands and the creation of a platform to mobilize workers in a revolutionary manner.

In the 1970s, the working-class struggle was characterized not only by the organization of area general strikes, but also by *plataformas reivindicativas* ("platforms of demands"). These demands were often supported by chains of solidaristic strikes or in coordinated, simultaneous waves of confrontations. They included uniformly detailed demands concerning wage increases, employment, working conditions, and political claims (free trade unionism, amnesty, the right to strike, the right to organize meetings in the plant, etc.). They provided a link between economic and political demands. This political aspect is expressed in the following call from the UGT for an area general strike in January 1976, which, following a lengthy exposition of the current struggle, declared: "Comrades, the UGT summons you to a general strike from the 12th to gain our *plataforma reivindicativa*, to free all political prisoners, to gain free trade unionism and all democratic freedoms."

The Government Response to Labor Unrest

The response of the Franco regime to the growing strength of the working-class movement and to the extension of industrial conflict involved a dual strategy of integration and repression. Integration consisted of partial reforms in the official trade union organization and in legislation on industrial relations. It included the legalization of the so-called economic strikes in 1962, a reform of the Penal Code in 1965, a constitutional reform in 1966, and the new trade union law of 1971. The new law introduced some degree of autonomy in worker representation at low levels and greater independence of workers and employers within the trade unions but they, nevertheless, remained "an instrument of the state," still vertical and compulsory.

This strategy should be viewed within the context of a wider attempt to reorganize the regime. The 1957–75 period of the Franco government can be characterized as capitalist development without democracy. Nonetheless, the regime sought to keep the economic aspects of modernization isolated from its political aspects, although some modifications were necessary to avoid a total loss of control over the increasing institutional incongruities. These crisis management policies followed a minimalist strategy, the intention of which was to limit institutional changes and maintain control over them. For instance, it was usual in official political writings to accept the need for "administrative" reforms as opposed to "political" reforms. This was also an important reason for the rise of a new technocracy to political power. From 1957 to 1974, the *Opus Dei*, a Catholic lay group, advocated and developed concrete policies for economic and administrative reforms.

The strategy of repression sought to isolate the clandestine organizations from the workers through political persecution. Repression against the organized working class movement was indeed massive. An analysis of information provided by the national press over the months of January and February 1974 reveals that 24,817 workers had their contracts and wages temporarily suspended, and that 4,379 were discharged from their jobs due to participation in strikes. The table on this page provides information on repressive measures by the firms and official trade unions during this period, but it does not include data on the third level of repression—police arrests.

Greater repressive measures against militant workers occurred in the Basque region, which reflects the importance of that area in the reorganization of the Spanish labor movement. In Madrid and Catalonia greater use of sanctions was employed against trade union representatives. The differing measures taken can possibly be seen as a rough indicator of the

Repressive Measures by Geographical Area in Spain
January-February 1974

	Suspension of Contracts and Wages		Dismissals from Jobs		Dismissals from Official Trade-Union Posts	
	N	%	N	%	N	%
Andalucia	2,890	11.6	962	22.0	5	7.6
Asturias	783	3.2	359	8.2	4	6.1
Basque Country	6,508	26.2	1,700	38.8	4	6.1
Catalonia	3,910	15.8	969	22.1	17	25.7
Galicia	3,772	15.2	90	2.1	—	—
Country of Valencia	2,583	10.4	53	1.2	6	9.1
Madrid	4,371	17.6	246	5.6	30	45.4
Total	24,817	100.0	4,379	100.0	66	100.0

influence of the infiltrationist strategy of the CCOOs in the two areas of Madrid and Catalonia and of the relative strength of the non-infiltrationist strategy of the UGT in Asturias and the Basque country. It also seems clear that, in terms of repression, the costs of the struggle remained very high well into the 1970s.

After the Death of Franco

What was the situation at the death of Franco in 1975 and how important were the resistance movements among workers and students to the gradual emergence of a quasi-democratic climate in 1976–77? There is clearly a reciprocal relationship between the struggle of these movements and the crisis of the dictatorship in the 1970s, especially after 1973. Increased repression after 1968 did not receive the support of important power groups. Repression was merely regarded as a temporary reprieve, manifesting the incapacity of the regime to move towards a different type of political system. Such a system was not viewed as necessary, due partly to the demands of Spanish capitalism and partly to the strength of the movements of dissent. It should be recalled that repression did not stop the working-class struggle—the number of strikes was higher than ever in 1970—nor did repression put an end to the clandestine struggle within the universities. Thus, the death of Prime Minister Carrero Blanco in a terrorist bomb attack in 1973 was seen by these sectors as an opportunity to increase pressures for reform. These included demands for the resignation of Franco. The death of the dictator in November 1975 led to the gradual dismantling of the dictatorial apparatus. The Suarez government continued the process after July 1975, following seven months of intense political confrontations.

The outcome of the general elections of June 15, 1977, the first to take place after forty years, have some interesting implications. It is, of course, obvious that there is no necessary correspondence between the militant capacity of an organization of the left and its electoral support among workers. However, these elections manifested the strong continuity of political forces since the Republican defeat in 1939, despite four decades of dictatorship. This continuity was particularly observable in the case of the Socialist party, whose success seemed to result from persisting ideological loyalties in working class communities, from lingering ideological allegiances within families, and from organizational policies.

Moreover, the geographical distribution of political cleavages also showed similarities with the political situation under the Republic. The most notable exception was Catalonia, where socialism and, to a lesser degree, communism have now become the most influential forces. Finally, the election results indicated that although Basque, Catalan, and Galician nationalism was a crucial political issue, it did not fragment the underlying ideological cleavages in the country as a whole or the unity of working-class politics. These seem to be relevant points, notwithstanding the basic differences between electoral competition and underground organized struggle, a difference dramatically underlined by the relatively poor electoral results of the Communist party, which had been such an important force in the clandestine struggle.

References

Amsden, J. *Collective Bargaining and Class Conflict in Spain.* London: Weidenfeld and Nicolson, 1972.

Anderson, C. W. *The Political Economy of Modern Spain: Policy Making in an Authoritarian System.* Madison: The University of Wisconsin Press, 1970.

Jackson, G. *The Spanish Republic and the Civil War.* Princeton University Press, 1965.

Romano, V. *Spain. The Workers' Commissions.* Toronto: The Canadian Committee for a Democratic Spain, 1973.

Romero-Maura, J. "The Spanish Case" in D. Apter and J. Joll, eds. *Anarchism Today.* London: MacMillan, 1971.

III

Worker Participation

Worker Participation

The German Experience

Gerhard Leminsky

TRADE unions were established in Germany during the 1860s largely
at the initiative of political movements of a socialist orientation.
Other political parties, influenced by Christian or liberal ideas, also sought
to exploit the unions for their political advancement. As a result, unions
representing these three ideologies continued to operate until the end of
the Weimar Republic in 1933. Thereafter, with the advent of the Nazi
era, trade unions were completely destroyed.

Following the conclusion of the Second World War, the unions were
reconstituted and a new pattern was established. Its most distinct characteristic was the abandonment of union organization according to political
ideology and adherence to the principle of one union—one industry.

Historical Background

EARLY TRADE UNION STRUCTURES

Many distinctive features of contemporary German trade unionism and
the development of worker participation schemes have their roots in early
labor organizations. Prior to World War I, Germany was an authoritarian
monarchy; the nobility, landowners, and entrepreneurs sought to defend

their privileges against the rising demands of the workers, their unions, and the socialist parties. By legal means and through government action, the organization of labor was suppressed, and the unions, therefore, had to operate illegally in an atmosphere of hostility and bitterness. Union leaders consequently came to the conclusion that the miserable situation of the workers could be bettered only through a revolution in the Marxist sense. At the same time they believed that only free parliamentary elections and a democratic state would make possible the existence of free unions.

But a contrasting development must also be taken into account. To discourage workers from joining unions, to counter socialist influence, and to strenghten the army, Chancellor Otto Bismarck established laws that marked a breakthrough in social policy (health and accident insurance and old age and disability pensions). These laws were enacted despite the resistance of the privileged classes. As the elected representatives of the workers, the unions participated in the administration of these pension funds. They also continued the pre-industrial traditions of craftsmen with their own mutual funds. Because of their Christian or paternalistic attitudes, some employers permitted a certain role for workers in the handling of these funds. Trade unions, because they were closely linked with political parties, were very ideological and believed that substantive changes in the life of workers required structural changes in society. Therefore, they never regarded themselves as acting in the interest solely of union members but of the working class as a whole.

Great economic and social changes took place in Germany between 1880 and 1910 and led to advanced industrialization, new technologies, and economic and social concentrations. Millions of workers were housed inadequately in overcrowded towns and worked under bad conditions made worse by the capitalist cycles of depression and boom.

Beyond ideological concerns, the unions sought to protect their members through collective agreements. There were strikes to improve safety conditions, especially in coal mining, and funds were established in case of sickness, unemployment, or strikes. Even prior to the First World War, unions possessed greater organizational strength than the Socialist Labor party, and collective agreements had been introduced in some sectors of German industry.

During World War I the unions gained, for the first time, a legal representational status in important firms devoted to public supply and war production, through white- and blue-collar councils. Employers complied with the law as a means of reducing unrest and the spontaneous strikes caused by bad working conditions, so that the government could achieve its expansionist goals.

THE WEIMAR PERIOD

In 1918 when a parliamentary system was introduced and the monarchy overthrown, works councils sprang up spontaneously, and some elements of this council movement found expression in the Weimar Constitution, which prescribed such councils at plant, regional, and national levels.

The constitution also recognized unions as the representatives of labor, and the collective bargaining agreement as the principal means to regulate wages and working conditions. In a 1920 putsch the unions called a general strike which saved the republic and the parliamentary system. They identified themselves with the democratic state, trusted the government, and pressed it to act for the well being of the workers.

In 1920, works councils at the shop level were introduced by law, giving restricted rights to the workers in the area of social problems and personnel policies. In 1922 the law was amended so that the works councils could appoint one or two members to company supervisory boards. On some executive boards of publicly owned companies the member in charge of social and personnel questions was selected through informal procedures by the union side. Though these activities do not represent a systematic process, they were the antecedents of the system of *Mitbestimmung,* or worker participation, that came into existence after 1945. (*Mitbestimmung* is a system which gives the workers an important voice in the operation of the company, through elected representatives on the company supervisory board and other means to influence company policy.)

Collective bargaining also became a widespread practice during the Weimar period, although compulsory arbitration by the secretary of state for labor also played an important role and labor courts were established. The democratic government was regarded as a vital defender of the common interest and undertook reforms in a direction desired by the socialists.

These changes were accompanied by severe conflict. Within the unions there were strong groups that opposed collective agreements because they feared integration into the capitalist system (an argument also applied today to *Mitbestimmung*). The unions in general distrusted the works councils because the councils regarded unions as part of the establishment. The unions feared that their goals of economic democracy through nationalization of key companies, self-administration of industries, and a framework for industrial planning in the public interest would be adversely affected by the works councils' collaboration with the company. Employers accepted collaboration with the unions only during the early phase of revolution. After 1920, once power was consolidated, changes by works councils or collective bargaining were strongly opposed. With the onset of inflation, the Depression, and mass unemployment, union influence declined, and by 1933 unions were dissolved by the Nazis.

Worker Participation after World War II

After 1945, the unions, which were one of the few groups in German society not identified with the Nazi regime, were restructured as industrial unions. Their ideology was based on the Weimar program of industrial democracy consisting of national planning, nationalization of key industries, and worker participation. Collective agreements were again established to regulate wages and working conditions, but an important change occurred concerning worker participation.

NEW PERSPECTIVES OF PARTICIPATION

The unions demanded equal status at the company level. Workers and their unions had been the driving force in the immediate post-war period for the reconstruction of many companies. They felt that they had demonstrated a proven ability to participate in the regulation of all labor problems in industry. In their view, this ability and their claim for participation could not be compensated for with money. They wanted real participation in industry. The unions also insisted that it should never again be possible to misuse economic power for political aims. They believed that Adolf Hitler had gained dominance in part with the help of big capital. Through the participation of workers and their unions in company supervisory boards and by the presence of labor directors on the executive boards such a misuse would be prevented in the future.

The Allied Forces, especially in the British zone of Germany, had already given the workers and the unions equal representation on supervisory boards and labor directors on executive boards in order to decentralize the Nazi system of production. In addition, after the war, company shareholders offered participation to the unions because they hoped to escape nationalization through such concessions.

For these reasons worker participation at both the shop and the company level was one of the principal union demands when the Federation of German Unions (*Deutscher Gewerkschaftsbund*) was founded in 1949. By that time, however, executives of German industry, who had been discredited by their collaboration with the Nazi regime, already had reconsolidated their power. They opposed both nationalization and participation at the company level. Only by means of strike threats did the unions gain a legislated worker participation plan in 1951 in the coal and steel industries. This plan gave labor equal representation with capital on company supervisory boards as well as an executive board member in charge of personnel and social problems who could not be elected without the approval of a majority of the labor representatives on the executive board. Worker participation, or codetermination, in the coal and steel companies became the outstanding innovation in the German industrial relations system. Other proposals for a new economic order advanced by the unions could not be realized. In 1952, works councils similar to those that existed during the Weimar period were established by law. In industries other than coal and steel, the unions achieved only one-third representation for the labor side on supervisory boards, not the parity obtained in coal and steel.

Further development of union activities has to be viewed within the overall political and economic context of the Federal Republic of Germany. The cold-war climate and Germany's division into East and West made West Germans highly distrustful of planning and nationalization, formerly important elements of the trade union outlook. Within the Federal Republic, the ideology of a social market economy gained a political majority and business was regarded as the main power center of the economy. The economic development initiated by the Marshall Plan and the reconstruction of the economy resulted in rapid growth, full employment, and rising incomes.

FULL EMPLOYMENT ECONOMY

These factors explain why workers focused their attention on codetermination at the company level. At the shop floor level, industrial relations had little importance, though the regulation of conflict by works councils was seen as useful by both sides. Collective bargaining produced substantial annual wage increases without a need for strikes. Workers were not much interested in politics after long years of inflation and depression; they preferred to pursue private concerns and live with some comfort.

Unions continued to seek the expansion of codetermintion, but they concentrated their efforts on demands for the forty-hour week, more holidays, increased incomes, etc., instead of structural changes in the economy and society. During the sixties, the first ideas regarding capital formation or capital sharing for labor developed. Through worker participation, the unions sought participation in the decision-making process at the company level. But they wanted some influence over the means for achieving a more just distribution of capital, which cannot be attained through collective bargaining. The issue of the unequal distribution of capital has received extensive public exposure.

CAPITAL SHARING

A generation after the end of the Second World War, scholars, trade union researchers, and churches began to decry the "scandalous distribution of capital" in Germany. The ensuing discussion of capital sharing developed under special circumstances. Because of the cold war, it was impossible to discuss planning and nationalization as an alternative to capital sharing. Possible solutions, therefore, were sought within the market economy, solutions that would not restrict worker participation at shop and company levels or collective bargaining at regional levels between unions and employers' organizations.

Collective bargaining could assure workers their part of the gross income of a national economy, but not of the investment funds. By definition, a redistribution of these funds would require that capital shares received by the workers would *not* be consumed.

In the late sixties the unions concluded that there should be a legal redistribution of capital. According to their proposal, employers would allocate part of their profits as capital shares to regional funds controlled by the workers. In this manner, employers would not lose money. The allocated worker shares would accumulate over several decades and become a substantial part of entrepreneurial capital. Although the individual worker would retain a relatively small number of shares, he could not, except under very restricted conditions, sell his shares. The term "capital sharing" for this process is misleading; it is more a form of industrial control by workers, which would allow them to influence general industrial policy without giving up a decentralized market economy.

The Federation of German Workers accepted an approach along these lines in 1972, but there was opposition from a strong minority, especially the metal workers. Opposition arose out of fear that capital sharing would block broader nationalization and a concern that there would be no monetary compensation for workers. It also was feared that capital sharing would eventually restrict the scope of collective bargaining.

This opposition and the present unfavorable economic situation have contributed to the fact that capital sharing is not a high priority of the Federal Republic. It should be added that the unions regarded participation at the company level and capital sharing not as alternatives, but as complementary elements. Participation focuses upon the internal decision-making process and the status of labor within the firm. Capital sharing and a fund system focus upon the relationship between the company and the market.

Employers strongly oppose these proposals. They advocate concepts of individual capital sharing as practiced in other Western countries.

A SHIFT IN UNION ATTITUDES

Since the second half of the 1960s, trade union activities concerning participation have shifted as a result of economic and political changes. When the Social Democrats came to power, first in coalition with the Christian Democrats and then with the Liberals in 1969, there was a widely felt need for economic and social reforms: civil rights, codetermination in industry, solutions to environmental problems, humanization of work, better education and training, etc. This occurred at a time of reduced growth rates, layoffs, structural crises in certain branches of industry, and later a deep recession. These developments severely tested the industrial relations system.

Although the works councils had won some additional power by the Works Constitution Law of 1972, their restricted influence (they had to bargain in "mutual trust" with the employer) soon became apparent, and they instituted much closer cooperation with labor at the company level, where important economic decisions were made. Moreover, collective bargaining, which heretofore had served as a mechanism for wage boosts, increased substantially in importance because strikes could be called on specific issues. The new emphasis on collective bargaining and other instruments of change was strengthened by the 1976 *Mitbestimmung* law, because it failed to give workers a truly equal voice in controlling company policies. The unions therefore began to reconsider whether it was advantageous for them to rely primarily on effecting changes through legal channels such as the works councils or participation at the company level. They concluded that political parties make decisions in the context of parliamentary relations, which are not always identical with trade union interests. The worker participation movement, therefore, came to be viewed as an element of trade union activities rather than as an isolated institutional mechanism.

The Institutional Framework of Worker Participation

Worker participation or *Mitbestimmung* is based on the works councils at the shop level. On the company level, workers have representatives on the supervisory boards, and on management boards they are represented by a labor director. Participation must also be related to the collective bargaining process. (Workers' influence on national economic and fiscal policy, however, is not dealt with in this paper).

WORKER PARTICIPATION AT THE SHOP FLOOR

At the shop floor level, worker participation is regulated by the Works Constitution Act of 1972. Under this act, a works council must be established in private enterprises employing more than five persons. The works council is elected for three years by all blue- and white-collar workers of an establishment; they may or may not be union members. The number elected to the council varies, depending on the size of the work force in the plant. Some establishments may have as many as thirty-five council members. Multi-plant companies must establish a central works council for the entire enterprise. Employers cannot dismiss members of the works councils while they are holding office or for one year thereafter. In larger companies with more than 300 employees, at least one member of the works council must be released from production work to devote full time to works council matters. If a company employs 10,000 people, twelve of them will be released for full time work on the works council.

The works council has various codecision, consultation, and information rights, vis à vis the employer, stipulated in the Works Constitution Law. These rights are to be exercised, as stated in the law, in a spirit of "mutual trust" with the employer; action is to be avoided that might disturb industrial peace at the shop floor; cooperation between unions and employers is required; and the precedence of collective bargaining agreements is to be observed.

The legal links between works councils and unions are relatively loose. The unions represented in a firm can visit the establishment, modify the structure of the works councils in minor aspects through collective agreements, and take part in the sessions of the works council in an advisory capacity if 25 percent of the members of the works council agree to their participation.

The most important general responsibility of the works council is to assure that all acts of parliament, regulations, safety rules, collective agreements, and works agreements are adhered to for the benefit of the workers.

The rights of the works council are specified for social and personnel matters, for the actual conduct of business, and—since 1972—for aspects of the structure, organization, and design of jobs, as well as problems of the industrial environment.

The works council has an equal say with management in social matters, unless otherwise stipulated by collective agreements, including:

- Job evaluation, piece rates, and wage structures.
- Working hours, overtime, short-time work arrangements, breaks, and holiday schedules.
- Financial compensation for those laid off and "social plans."
- Training, accident prevention, and welfare schemes.
- Allocation of houses and apartments provided by the employer.
- Workers' conduct on the shop floor.

If agreement on these matters is not reached or should a deadlock occur between employer and works council on matters where the works council is entitled to codetermination, either side can bring the case before an internal joint arbitration or conciliation committee with an outside chairman. Where statutory rights are involved, the final decision lies with the labor courts.

In other areas, the works councils have rights of information, consultation and control, and an equal voice within certain limits.

In matters concerning working conditions and industrial environment, the works council must be informed and consulted regarding the structure, organization, and design of jobs as well as environmental changes contemplated by the employer. The works council has the right of codetermination concerning consideration of "established and accepted findings of ergonomics;" if an agreement cannot be reached the decision is referred to a conciliation committee.

In personnel matters, the works council has extensive rights of information and consultation concerning manpower planning, guidelines for selection in recruitment, transfer, dismissal, training, hiring, and firing of individuals.

In the case of hiring and firing, promotion, allocation of work, and transfers, the advance consent of the works council is required. If, for example, an employer wants to hire someone from the outside to fill a certain post, the works council can insist that someone should be promoted from within the company.

An employer who wishes to dismiss a worker must consult the works council first and explain the reason for the dismissal. Any dismissal without such consultation is against the law. The works council even has the right to object to a dismissal, for instance, on the grounds that a "social hardship" would result for the worker or that a dismissal violates the law.

Unresolved differences are referred to the labor courts. In general, the works council cannot develop its own policy on personnel matters, but it can affect the policy of the employers in this field by assuring that they conform to legal provisions, regulations, and collective agreements. The council can also extend this form of monitoring to planning, recruitment principles, and guidelines for promotion.

One of the principal union demands is not only to have an equal say in social matters but to extend codetermination to personnel matters as well. In matters affecting the actual conduct of the business, the powers of the works council are more limited. In companies employing more than 100 workers, the council must appoint an economic committee, which is entitled to information concerning the economic and financial situation of the company, production problems and the market situation, reorganization, alternatives in the scale of production, and intended staff cutbacks or shutdowns.

In the case of major changes which would result in the loss of jobs, the employer must jointly establish with the works council a plan that would provide employment elsewhere in the firm, retraining, or severance pay for the workers affected ("social plan"). In case of conflict, the issue is referred to the company conciliation committee or to the labor court.

The works council cannot change the employer's decisions in the conduct of business, but it can influence consequences for the workers, especially in terms of financial compensation for lay-offs. Works council members also may influence business matters through their representation on supervisory boards.

In recent years, unions have emphasized the election of union shop stewards as a countervailing force to the works council. Union rights and duties are regulated by collective agreements. The shop stewards have no legal powers, but explain union activities at the shop floor level and report to the unions. The shop stewards can influence the works council, because they serve as a source of recruitment for candidates on the works council. In many unions, the function of a works council member and a shop steward are compatible. Employers strongly oppose the elections and functions of shop stewards because, in their view, the workers should be represented at the shop and company level exclusively by the works councils and not by the unions.

It should be noted that, on the average, more than 80 percent of the works council members are union members—particularly where a Federation of German Unions industrial union is represented in the company. Even in plants where the union has only a low rate of membership, the majority of works council members are usually union members.

German collective bargaining cannot be discussed separately from the works councils because the councils deal with problems that are within union jurisdiction in many countries.

WORKER PARTICIPATION AT THE COMPANY LEVEL*

Worker participation at the company level was introduced during the Weimar period more than fifty years ago. At that time, one or two members of the works councils were empowered with equal rights and duties to serve on supervisory boards; in some state-owned companies, executive board members in charge of personnel matters were elected following consultation with the unions. These were forerunners of the present labor directors. Since 1945, worker participation at the company level has become the increasing focus of trade union activities, although the works councils and collective bargaining have been much more practical as a way to increase workers' status and union influence.

An industrial company, in the union view, consists of three elements: employees to perform the work, capital owners to provide equipment, and management to combine labor and capital into a profitable unit.

---

* The framework of institutional participation presented in this paper does not conform to legal technicalities but rather to substantive structures. For example, when it is stated that capital and labor elect representatives in coal and steel on a parity basis, in terms of substance this is correct but not so from a legal point of view because the Act of 1951 prescribes the formal election by the general assembly of the company. Although this is a formal requisite, the assembly must abide by the proposals submitted by the labor side.

The unions view a company not merely as an economic unit, but also as an institution where thousands of people spend a large part of their lives. These people's aspirations and dignity must be looked after by the unions and their representatives, the unions believe. Therefore, management, which is the power center of the company, must be jointly controlled by capital and labor. Because employees are an essential part of the company, staff matters and personnel problems should be treated by management with the same regard given to investment policy, financial planning, or marketing strategies.

The union concept of *Mitbestimmung* at the company level is based on their interpretation of the relationship between capital, labor, and management.

German companies have three main institutional groups: the general assembly of shareholders, the supervisory board, and the executive or management board. The supervisory board, which meets about four times a year, serves as a link between the shareholders' assembly and the executive board. The supervisory board appoints the members of the executive board, supervises and approves their activities according to the by-laws of the company, and makes decisions of major importance such as financial planning, investment policy, major changes in production, etc. At the supervisory board level, various interests bargain to reach a workable compromise that assures the survival and expansion of the company.

The unions seek equal representation of labor and capital (parity representation) on supervisory boards because both are of equal importance in company operations. Less than equal representation, evidence has confirmed, can only be classified as consultation. Only parity representation on supervisory boards guarantees that management will give both sides equal weight in decision making. Equal representation, in the union view, should not be restricted to private companies; the principle of equal representation holds whether the property is private or public. In addition, unions claim that works council members on supervisory boards bring the point of view of the shop floor into the decision-making process. But, since they tend to view company policy from the perspective of their specific shop or department, it is necessary to include trade union officials on the boards, because they can relate company policy to the broader perspectives of labor in industry and the total economy. Thus trade union officials bring the support and solidarity of the unions into the supervisory boards. Because they are not dependent on management boards or specific groups of employees in a firm, they find it easier to discuss unpopular issues on behalf of representatives from the shop floor. In addition, they bring to the boards a wide range of qualifications and expert knowledge that the shop floor representatives do not possess. This is of importance at a time of increased planning and multinationalization of company policies.

This scheme of worker participation is based on the principle of industrial unionism: one industry, one company, one union. The union official acts as the spokesman and is also accepted as a mediator in case of sectional conflicts betwen different labor groups within a company.

The executive board conducts the day-to-day business and is the true power center of the company. The unions do not wish to destroy this management function but do insist that its structure reflect the social responsibilities of the company. Therefore, unions say, the problems of labor are to be accorded a weight equal with financial, investment, or marketing problems. The institutional expression of this concept is the labor director, a full-time member of the executive board who is charged with staff matters, personnel, and social problems within his overall responsibility for company policy. The labor director, in the union view, is considered a board member with equal status. But to assure a better understanding of labor problems, he should be elected by a majority vote of the labor members of the supervisory board, which is the practice among coal and steel companies.

Worker participation, as described here, is a network of relations, all elements—works councils, labor directors, supervisory board representatives—working together and connecting at several points with the collective bargaining process.

German trade unions have attained a greater degree of participation at the company level than unions in other countries, but less than they have sought. Since the adoption of legislation in 1951, equal representation of capital and labor on the supervisory board has been in effect for the coal and steel industries. All boards contain an odd number of members, either eleven, fifteen, or twenty-one. A supervisory board composed of eleven members, for instance, has five members appointed by the shareholders and five by the workers. The eleventh man, known as the "additional member," is chosen by both sides.

Members on the workers' side are chosen in three ways. For example, where there are five worker members: Two are proposed by the works council (as a general rule, these two are the chairman and his deputy, representing the blue- and white-collar workers). Two are delegated by the trade unions from outside the company, after consultation with the works council. The fifth or "additional member" is nominated by the Federation of German Unions (not a direct union representative, but someone with a pro-labor bias such as a banker from the labor bank, an expert from the academic field, or a representative of community interests).

Shareholders can elect four of their five members, usually at a general assembly. The fifth member, also called an "additional" member, must not have direct capital relations to the firm, but usually does have a bias toward the management side.

These ten members select the eleventh member by a majority vote of each side, and a majority vote of the ten members. This member is often referred to as the "neutral member." The chairman of the supervisory board generally is from management, with the vice-chairman from labor, normally an official of the industrial union or the chairman of the works council.

On a supervisory board with parity representation, there are three additional members who are intended by law to represent the public interest.

On the management board of coal and steel enterprises, a labor director must be elected by a majority vote of both the supervisory board and the labor side. He shares similar responsibilities with the other executive directors and is entrusted with wages, staff matters, personnel, and welfare questions.

The unions have sought to extend the model of participation that exists in the coal and steel industries to all large companies with more than 2,000 employees. After protracted controversy, legislation was enacted in 1976 (*Mitbestimmungsgesetz* 1976) by an overwhelming majority. Labor, however, has regarded the law as "a step in the wrong direction." No real parity of representation is provided by the new law. It is the product of conflicting interests between the Social Democractic party and the Free Democrats, who compose the present social–liberal government coalition. Compared with participation in the coal and steel industries, union influence under the new law has been weakened. There is no real parity for the labor side; the number of union representatives from the works councils is reduced; the procedures to elect members tend to split up worker solidarity; and the labor director does not have to have a special relationship with the labor representatives and can even be elected over labor's opposition. If a supervisory board is composed of twenty members, ten are chosen by the labor side. Seven of the ten members must be from within the company, and only three are trade union officials. Among the seven labor representatives, one is elected by a small group of senior executives, and this member generally tends to assume a pro-management attitude. In addition, the chairman, who in fact is chosen by the shareholders (if we leave aside legal technicalities), can cast the deciding vote in case of a deadlock. Election procedures are very complicated, and small groups of employees can also submit lists of candidates. If a company is not strongly unionized, there is a danger that different groups of employees and even non-union members will compete and thus weaken workers' solidarity. A labor director is prescribed by law, but his election merely requires a majority of votes and it is possible for him to be elected solely by shareholders.

Despite the law's pro-management provisions and its nearly unanimous acceptance by parliament, the German Employers Federation appealed to the Constitutional Court in July 1977, asking that the law be declared unconstitutional on the grounds that it was incompatible with the basic rights of the constitution, namely the rights of owners of private property to dispose of their property as they wish and the rights of collective bargaining between equal and independent parties.

At a hearing before the Constitutional Court from November 28 to December 1, 1978, unions, employers, and the government reiterated their positions. Although critical of the law, unions were not eager to see it declared unconstitutional. They were concerned about a recent tendency by the Constitutional Court not to restrict itself to ruling on the constitutionality of laws but to intervene in the political process. The court could bar any possible future development of *Mitbestimmung* by declaring, for example, that the present status of the labor director was unconstitutional. It can be assumed that the employers' intention was not to eliminate the 1976 law, but to use the appeal as a means for blocking any future expansion of *Mitbestimmung*. The unions were cognizant of the court's ambitions and feared a shift of power from parliament to the Constitutional Court, which would place constraints on the political process. The court rendered its decision in the spring of 1979.

The court rejected the employers' arguments and stated that the law does not bring real parity of influence for labor at the supervisory board level and that the labor director can, in fact, be appointed against the labor side. It declared that participation and collective bargaining are compatible and stressed the positive function of trade union officials in supervisory boards.

But the court also said that parliament was within its constitutional limits. Participation should not lead to a situation in which decisions about investment of capital are made against the will of shareholders or in which the owners of capital lose control over the selection of top management and final decision making.

Employers have interpreted this decision to mean that if a law gave labor real decision-making powers over investments, selection of management, and company strategy, such a law would be unconstitutional. Many German observers have concluded that the decision of the Constitutional Court reflects a political compromise that leaves the way open for further legislation in the field of participation but sets down some ground rules that must be followed.

The effects of the new law cannot yet be evaluated totally. But many companies have shifted policy-making authority away from the supervisory boards. In some cases labor directors were elected prior to the establishment of the new supervisory boards, or against the labor side; other legal and illegal means have been employed to weaken labor influence. Although in most cases between 80 and 90 percent of the labor members of supervisory boards are union supporters, they do not have equal voice with others on the supervisory boards. Unions, therefore, fear that this "illusion of participation" might be deeply disappointing at the shop level, when workers realize that the new law, discussed over years in parliament, does not bring any real advantage for labor.

PARTICIPATION AND COLLECTIVE BARGAINING

The institutional arrangements for worker participation at the shop and company level are often regarded as separate from the collective bargaining system, because they possess different legal foundations and regulations to resolve conflicts and have different relations to the unions. But collective bargaining and participation should be viewed as integral elements of a system of industrial relations. Collective bargaining concentrates on the regional levels of an industry and deals primarily with wages and working conditions. Some of the problems that in other countries would be dealt with through collective bargaining agreements are handled by institutions such as the works council in the Federal Republic. These institutions have to observe the precedence of collective bargaining, but there is no doubt that their mere existence has implications for the structure of collective bargaining. Empirical studies have established that participation does not have a negative effect on collective bargaining.

Experience with Worker Participation

A valid evaluation of worker participation is possible only if the various elements are viewed within a proper context. In this instance, the issue is whether participation and collective bargaining—the two main ingredients of the German industrial relations system—do promote the workers' interest.

UNEMPLOYMENT AS A RESTRICTIVE FACTOR

In Western industrialized countries labor has similar goals: stability of employment and income, humane working conditions, a real voice in matters that affect workers, education and training facilities, etc. It is evident that achieving these goals through collective bargaining or participation is partly dependent on outside factors that are beyond the power of unions to control. The most essential is full employment. The Federal Republic had, for three years (1974 to 1977), one million unemployed people. This 5 percent rate is merely the tip of the iceberg, because it is accompanied by steady pressure for streamlining industry and laying off workers deemed to be superfluous. In such a situation, there is strong resistance to any extension of participation; labor is generally in a defensive position.

PARTICIPATION, COOPERATION, AND CONFLICT

Experience has shown that participation does not necessarily mean cooperation, nor does collective bargaining mean conflict. In a broad sense, it is natural for workers to bargain with employers over differing interests to reach a workable compromise.

Unquestionably, a collective agreement can be reached more effectively through a strike. But the works council, which is not allowed to strike by law, has other means of exerting pressure such as reducing cooperation, inciting workers to spontaneous protests over the employer's unwillingness to concede change, or bringing issues before a conciliation committee or a labor court. Furthermore, labor members of the supervisory boards can trade their support of a decision desired by management for concessions to labor demands. Thus there are numerous means of exerting pressure short of a formal strike.

The final outcome of a bargain in each case is dependent upon the actual power relationship of labor and capital, irrespective of the legal form through which this influence is exercised. Therefore, arguing about whether participation or collective bargaining is the "right way" is not very useful. It is more helpful to discuss how the problems of employment, income, training or working conditions, etc. in each system are dealt with and to learn from different approaches.

POSITIVE AND NEGATIVE EFFECTS OF INSTITUTIONAL PARTICIPATION

A broad agreement on bargaining does not exclude the possibility that the works councils can have their own specific effects. For example, the tendency of German unions to advocate state intervention and industrial relations laws has given the system a high degree of stability. Pension schemes, accident prevention, unemployment benefits, and retraining are legally guaranteed to all workers; these guarantees have produced much greater acceptance of technical change in Germany than in other countries. Maintaining an adequate standard of living is not solely dependent on holding a given job. Industrial life in the Federal Republic is administered by a network of rules, more by law than collective agreements. But it must be observed that the government has sought to make this network compatible with existing structures and to promote stability in industrial relations. The works council must bargain in "mutual trust" with the employer; participation at the company level is possible only in the interests of the company as a whole. The German federal labor courts try to restrict open conflicts in collective bargaining.

The impossibility of strikes at the shop level has widened the scope of conciliation committees. The regulation of conflicts by such an institutional mechanism makes much industrial conflict "invisible" to the foreign observer, who is used to regarding strike statistics as a main indicator. Institutional stability, the bureaucratic machinery for resolving conflicts, alienates the worker from his union unless the union counteracts this tendency by, for example, strengthening the network of shop stewards and maintaining close contact with their members. The advantage of such a structure is that there are established channels of information and communication, and regulations for resolving conflict, which are also useful in handling difficult problems during times of recessions. The more that is accomplished for the workers, the more they are willing to back their representatives in forms of protest that employers consider acceptable.

THE ROLE OF COLLECTIVE BARGAINING

Since 1945, innovations have been made in participation schemes, but not in collective bargaining. Although the laws give precedence to collective bargaining agreements, the existence of the works councils has tended to exclude shop problems from the bargaining table. This tendency has been strengthened by the desire of the powerful German employers associations to separate the shop floor from union activities. But in recent years, because of problems with the economy, relations between workers and employers have deteriorated, and problem solving is shifting from works council activities to the collective bargaining table.

Heretofore disputes have centered on the nature of institutions; now, however, specific problems, such as employment, incomes, and vocational training, are the focus. Institutions are now viewed in terms of the contributions they can make to solve these problems, and the relationship between participation and collective bargaining is seen in a new light. Collective bargaining, as the autonomous action of unions, establishes minimum standards in the field of employment, income, or working conditions. Participation at the shop and company level implements and adapts the rough indicators and criteria of collective agreements into the reality of a specific enterprise. Participation can provide the tools for the direction of industrial labor by developing manpower planning, new forms of work organization, work safety, training schemes, etc. Successful experiments at the shop level can be applied by management and by collective agreements to an entire region and may even eventually find expression in law.

Nevertheless, collective bargaining remains the most flexible instrument of the industrial relations system and after decades of discussions over participation by law, the unions have rediscovered the broad scope of issues that can be taken up at the bargaining table: working conditions, employment guarantees, branch funds for compensation in case of unemployment or short time work, training facilities, etc. Many new ideas concerning collective bargaining in the last three years have come about because the works councils alone are no longer strong enough to guarantee employee standards.

INTEGRATION OF PARTICIPATION AT THE SHOP AND COMPANY LEVEL

For a long time, participation at the company level was considered to be quite different from participation at the shop level. Since the advent of economic crisis and high unemployment rates, the works councils have had to deal with layoffs, reorganization of work, new technologies, mergers, and closures. They have realized that they have little power to control these processes, which are planned at the company level. Therefore, cooperation and coordination between works councils, labor directors, and labor representatives on supervisory boards has become much closer now than in former years. At the company level, efforts are being made to abolish dismissals as the usual short-term management reaction to economic crisis. Personnel planning has been introduced and the consequences of investment policy on employment have been studied. Some success can be reported: the reduction of employment in the German steel industry was markedly lower than in other industries in proportion to the decline of production. But *Mitbestimmung* at its best can only protect those who have a job. It would be unrealistic not to admit that participation is dependent upon the situation of the company and, in case of a crisis in an industry, the problems can be solved only by measures beyond the scope of individual firms.

PARTICIPATION AS A MEANS OF INFLUENCING CORPORATE PLANNING

If workers want to control their situation in industrial life, they must be able to influence company policies. To influence such policies means taking part in the planning process of the company. The German experience clearly shows that participation has evolved more and more toward corporate planning. Works councils cannot merely deal with staff matters such as hiring and firing; they must also concern themselves with manpower planning and recruitment principles. They cannot merely concern themselves with monotonous jobs and monetary compensation for inhumane working conditions, they must also influence industrial environment policies and job design.

Similar problems can be studied at the enterprise level, where it is equally essential for labor to bargain for employee concerns in corporate planning and investment policy. Unions must develop instruments to deal with corporate planning. Participation is one way. The German experience has shown that to influence the planning process in the interest of the employee, all company activities should be scrutinized. Effective and constant communication is necessary so that problems can be fully discussed at all levels of the company and the shop.

SOCIAL CONSEQUENCES OF ECONOMIC DECISIONS

In theory, parity of representation on supervisory boards provides a way for labor to be involved in discussions of all elements of managerial activity. But in practice, labor representatives concentrate their efforts on the social consequences of economic decisions. If management presents a new investment plan, what does it mean for the employees? If there is a closure accepted by labor, how can the affected workers be employd at other jobs within the company? If a new technology is to be introduced, what does it mean for the job classification structure? Thus worker participation at the company level is a political function in which the interest of the workers serves as the main guideline: stability of employment, stability of income, better working conditions. In these areas, participation has truly been innovative.

INFORMATIVE DECISION MAKING

When workers gained equal representation at the company level in the coal and steel industries, it was feared that deadlocks and confrontations might occur. But in reality nearly all decisions have been unanimous when they have reached the formal agenda of the supervisory boards.

Management boards bring an issue to the supervisory board meeting only after prior agreement has been reached informally. The chairman of the works council and the industrial union officer play the most important labor roles in the final outcome of the bargain. This is an important feature of the decision-making process under *Mitbestimmung*.

Unions and Worker Participation: A Comparative View

Through history and ideology, the German unions have promoted legislation in the field of participation as a useful instrument for the regulation of conflict between workers and employers. In contrast to the labor movements of other countries, German unions view participation and collective bargaining as compatible. However, attitudes toward the function of these labor tools are now shifting, as previously noted. It is clear that a union which follows a Marxist approach or one that adheres to American union philosophies cannot accept participation as an element of union policies.

The structure of unions also plays an important role. Whether there is a multi-union structure at the company level with craft, industrial, or general unions as in Britain, or an ideologically fragmented union structure as in France or Italy, it is difficult for unions to speak with one voice. The German structure of industrial unionism has tended to favor approaches such as works councils or representation of workers at the board level.

The comparative weight given to collective bargaining and participation within the unions should also be cited. A bargaining structure concentrated on the regional level of an industry obviously favors the establishment of participation mechanisms such as the works councils. But the institutional presence of works councils will influence the extension of collective bargaining and vice versa. In Germany it is much more difficult to establish strong union activities at the shop floor level than it is in countries which lack a legal machinery for participation at shop and company levels. But the results achieved by collective bargaining systems such as those in Britain or the United States still might be achieved in Germany through the coordinated effects of collective bargaining and participation.

The structure of German companies is favorable to worker participation because the functions of legitimation and control can be separated from the conduct of day-to-day business. Workers and union representatives on the boards can abstain from an undue involvement in management.

It should be underscored that coordination and cooperation between works councils and unions are very strong. Most works council members, even if initially non-union, join a union. They soon realize that support of the unions, with their training facilities, organizational strength, and expertise, is indispensable for them. As previously noted, the works councils are identified with the unions at the shop floor. Evidence reveals that works councils separated from the unions are weak and tend to become perverted to instruments of management. The presidents of works councils in large companies are nearly without exception also serving in important trade union positions.

Capital Formation

Through Employee Investment Funds

A Swedish Proposal

Rudolf Meidner

FOR many years the problem of wage earners sharing in capital accumulation has been discussed in a number of West European countries. It is not too difficult to point to some of the reasons for such a debate.

After the ravages of World War II the European economies had to be rebuilt by the joint effort of all groups. The restrictiveness in wage policies exercised by the unions was a necessary precondition for the process of reconstruction. But, as a consequence of these moderate wage policies, wealth increased and became strongly concentrated in the hands of capital owners. A development that was considered tolerable as an act of national solidarity—still in the spirit of war time emergency—during the period of reconstruction was eventually seen as socially unjustifiable. Not only labor unions but also liberals, progressive economists, and religious groups asked for measures aimed at leveling wealth. Profit sharing was deemed to be an appropriate method of spreading wealth among wage earners.

Company profit-sharing schemes, designed mainly to increase productivity and employee loyalty to the firm, had been in existence in both West Europe and the United States for about a hundred years. During World War II in Great Britain, John Maynard Keynes proposed that part of a worker's wage (or company revenue) be deferred, placed into

161

a special savings fund in a worker's name, and not released until after the war. This plan was designed to reduce wartime inflationary pressures, as well as to protect the employee's equity. It would also have served as a kind of accumulation of assets for workers.[1]

What was new in the debate after World War II was not the technical concept of profit sharing as such but a change in the character of profit-sharing schemes. The paternalism of earlier schemes was replaced by an idea of social justice and a feeling that employees ought to have a greater role in managerial functions. Profit sharing became more and more an issue with a clearly ideological tone.

For historic reasons the debate on how to give employees a share in capital formation was particularly intensive in postwar Germany, a country committed to rapid and high capital accumulation, voluntarily restrictive wage policies, and, consequently, an extremely uneven wealth structure. By the mid-fifties a German union economist proposed the formation of collective "social funds," financed by company profits and administered by the unions (the "Gleitze Plan").

More than fifteen years later the main elements of this plan were adopted by the German labor movement. At their 1972 convention the German Federation of Trade Unions (DGB) endorsed a proposal for regional employee investment funds, financed by profits from the larger companies. It was explicitly stated that the purpose was two-fold: to support wage policies and to counteract concentration of private wealth and power. Shortly thereafter the Social Democratic Party (SPD) adopted a similar scheme. The debate lost momentum for several reasons: the coalition government had to find a compromise, the proposal was criticized within the trade union movement, and, finally, the economic situation deteriorated. At present profit sharing by collective schemes is no real issue in West Germany, although individual workers in a number of companies (and notably in the construction industry) do participate in a form of individual saving and profit-sharing plans that receive limited tax-incentive encouragement from the German government.

In France as early as 1967 Gen. Charles de Gaulle initiated a compulsory profit-sharing scheme, without the support of the unions or, of course, the employers. The scheme can be seen as part of the Gaullistic idea of harmonious industrial relations. It did not, however, result in any increased influence for the unions. Immediately before the 1978 election, a government commission delivered a report proposing new incentives for employee shareholding. The report stated that the compulsory system of employee capital sharing covers nearly five million workers in over 11,000 firms, while in contrast, the various voluntary schemes have awakened little interest.

In recent years various forms of profit sharing have been discussed in the Netherlands and Denmark. In the Netherlands a social democratic–liberal coalition was very near to an agreement on a compulsory scheme for employee funds, financed by excess profits, when a nonsocialist government took over. However, the new government has announced a bill that, with some modifications, seems to build on the original ideas of excess-profit sharing and the formation of a number of wage earner funds.

In Denmark various profit-sharing schemes have been discussed for nearly ten years, and in 1973 the government proposed a compulsory wage earner's investment fund financed by payroll taxes. The bill failed to pass in parliament, but the Danish labor movement still advocates the idea of collective employee funds to achieve "economic democracy."

Finally, it should be mentioned that some experts within the European Economic Community have recently shown an interest in profit sharing.

The Swedish Scene

It is noteworthy that the debate on profit sharing that took place in a number of West European countries, among them Denmark, did not influence public opinion in Sweden. In fact, in comparison with other countries, in Sweden the number of profit-sharing schemes for individual firms was small, and the endeavors of the nonsocialist parties to stimulate such schemes by special tax rules and other measures did not meet any positive response in the Swedish labor movement.

Sweden finally entered the scene, and a debate on profit sharing was started. However, the debate differed from debates carried on in other countries. The fact that the Swedish trade union movement is exceptionally strong seemed to guarantee a fair share of the national product to the wage earners and to make profit sharing—an addition to wage increases—unnecessary. When codetermination became an issue at the end of the sixties the strength of the unions, supported by new labor laws, was regarded as sufficient to enforce union claims. Neither was a need felt, as in Denmark, to make a collective form of profit sharing an instrument of capital formation. At the beginning of the sixties, Sweden had introduced a system of collective pension funds that entailed a large volume of savings and thus facilitated high investment activities. Social injustice, which was the driving force behind the German debate on profit sharing, was not a central issue in a welfare state. For many decades governed by Social Democrats, Sweden was a country known for having a progressive tax system, an equalizing wage policy, and, consequently, a relatively equal income and wealth structure.

Although there were good reasons to expect Sweden to stay outside the European debate on profit sharing, still, to the surprise of many, just the opposite occurred, but certainly not by chance.

The historical roots of the present Swedish debate must be traced back to the Swedish wage policy of solidarity, which is aimed at equalizing the wage structure. "Nature of work" is the criterion for wage setting, without regard to differences of profitability in various trades or in individual firms. Under this so-called solidarity wage policy of the Swedish Federation of Trade Unions (LO), the same job in different industries (or companies) should pay approximately the same wage.[2] By the end of the sixties this policy proved to be successful, and wage differentials clearly narrowed. On the other hand, a solidarity wage policy favors firms with an unused capacity to pay higher wages. This results either in an increase in wealth for the shareholders of these firms, or in "wage drift," i.e., local wage increases for categories already well above the average level. Both alternatives are equally undesirable from the union view, the first because it enriches the wealthy, the second because it undermines the solidarity between groups of wage earners.

For decades the Swedish trade unionists have felt unhappy with these consequences of their own wage policy and have tried to find a solution to the dilemma posed by the solidarity wage policy and to achieve fair income distribution between wage earners and capital owners. The primitive idea of a "wage pool" financed by excess profits in highly profitable firms from which income would be redistributed to low income groups was early rejected as incompatible with the idea of a dynamic and growing economy. More sophisticated proposals to create branch or branch streamlining funds out of excess profits and to use these funds for research, union educational work, and streamlining activities in weak trades were rejected or neglected by union congresses held in the sixties.

The turning point came with the LO congress in 1971. This time the powerful union of metalworkers put forward a number of motions, in which it invited the LO executive to initiate a thorough examination of the problem of how the union movement could continue to carry on its solidarity wage policy without increasing profits in already profitable firms. At the same time the union felt that the concentration of wealth in the hands of a few capital owners, mainly as a consequence of industrial self-financing, should be neutralized and the influence of employees over the economic process increased.

The time was ripe to solve a problem which for decades has been a serious concern for the union movement. The 1971 congress adopted the motions, and the LO executive decided shortly thereafter to appoint a working group with the aim of studying the following three questions: How to complement the wage policy of solidarity so that further increases in capital in firms with high profitability could be avoided? How to counteract the concentration of wealth which stems from industrial self-financing? How to increase—in addition to what the new labor laws could achieve—employee influence through co-ownership of productive capital? (In 1972 the parliament had passed a law providing for employee representatives to be appointed on the boards of directors of large Swedish corporations. A 1977 act on collective bargaining also extends employee and union participation in enterprise decision making.)

The 1976 LO Proposal

In its report to the 1976 LO congress, the working group tried to answer the three questions by proposing a scheme for collective capital formation through wage-earner investment funds. To cover such large questions the report had to be somewhat complex and technical. At the same time it was rather sketchy, with numerous problems unsolved or only hinted at.[3]

In short, the LO report suggested that 20 percent of a company's pretax profit should be transmitted to an employee fund. This money should not be allowed to leave the firm but should remain as collectively owned stock capital administered by the employees through their representatives. Differing from proposals put forward in other countries, the LO scheme did not give any benefit to the individual shareholder. Control over the larger, more profitable companies was to be successively exercised by wage-earner funds that would use their increasing voting rights at the meetings of shareholders to elect board members to represent employee shares.

The 1976 LO congress did not endorse the report in all its technical details but adopted a few principles, leaving it to further discussion and examination to transform a sketchy proposal into a concrete and technically consistent scheme. These principles, as formulated in a statement issued by the LO executive and adopted by the congress, were the following: (1) The fund capital ought to be accumulated out of company profits. (2) The benefits of the scheme ought to accrue to all employees, whether or not they are employed by firms which contribute to the funds. (3) The fund capital should be built up by the appropriations of "wage earner shares" corresponding to some portion of the annual profits. The capital may not be withdrawn from the firm, and, consequently, no individual is entitled to receive any part of the fund capital. (4) Since the proposed program is part of the LO's ongoing effort aimed at democratization of industry and codetermination of enterprise decision making, strong local employee influence was to be ensured by assigning a considerable part of the voting rights to local unions.

Wage-Earner Funds in the Swedish Debate

The LO proposal was similar to schemes discussed intensively for decades in a number of West European countries—if one leaves out the feature that the individual wage earner would derive no personal benefit from the collective capital. However, the Swedish public was not prepared for a matter-of-fact debate, especially as the proposal was introduced a few months before a general election. With the vast majority of the electorate ill-informed, with no clear position taken by the Social Democratic party, and with heavy criticism from all nonsocialist parties and representatives of industry and management, the debate was unavoidably confused and vulgar, dominated by slogans more than by rational arguments. Charges were made that profit sharing would lead to lower returns for stockholders, a withdrawal of investment from industry, and even to a collapse in the stock market. Flight of capital from the country was also mentioned.

According to some observers, the fact that the LO proposal was launched during the election campaign and without coordination between the unions and the political branch of the labor movement contributed to the defeat of the Social Democratic party in the 1976 election. Although it can hardly be proved, this hypothesis sounds far from absurd.

Since 1976 when the LO report was published, the public debate has circled around the question of whether there is a real need for some kind of wage-earner fund, and, if so, how such funds should be designed. As in the German debate some decades earlier, all political parties, labor market organizations, and private groups have produced plans of their own. As time passes, there is a tendency no longer to question the needs addressed in the 1976 LO report but to formulate alternative methods to meet those needs. There are two exceptions to this general attitude. Both the Conservative party (part of the 1976–78 coalition government) and the Swedish Employers' Confederation are strongly opposed to the idea of employee funds as not only dangerous for the Swedish economy but also as totally superfluous.

Practically simultaneously with the LO, the Swedish Confederation of Salaried Employees (TCO) published a report entitled "Wage Earner Capital through Share in Excess Profits." The report emphasized the need for sufficient capital formation but suggested a scheme for wage-earner funds similar to the LO proposal.

One decisive difference between the two proposals was that the TCO proposal suggested sharing excess profits, i.e., profits after deduction of a certain normal yield to the old shareholders. Generally speaking the TCO report was written in a much more vague and circumspect tone than the LO report. It is also obvious that the TCO, which is not connected, as the LO is, with the Social Democratic party, had no reason to stress the ideological aspects of the scheme.

The business world's point of view is reflected in the Waldenström report, a report from a working group made up of leading industrialists and some professional economists and named after its chairman. The report contains heavy criticism of the LO scheme, which is said to result in the confiscation of at least part of the shareholders' property, as well as losses in economic efficiency and difficulties for foreign companies operating in Sweden and for Swedish multinationals. In the long run the proposed scheme may, the report argues, jeopardize the Swedish market economy and introduce a new and, for the traditional Swedish view, strange economic system.

The business world's alternative to the LO (and at the same time to the TCO) proposal is a state-subsidized voluntary savings system. The savings are paid into different investment funds run by the wage earners collectively, but savings must remain there for a stipulated minimum period.

The Centre–Conservative–Liberal government has effected the main ideas of the Waldenström report by submitting to parliament (in March 1978) a bill aimed at stimulating private savings by tax reductions and premiums. According to the bill a monthly saving of 75 Sw. Cr. as a minimum and up to 400 Sw. Cr. as a maximum entitles the saver to receive a tax reduction of 20 percent of the amount saved. The interest paid on the special savings accounts (or dividends paid for shares bought within the savings scheme) is tax free. The stipulated saving period is five years, and tax advantages are lost if savings are withdrawn before the period has expired.

At the beginning of 1978 a number of new and revised schemes were proposed, and, consequently, the debate blazed up again after a relatively quiet period. The LO, the TCO, the Liberal, and the Conservative parties have all made contributions to the already considerable number of plans, schemes, and proposals.

The most concrete scheme is presented in a report, jointly produced by a group of trade unionists and representatives for the Social Democratic party, and published in February 1978 under the title, "Wage-Earner Funds and Capital Formation." The three motives for the earlier LO report were accepted, but a fourth was added: the need for greater capital formation. The goals were said to be two-fold: to develop economic democracy and to contribute to expanding competitive industrial production.

As in the LO report, a profit-sharing system is suggested, but only firms with more than 500 employees are included in it. The system entails the appropriation of 20 percent of the annual profits to collective wage-earner funds. The voting rights for the shares owned by the funds are divided between the employees and a number of regional union bodies. The majority of private firms are left outside the scheme but have to pay 1 percent of their payroll as a tax into a "codetermination fund" aimed at financing union activities for the democratization of the economy.

In addition to the profit-sharing part of the system, the group proposed the establishment of two large national development funds (one dominated by the government and the other one with a majority elected by the employees) and a large number of regional funds administered by local government authorities. The main function of these funds is to supply the competing part of Swedish industry with financial resources for technical development. The LO–Social Democratic party working group

argued that total savings and investment in Sweden have drastically decreased in recent years; consequently there is a great need to restore equilibrium in the Swedish balance of payments, to develop and upgrade industrial capacity, and to create new job opportunities. This development
fund capital is to be raised by a 3 percent of payroll tax, made available
by a reduction in future wage increases.

It can be easily seen that the revised proposal differs considerably from
the original LO proposal. As part of an extensive study campaign, unionists and party members have been invited to send written comments to
the group. On the basis of these comments the executive of the Social
Democratic party formulated a statement, which was submitted to the
party congress in September 1978. The congress has to make the final
decision on which way the Swedish labor movement will handle the question of wage-earner funds in the September 1979 election campaign.

This new LO–Social Democratic revised proposal, since it involves
only large companies, seems more acceptable to the TCO. The TCO itself
also brought out a revised report in February 1978. Increased capital
formation and profit sharing are the two components. The goals are thus
almost identical for both confederations. A number of wage-earner funds,
financed by payroll taxes—or by some portion of the firms' value-added
tax—and by excess profit sharing, would provide industry with capital,
either as credits or by investment in stocks. In the initial stage, when
stock ownership would be small, the voting rights would be delegated to
the local unions. There would be no individual ownership of shares. On
this crucial issue the two large confederations take the same view—in
clear contrast to the three nonsocialist parties who advocate individual
shares or, at least, some kind of "individual connection."

Both the Liberal party and the Conservative party have published reports
on the question of employee funds and capital formation. The Liberals
confined themselves to presenting various alternatives as a basis for discussion among party members and for final decision at the party's congress in late 1978. The group agrees that the need for increased capital
formation can only be realized at the expense of total consumption. The
system must be adjusted to the present market economy but must also
promote the democratization of working life. The Liberal's report is
compatible with the main principles of the TCO report.

On the other hand, the report issued by a working group from the
Conservative party argues against every kind of collective capital formation or profit sharing. Wealth should be spread among as many indi-

viduals as possible, and private savings stimulated by tax reductions and premiums. The minister of finance—at the same time chairman of the Conservative party—designed the aforementioned bill on state-subsidized voluntary saving exactly along these lines. The bill is strongly opposed by the unions and the Social Democratic party.

The Outlook

With a great number of alternative schemes being put forth and a bitter fight between the Social Democrats and the unions on one side and the nonsocialist parties, together with industry and employers, on the other, the situation is confused and intriguing. It has been said that the LO proposal—and for that matter the proposal put forward jointly by the LO and the Social Democratic party—would change the Swedish economic and political system in an almost revolutionary way. The advocates of the LO scheme have admitted that a change was exactly what they were aiming for but insist that such a change is consistent with the "Swedish model," a mixture of market economy and state planning.

Swedish politics are, as a rule, very pragmatic, and major changes are always the result of careful and often time-consuming analyses by royal commissions. Typically enough, a royal commission had been in the process of examining the whole issue and illuminating it from different aspects. The commission, appointed by the previous Social Democratic government and chaired by Hjalmar Mehr, a former governor of Stockholm, worked behind the scenes, far from the noise of the battlefield.

The commission, with representatives from all political parties (except the Communist), the unions, employers and industry, not only has to analyze the various schemes and to examine their possible effects, but also has to make an attempt at finding a solution that can be accepted by different groups. In spite of large divergencies of opinion it seems that a common basis exists for continuous discussions in this area. A recently published government report has indicated that Sweden has an urgent need for capital formation, and everyone knows that such a need can be met by collective savings. There is enough agreement in broad terms on the basic elements of a system so that a solution can be reached by the commission if it works long and hard enough. The commission's time schedule indicates that no report can be expected before the elections in the fall of 1979.

Earlier it was mentioned that Sweden entered the debate on employee participation in wealth and capital formation later than other West European countries. In many of these countries this debate has come to an end without any evident results. Sweden may be a different case. It is a Swedish tradition that formal decisions taken by union and party congresses determine future policies. We may remember that after a long period of bitter political fights nearly twenty years ago the Swedish pension fund system was introduced. Now it is no longer a controversial issue. It is not too hazardous to guess that some time in the eighties Sweden will launch a system of collective employee investment funds, which, eventually, will be accepted as an integrated part of the Swedish welfare state.

Notes

[1] John Maynard Keynes, *How to Pay for the War: A Radical Plan for the Chancellor of the Exchequer* (New York: Harcourt Brace & Co., 1940).

[2] Landsorganisationen i Sverige (LO), *Trade Unions and Full Employment, Report to LO Congress, 1952* (Stockholm: Landsorganisationen, 1953); Rudolph Meidner, *Co-ordination and Solidarity: An Approach to Wages Policy,* edited and translated by T. L. Johnson (Stockholm: Prisma, 1974); Meidner and Berndt Ohman, *Fifteen Years of Wage Policy* (Stockholm: Swedish Trade Union Confederation—LO, 1972); and Derek Robinson, *Solidaristic Wage Policy in Sweden* (Washington, D.C.: Organisation for Economic Co-operation and Development, 1974).

[3] The report has, with some abbreviations, been translated into English: Rudolph Meidner, *Employee Investment Funds* (London: Allen and Unwin, 1978).

Changing Life at Work

Current Trends in France

Yves Delamotte

RECENT movements to "humanize work" and "reform the enterprise" have long antecedents in France. The questioning of Tayloristic principles* and some of the dogmas of scienic management began even before World War II, when Hyacinthe Dubreuil advocated experimentation with work in small groups. Right after the war, Georges Friedmann called attention to some interesting experiments in job enrichment. What seems relatively new is that now *many* changes are taking place in industrial plants and in offices and there is an awareness that different "organizational choices" are possible, on a practical level. It is difficult to forecast what the future of this movement will be. Thousands of engineers are still trained by traditional methods, whose efficiency has been established. Many of the so-called "experiments" remain fragile, and many changes are associated with the enthusiasm and faith of one man or one team. The advocates of traditional organization are opposed to this "personalization" of organization, preferring instead general and abstract rules, which anyone can understand and implement.

---

* In his noteworthy work, *Scientific Management* (1911), F. W. Taylor advanced the idea that determining work methods is too complicated a matter to be left to workers' discretion. In plants, this should be handled by specialists able to define the "one best way" that workers must follow. The simpler the tasks are, and the more they are repeated, the greater the chance they will be performed in the best way.

However, in France as in most industrialized countries, many people share the belief that life in many work places remains anachronistic. The physical environment in many plants is not very different from what it was 100 years ago. Social relations are still strongly marked with authoritarianism. However, even if the enthusiasts of the "quality of working life" were a little too optimistic when they foresaw the end of the assembly line, it is certain that important changes are under way, and that many more changes could occur in France, especially if the left were to gain a general election victory. This article deals with attempts to change the traditional organization of work, and tries to show how they are part of a wider context of change.

The Crystallization of Attitudes on Working Conditions

The year 1968 was a very special one for France. Words and feelings which had been stifled exploded at the surface. Society was made aware of its problems, mainly of the problems of young people, either in universities or in factories and offices. The subject of "working conditions" appeared in newspaper articles and political arenas. "Working conditions" refers to all aspects of life at work: the physical environment, safety and health hazards, length of working time, pressures associated with wage systems, frustrations associated with the nature of the work. It is not meant to designate only those problems related to repetitive and fragmentized tasks. However, assembly line workers were the subject of special interest. Strikes took place in different areas of France, and these were usually interpreted as the reactions of young, educated workers to frustrating jobs.

Although absenteeism and turnover were not as high as in Scandinavian plants, many employers realized that working conditions had become a real issue that had to be tackled, or at least studied. In 1971, the National Council of French Employers (CNPF) issued a report which focused upon the problems of semi-skilled workers (working conditions, pay, training, and promotion opportunities).

In 1972 two of the main workers' unions in the private sector (Confédération Générale du Travail—CGT and Confédération Française Démocratique du Travail—CFDT) issued documents which highlighted the most important problems in various industries as well as in office work, and proposed some remedies. These documents were widely circulated. In

February 1972, a televised debate between the minister of labor and the general secretary of the CFDT, where each debater presented a short film on working conditions, drew national attention. There was also some interest in job enrichment, semi-autonomous groups, and so on. Crowds of managers gathered to listen to Frederick Herzberg when he came to Paris in 1972 to deliver a lecture in which he explained his well known theory of motivation. According to Herzberg, motivation can only be found in the content of work. Managers should try to enrich the jobs of their employers so that their jobs become more motivating and lead to self-fulfillment and work satisfaction. The period 1969–72 was one of speeches, debates, and reports, followed by a period of less abstract innovations.

Developments in Government Policy, 1972–75

Since working conditions had come to be recognized as an important national issue, the government thought that a bill should be prepared on the subject (a typical French reaction). The bill became the Act of December 27, 1973, on working conditions.

The Act of 1973 is made up of four parts. The first determines how the works council, a consultative body at the plant level with elected representatives of all employees, should be informed by management concerning developments in working conditions. Once a year a report, drafted by management and describing the measures taken during the previous year, is submitted to the council with a detailed program of the measures foreseen for the coming year. The works council gives its opinion on the report and the program and can request the inclusion of measures that had not been considered by management. The second part of the act deals with occupational safety and health and provides for some improvements of existing regulations. The third part is designed to eliminate legal obstacles that hindered the development of flexible hours and part-time work.

The fourth part of the act established a new institution: the National Agency for the Improvement of Working Conditions. A public body with a tripartite board, its tasks are "to gather and distribute all information which would help to improve working conditions" and "to contribute to the development of research, experiments or actions in view of improving working conditions."

As can be seen, the 1973 act is not a major, comprehensive law defining an overall policy. It should be noted, however, that a clear relation is established between improving working conditions and workers consulting with management. An implication of the act is that such improvements should be discussed with the people concerned (or at least their representatives). In 1975, the Sudreau report adopted this same approach and strongly emphasized the idea that giving workers more influence over their working environment was a way to "industrial democracy."

The limited scope of the act can be explained by the fact that, when the bill was under preparation by the government, collective bargaining at a national inter-industry level had already begun between the employers' union and the main workers' unions (in France collective bargaining usually takes place at the branch level, but some issues such as job security, adult training, and now working conditions are subject to such "summit" agreements). The government set limits on its own intervention to avoid interfering with the progress of these negotiations and to preserve the freedom of both parties to set new rules. The agreement that resulted from this bargaining was signed in March 1975. It deals with work organization, working time, wage systems, health, and safety, and sets guidelines and principles rather than binding rules. For instance, the section on work organization states that "the number of tasks to be carried out, the number of machines to be operated . . . must not require undue exertion." Job enrichment and semi-autonomous work groups are recommended as interesting possibilities. However, they should not lead to an excessive work load; and "any additional skills that may result from job enrichment must be taken into consideration where wages and, if necessary, grading (job classification) are concerned."

There was nothing in this national inter-industry agreement which was binding for enterprises (which are already subject to very elaborate regulations in the area of hygiene and safety). For the employers' organization, the agreement seemed a useful and comprehensive set of guidelines which individual employers might follow; it was also expected to be used as a starting point for negotiations at the branch industry level. These negotiations developed in various industries and at this level some more precise rules were sometimes defined, for instance in the chemical industries, concerning shift work. But by the end of 1975, it was clear that neither the 1973 act nor the 1975 agreement would be very influential, and that concrete policies for better working conditions would stem mainly from the enterprises themselves; something had to be done, it was believed, irrespective of agreements at the top. However, there was still room for the government to take another step.

The Sudreau Report

After the election of Valery Giscard d'Estaing as president in May 1974, a new phase began in French political life. Throughout his campaign he had emphasized the need to renew French society. But what could be done or should be done about working conditions was not clear; a preliminary investigation was required.

The president established a "Commission for the Study of the Enterprise," consisting of eleven persons under the chairmanship of a former cabinet minister, Pierre Sudreau. The Sudreau Committee sat from September 1974 to January 1975. It heard evidence from employers' and workers' organizations, individual entrepreneurs and experts. Tremendous activity was sustained during this short period. The report was presented to the president on February 7, 1975, and was distributed a few days later.

"Reforme de l'entreprise" is, in a way, the French equivalent of what has been termed "industrial democracy" in other countries. But the *reforme de l'entreprise,* as conceived in the report (and this is one of its original features), deals in fact with the many problems facing enterprises. There is a chapter entitled "Encouraging the Creation of New Types of Enterprises," and another called "Strengthening the Rights of Shareholders." In fact only a small fraction is related to "industrial democracy," strictly speaking. Top priority is given to the improvement of working conditions. There are, in other parts of the report, some proposals dealing with worker representation on supervisory boards and the extension of the works councils' duties, but one of the assumptions which underlies the report is that these structural changes would be of little value to workers themselves if the day-to-day life in the plant is not changed. The first chapter, "Transforming Day-to-Day Activities in Enterprises," deals with working conditions. Improvements in this area should not be limited to the prevention of accidents and to physical facilities. They should also aim to give workers more varied and challenging tasks as well as increased responsibility and autonomy. Working conditions are presented as an area where improvements should be discussed with workers, or proposed by them, rather than being imposed upon them. It is suggested in the report that all employees should have the opportunity to *express* themselves on the content and conditions of their jobs. Here the relation between working conditions and industrial democracy is made very apparent.

Of course this was just another report, well done and clever though it was. The interesting point is to see how many of its proposals were implemented by the government. The economic situation in 1976 did not make for a favorable context and many of the proposals simply were dropped.

In assessing the practical consequences of the Sudreau report, we can detect at least three areas where some progress has been made:

1) A law on social indicators *(bilan social)* was passed in July 1977. According to this law, the management of an enterprise must submit to the works council an annual *bilan social,* an analysis of the situation within the enterprise in areas such as employment, health and safety, physical environment of work, length of working time, wages and salaries, and training. Decrees annexed to the law enumerate in a very precise way the items which should be covered under each title and the corresponding indicators (for health and safety, for instance: number of accidents with work stoppage, number of days lost for accidents, number of death casualties, sums spent by the enterprise to improve safety, etc.). Using these indicators it should be possible to follow the evolution of the situation within the enterprise from one year to another, to determine the areas where improvements are necessary, etc. The data are given for the last three years. In 1979, all companies with at least 750 employees are subject to the law which, in 1982, will cover all companies with at least 300 employees. As can be seen, the objective of this law is to furnish management and the workers' representatives in the works council with precise data for their discussions. Such an idea was already present, in a more diffuse way and for working conditions only, in the 1973 act.

2) A fund for the improvement of working conditions *(fonds pour l'améloriation des conditions de travail)* was established in 1976. Through this fund the Department of Labor can allocate subsidies to companies that submit interesting projects in different areas: safety, working environment, work organization. The project must be approved by the works council. The amount of the subsidy can be as high as 30 percent of the total cost of the operation. In October 1977 seventy-three enterprises had received some assistance, while seventy-nine others had their projects under scrutiny. Those companies which receive a subsidy must give all relevant information about the operation to the fund, whose mission of gathering and diffusing useful knowledge in the area of working conditions is thus facilitated. The fund's initial grant amounted to $5 million.

3) A policy to upgrade manual workers was defined. This policy interferes in a way with the policy for the improvement of working

conditions, which mainly concerns manual workers, but some emphasis was also placed on the wages problem (manual workers in France are poorly paid) and on vocational training. A law of December 1975 allows manual workers who have held certain kinds of strenuous jobs for five years to retire on full pension at age sixty instead of sixty-five. Another law, passed in 1976, provides for compensatory rest (and not just more money), when a stipulated amount of overtime has been worked.

Developments Taking Place in Enterprises

As early as 1970, many enterprises began to improve working conditions without waiting for legislation or for the financial aid offered by the Labor Department fund. These improvements dealt with accident prevention, redesign of workplaces, improving the physical environment, working hours, and shift work. Some data were gathered by the National Agency for the Improvement of the Working Environment in 1976 concerning actions taken in the area of work structuring. Approximately 100 companies were covered by the survey. Some of them followed a well-defined, comprehensive social policy and tried to include all the workers. The majority of them proceeded cautiously, using a small percentage of their employees to experiment with changes.

The steps taken have been very diversified. In some enterprises there has been an increase in the number of individual work places where one person can assemble a complete product. In others, job enrichment has been sought by merging various production and maintenance tasks. But on the whole groupings seem to be the most widespread approach. Often these groups consist of a handful of workers taken out of an assembly line; the nature of their jobs changes little, if at all (there is simply less pressure). In other cases groups have been established whose task is to assemble a whole complex product. In this case a change may have been required in the layout of the machines, and, because the tasks required became more complex and involved more skill, some additional training was given to the workers.

Few data were collected about the effects of these changes on absenteeism, worker satisfaction, or productivity. But it is clear that some companies found it necessary for technical and economic reasons to move from the assembly line to production in groups, owing to the greater flexibility of this system, which allows for the rapid adjustment of production to demand. It was mentioned too, by nearly all the enterprises covered, that improvements in product quality were noticeable.

The changes were sometimes unilaterally introduced by management, without informing the works council and without the participation of workers. In many firms, however, there is a growing conviction that such operations must be achieved in close association with the workers concerned, along the lines recommended by the Sudreau report.

An enterprise in the Paris area went rather far in involving the workers. About 300 people work there, among them 120 semi-skilled workers, mostly women. They make lead and aluminium tubes for pharmaceutical products and cosmetics. In 1971, the head of the plant decided to try something new. He knew that he did not like the Herzberg approach, which he found too unilateral and authoritarian, but he wanted to improve conditions for the semi-skilled workers. He thought that the best way to find out what could be done was to let them express themselves (not necessarily an easy task). He had discovered, even before the Sudreau report, that workers should be helped to "express themselves."

With the assistance of an outside consultant, some steps were taken in order to foster discussion. Three groups, of twelve to fifteen people each, were formed. The groups would meet two half-days each week on paid time. No member of management was present, but a psychologist, brought in by the consultant, would assist the discussions. Four themes were proposed: improvement of working conditions, training, extension of responsibilities, and changing the wage system. The groups were invited to select a theme; when proposals were ready, they would be examined by a joint committee composed of an equal number of management's representatives and of members selected by the workers' representatives.

In fact, discussions focused rapidly upon the *quality* of the tubes made by the workers. The workers were pressed by foremen to work quickly and not to bother about defects; this was the job of quality control. For the workers, affirming the priority of the quality issue was a way to assert themselves with management.

The groups' members asked to see the complaints of the customers; then they undertook the long and arduous task of making an inventory of all possible defects. When the work was finished in May 1973, more than 5,700 hours had been spent in group meetings.

The next phase was to define the controls to be effected at the place of work. The type of control and the time to do it had to be determined from the analysis made in the first phase. The help of a statistician was required. It was found, too, that the controls should be made by the workers themselves and that the workers should have the right to stop the machines when certain defects were detected. Earlier this had been the foreman's prerogative.

The next phase was the discovery by the groups that quality control could be facilitated if they knew of customers' orders in advance and could plan their work accordingly. Through *ad hoc* committees, the workers were now able to discuss with the planning service the order in which various series of tubes should be produced.

This is not the end of the story; but enough has been said to show that a kind of creativity developed among the workers when they realized that things had changed, and that they might be listened to when expressing proposals for change. Of course such a policy can be developed only within well-defined limits and well-accepted rules of the game. At the beginning two things had been accepted by the workers: they should not demand the replacement of old machines with new ones, and their proposals would be checked by the joint committee.

Such an experiment might seem expensive because of the time spent in discussions. But according to the head of the plant, the discussions are not considered as necessary now as in the beginning because the groups are satisfied with what they have done. New procedures have been found. A new type of organization has been determined. Moreover, quality has improved.

Such an experiment, which is bold in some respects, raises the important issues of the long-term impact of such changes and of adjustment to the new situation. The question can be raised: What next?

Trade Unions and Organizational Changes

All the developments which have been mentioned are taking place in a society where trade unions are usually seen by foreign observers as highly political bodies, ideologically oriented, and weak at the plant level. In a way the "experiments," run by management in the area of work organization, clearly reveal the ideological orientation of the unions and the difficulties they have in organizing action at the plant level.

The two largest workers' unions, the CGT and CFDT, are both strongly influenced by Marxist views of class conflict. They hope for a general societal change and for the victory of the Left in French national elections. But the CGT has strong ties with the Communist party, while the CFDT, many of whose leaders have informal ties with the Socialist party, is hostile to any form of centralization and bureaucracy. One of the keynotes in the CFDT's platform is self-management *(autogestion)*. This means giving more autonomy and power to the workers themselves, and encouraging them to seek and impose their own solutions at the shop-floor level.

At the national level both the CGT and the CFDT had to define their position on management experiments.

The CGT is not opposed *a priori* to these experimental changes when they are aimed at reducing the monotony of work or at developing skills. But such changes should not mean a reduction of the work force, nor an increase of the work load. They should allow the workers concerned to accede to higher classifications and better wages. Each experiment should be studied carefully by the unions with the workers themselves. Of course this pragmatic approach does not mean that the CGT places too much hope in these changes. For the CGT, it is clear that the main objective of the companies is more profit, as usual. These experiments take place in a capitalistic society where workers are exploited. According to this outlook, it is only when the society is changed, when the most important firms have been nationalized, that the real problems can be solved and that the exploitation of workers will come to an end.

For the CFDT, questioning the traditional organization of work is quite justified. Changes should not be opposed; on the contrary, they should be supported. But precise guarantees should be obtained about job security, higher classifications, wages, etc. It should be certain that these changes do not stimulate competition between individual workers or groups of workers, as can often be observed. And these changes should be part of an overall policy that seeks better working conditions (safety at work, reduced working time, suppression of piecework and other incentives, and better physical environment).

The CFDT sees these changes as an opportunity for the workers to learn and to gain more and more responsibility and power. Groups of workers should be able to define how the work should be organized and planned. Instead of being isolated and passive, they should become the controlling power in their own environment. Thus the Taylorian dichotomy between conception and execution would be effaced and workers could at last "express themselves" by way of concrete changes they themselves would have determined. These changes would pave the way to self-management, which is one of the main (if somewhat ambiguous) goals of the CFDT.

What is the practical impact of these positions at the plant level? While in the United States all the workers of the bargaining unit are represented by one union, in France workers may choose between unions or decide not to join any union. This is a matter of personal choice. In a private sector industrial plant in France, it is quite common to find a majority of non-union workers; of the minority who belong to a union, perhaps 60 percent will be members of the local CGT, 30 percent members of the CFDT, and 10 percent of another minor union. In large plants the majority of the workers may be unionized, but they rarely belong to the same union. In most of the large plants the CGT has the highest membership; in some of them, however, the CFDT is the major union.

In the case of changes decided by management, which are supposed to improve the quality of working life, the different local unions may have different reactions, reflecting more or less the positions taken at the top. Initially, these positions remain mainly abstract and permeated with ideology. If there is opposition to the changes, it is mainly verbal and no active steps are taken. A kind of wait-and-see attitude is found frequently.

It is in the works council, where the manager of the plant and the elected representatives of all the employees sit together, that some information is exchanged about forthcoming changes; it is here that the representatives, elected on union slates, can express their views. But unions also have some appointed representatives in each plant, and views can be expressed through this channel as well. There is never formal bargaining about the change, since, as has been pointed out, few agreements are signed at the plant or employee level and collective bargaining takes place at the industry level. This means that management faces different unions, acting through different channels (works council and unions' delegates). The situation is much more complex and ambiguous than in some other countries, where management faces only one union and handles problems with this union through collective bargaining. In France the chance is great that the positions expressed by the different unions, through the various channels, will be diversified: this affords leeway to management, and it can go forward without much opposition.

Another reason that opposition to management's changes is usually not strong in the first phase is that the unions have to take into account the reactions of the workers themselves. If they seem to be satisfied with the change, it would be dangerous for any union to oppose it, for their influence could be impaired to the advantage of another union in the plant. However, if, while the change develops, some concrete problems arise (on classifications, wage system, work load), the unions find themselves on safer ground and thereby drop the wait-and-see attitude. Some issues may be raised in the works council, or some bargaining may take place upon the points at stake.

Because of these complications, it is very difficult to foresee what will happen at the plant level when management changes are introduced. Each case is different, since there are so many variables that intervene. Maybe the most determinant factor is the position of the workers themselves, more important for the survival of the local union than adherence to guidelines coming from the top (This is why there is reluctance at the top to give guidelines.)

Though each story is different, there are some scenarios that are never enacted. It never comes about at the outset that the unions agree to join forces to obviate the change, nor do they ever agree to cosponsor it with management.

The recent movements for work and enterprise reform have, then, had varied and somewhat fragmented results. It is, as yet, difficult to foresee what may be their wider impact or significance for French work life in the future.

The Work Humanization

Movement

U.S. and European Experience Compared

Jack Barbash

THE vocabulary of the "work humanization" movement includes the terms "work reform," "quality of work," "job life," "job design," "job enrichment," "work environment," "work restructuring," "alienation," "ergonomics," and, undoubtedly, many others. There is no generally accepted terminology, but for the purposes of consistency I will use "work humanization" as the inclusive term. In the United States and Western Europe, the work humanization movement is divisible into three narrower themes:

1. Work reform—schemes for enhancing individual discretion in the work situation (job enrichment is the most prominent).

2. Work environment—improvement of health and safety at work.

3. Codetermination—worker representation in enterprise decision making.

The seeds of the work humanization movement are found in the work of Elton Mayo, a transplanted Australian. Mayo's human relations replaced Taylorism as the dominant management ideology, although management practice is probably closer to Taylor. Taylor's economic man was interested only in money, but Mayo described a social man interested in work as a collaborative experience.

Mayoism emerged in the United States when dominant work patterns were in the process of changing from hard physical labor to mechanized labor and labor in the office. The work humanization movement is the latest stage in that evolution. Although it, like earlier movements, is necessarily constrained by enterprise cost and efficiency, work humanization goes farthest in pressing the claims of "self-actualizing" man.[1]

Work Reform

Work reform is a product of the recent full employment era in two senses: First, the idea of improving the *quality* of work would have been impractical if a measure of minimum adequacy had not already been achieved in the *quantity* of work. Second, work reform seems to offer remedies to many of the problems associated with full employment, i.e., a weakened work ethic, indiscipline, absenteeism, turnover, ethnic segmentation and its counterpart in Europe—the massive importation of foreign workers. The alienation strand in the work reform movement was inspired by Karl Marx. Somewhat earlier the young Marx's "alienation manuscripts" had been rediscovered in leftist circles and became a major intellectual influence.

In short, a combination of labor market conditions and new styles in ideas created the work reform movement. The movement has generated what I call a management ethic—an ethic distilled from the basic aims of various programs associated with work reform: autonomous work groups, job enrichment, "flexitime," worksharing, and the earlier notion of management by objective. The traditional work ethic tried to indoctrinate workers in the faith of a "fair day's work for a fair day's pay." Under the management ethic, spurred by relative labor scarcity, it is the employer who now needs to prove that he has earned the right to demand a fair day's work by constructing a work situation worthy of a fair day's work. The management ethic is more a set of values than a prevailing practice. Above all, the management ethic is informed with a spirit of flexibility and adaptability.

The basic elements of the management ethic can be briefly described. *Job design* essentially means suiting the job to the worker rather than the other way around. This is a simplification of the Tavistock socio-technical systems approach. In the words of Louis E. Davis, a leading American Tavistockian, job design is the "specification of the contents, methods and relationship of jobs in order to satisfy technological and organizational requirements as well as the social and personal requirements of the job holder."[2] *Decentralization* and *participation,* in work reform theory, bring practical decision making closer to the workers who have to live with the decisions and encourage a more satisfying as well as a more productive experience. *Despecialization* and *choice* allow for a freer and more personal adjustment to work. *Deinstitutionalization* replaces bureaucracy with more informal relationships. *Trust,* the ultimate object of the management ethic, builds a relationship based on mutual regard rather than solely on the coerciveness of power.

Reform of the Work Environment

In some respects an aspect of work reform—in others a quantum leap in its evolution—reform of the work environment has become a powerful movement in its own right and is distinguishable from work reform. It has evolved from a concern for the safety and health of workers to a "total view of the work environment."[3] "Safety" used to mean safety shoes, hard hats, safety goggles. Reform of the work environment now carries with it a strong preventive emphasis, particularly in respect to toxic substances, noise, lighting, radiation, and climate in the work process.

"A good working environment is characterized not only by the fact that illness due to working conditions does not occur but by the fact that the working environment also has a socially inspiring effect,"[4] wrote the Norwegian labor specialist Harry D. Hansen. In Sweden, a proposed law urged by the labor movement would require that "working conditions shall be adapted to the physical and psychological abilities of human beings."[5] A U.S. union resolution defines the scope of reform of the work environment to include "changes in traditional work patterns, working days and job elements and structure which contribute to destructive boredom, alienation, threaten emotional stability and render impossible a calm and stable home and family life, especially if wives as well as husbands are working."[6]

Codetermination

Codetermination and industrial democracy are the more popular terms for the effort at democratization of the enterprise, which includes employee or union representation at the level of the corporate board of directors; works council representation on the shop floor; an employee/ union voice in personnel administration; wage earners' funds for capital formation, ownership, or profit-sharing;[7] and the social contract—negotiation of the macroeconomic terms (somewhat beyond the context of this paper).

Codetermination is largely a Western European phenomenon. It partially fulfills the historic socialist demand for the social ownership and control of the means of production. Codetermination belongs to the work humanization movement because, its protagonists assert, ownership and control of the means of production by the workers themselves reflects the ultimate job satisfaction.

Management Attitudes Toward Work Reform

There is probably no substantive difference between American and European management attitudes to work reform. American reform practices are more developed because the professionalization of management is farther advanced. Employer paternalism, which is, in some respects, the negation of work reform, is still more important in Europe than in the United States. University and independent consulting and training resources, which are major elements of professionalization in the United States, are still in rudimentary stages in most Western European countries.

Work reform in both settings is essentially a management movement and largely in an experimental stage of development. It does not represent a groundswell of sentiment either from the rank and file or their unions. In the United States, the more systematic work reform programs are found largely in nonunion situations.

Union Attitudes Toward Work Reform

Union attitudes toward work reform programs in Europe and the United States differ markedly. In Europe, there are more instances both of collaboration and total ideological rejection than in the United States. There is nothing in the American experience, for example, to compare with the sizeable commitments that the national labor centers in Sweden and Norway have made to their respective work reform experiments. In the United States, there are only a handful of experimental enclaves in the same class, and they are rather more cautious and less ideological. The United States and Scandinavia have this much in common: in neither are trade union staff the prime movers. In Swedish Volvo AB it has been an enterprising management, and in Norway and the United States, creative and gifted "change agents" who are the activists.

Both Norway and Sweden have integrated work reform policies into their collective bargaining through authorizing legislation. For example, in Norway the Basic Agreement has "framed rules aiming at adjusting conditions for good cooperation between the [employer and union] organizations and between the undertaking [company] and the employees. To the individual person it is of the greatest importance that the feeling of unity between him and the undertaking is strong and alive." The agreement commits the parties to cooperate "in increasing efficiency, reducing production costs, improving the competitive capacity of the undertaking, and [designing] a more satisfactory place of work and a working organization which is both efficient and meets the needs for self-development."[8]

The other extreme in labor movement attitudes to work reform is found in France and Italy, where it is perceived as a means of dealing with ills inherent in capitalism and solvable only under socialism. Trade unions may properly lodge demands for improvements, but if some changes are forthcoming it will be as a consequence of trade union power, not of worker co-optation of the work reform variety.[9] In between these extremes are many European unions that express apprehension more than outright rejection because they have had so little direct experience with work reform programs.

American and many European unions criticize work reform programs from the conviction that they are either a substitute for, or a rival of, collective bargaining. This image is reinforced by the non- (if not anti-) union settings in which most of the work reform experiments are found. American unions see work reform as a modern incarnation of Taylorism's anti-unionism.

More specifically, work reform programs are seen as a challenge to job security and union power and ideology. The work reform movement is inimical to union power because the flexibility necessary to enrich or enlarge jobs jeopardizes the work rules that are the foundations of union power at the work site. Job security is endangered, in the union view, because the real purpose of work reform is to cut the number of workers and to get those who are left to work harder without commensurate compensation. The collaborative spirit which underlies work reform is really a device to co-opt workers into the managerial power structure. What is the purpose of the autonomous work group, unions say, except to get the work group to do management's dirty work?

Work reform is viewed as a challenge to union ideology because its real objective, in the union view, is to make the union redundant in the manner of Taylorism. For the union's adversary attitude the work reform movement seeks to substitute cooperation which, from the American union interest, is really co-optation.

The United Auto Workers work reform experiments in the Bolivar, Tennessee, plant depart at several points from the mainline trade union position as set out here. Collective bargaining and work reform need not be mutually exclusive. Coexistence is possible if workers retain their traditional adversary role in bargaining collectively for wages, hours, and working conditions and use work reform as a proper field for collaboration on a "win–win" basis. At some future time it may even be possible to fuse the two approaches.

For collective bargaining and work reform to coexist, the latter cannot be equated solely with a narrow job enrichment definition designed mainly to get more efficiency out of the worker. According to Irving Bluestone, the United Auto Worker's vice-president, who has been influential in the movement, work reform's essence must lie in "creating heightened job satisfaction and democratizing the work place" for it to be compatible with collective bargaining.[10] Thus, work reform policies may properly include consideration of problem-solving techniques, plant layout, tools, methods of production, utilization of time and space, and improvement in product quality. Coexistence is not possible, however, if work reform is mainly focused on increased work-pace and labor cost-cutting.

In contrast to the essentially unilateral character of conventional work reform, work reform in a collective bargaining environment, according to Bluestone, should be "designed, developed, and implemented by agreement between the parties to bring greater dignity and self-respect to the role of the worker through his participation in the decisionmaking process at the workplace." [11] Third party assistance can be helpful in providing experts and dispelling mutual suspicion. But the third party can't be a permanent crutch. "Those directly affected must be left to find their own way with the assistance, if requested, of professional experts who act as catalytic agents." [12]

Work reform is criticized by the European labor movement in sharper terms than it is by American labor.[13] The unions, with some exceptions, are critical of the work reform concept on the grounds that it is a disguised method of exploitation, a tactic of union substitution, and a co-optation of the union into the management power structure. Its exploitative objectives are achieved by playing down the importance of workers' economic security and occupational health and safety through a kind of utopianism and "abstract humanism" that seems to assume that these problems have been largely solved, when from the union and workers' standpoint these needs are still urgent.

Worker participation through work reform programs is participation without power—a form of participation which emanates from the top down—and fragmentation of the larger solidarity through the mystique of the small group. Work reform plans typically do not accord a legitimate co-equal place to the union, which is perceived largely as an outsider or as a frictional interference in the naturally collaborative relationship between worker and management. The trade unions fear co-optation on the ground that collaboration with management will impair their thrust as a protective institution of the workers.

Labor movements in the socialist tradition charge that work reform programs deny the capitalist–socialist dichotomy by assuming that there is an inherent economic mutuality between workers and management; by refusing to admit that the industrial power is intrinsically authoritarian; by ignoring the fundamental changes essential to deal with large-scale, technological unemployment and the deterioration of working conditions; and by glossing over the profit system, which determines pace and the direction of change and ignores the workers' own interests in change and the trade union's role in articulating change. The conduct of the enterprise according to the profit system is, in any case, *prima facie* against the interests of trade unionists, and the trade unions are justified in resisting changes "unless and until negotiated mechanisms and measures exist which guarantee re-employment of displaced workers on acceptable terms." [14]

However, some union sympathizers and unionists (including unionists involved in work reform), feel that properly perceived, work reform programs can be a source of strength to the union. Conventional collective bargaining may be sufficient to regulate wages, but there is more to working conditions than wages; to offer maximum protection over the whole range of workers' problems, the union needs to work from within the management structure. It is insufficient for the union to function only as a veto influence; it must also act positively to influence design systems, to exert a genuinely radical effect on work, and incidentally to offer practical alternatives to the appeals of the left. Union involvement in work reform may help to shore up the shop floor's faltering support for the union.

Union Attitudes

European trade union attitudes on codetermination are not altogether of one piece. In the Scandinavian countries, codetermination is assimilated into the collective bargaining relationship; a similar situation will occur in the United Kingdom if codetermination ever comes to pass. There are strong dissenting views among United Kingdom unions as to the merits of codetermination in general, largely on the grounds of displacement of collective bargaining and co-optation.

American unions reject codetermination by maintaining that owning and controlling the means of production are unnecessary as long as they can bargain with those who do. However, bargaining effectiveness, which is the union's main business, may, in fact, be impeded by codetermination since the capitalists are unlikely to want to negotiate their own dissolution.

In the American union view, bargaining effectiveness is better enforced through countervailing power rather than through the kind of integration in the management system which codetermination imposes. For one thing, the unions fear that co-optation into the management system will blunt the force of their adversary role, which underlies bargaining effectiveness. For another, unions lack the technical resources to cope with the vast amount of technical information that management feeds on. The union can do more for its members as a "griever" than as a partner. Finally, American unions lack the socialist commitment that is the mainspring of codetermination. The point isn't that American unions are pro-capitalist; it is simply that they are not persuaded that codetermination and its variants, including socialism, will enhance union bargaining effectiveness.

European employers are opposed to codetermination but at different points and in different ways. They are uniformly opposed to union representation in the board room, because it dilutes power and injects union intervention without responsibility. Employers generally favor voluntary shop floor and plant council schemes of consultation. [15] A team of British metal industry employers concluded: "German codetermination is successful but . . . it depends heavily upon there being a limited number of strong, reliable and responsible unions; legally binding agreements; labour court redress; and the works council system. It certainly does not prevent conflict but aids the rapid solution of grievances." [16]

In the United States, the catalytic agent in improving the work environment has been the enactment of the Occupational Safety and Health Act in 1970. This act pushed health and safety forward as a major collective bargaining demand by the heavy industry unions. It also aroused management to defend management rights against both union and government penetration as nothing has in recent times. Since its enactment, the Occupational Safety and Health Act has spurred administrative and technical insights which have been avidly watched by the Europeans.

My impression is that in Europe efforts to improve the work environment are a spin-off from the work reform movement. Work environment indeed may have already outstripped work reform in its importance in union calculations, judged by the effects on legislation and collective bargaining demands. The work environment route seems to be preferred by unions because it is concrete and tends to favor union power. Employers are less enthusiastic about the work environment movement pre-

Polarized and Integrated Industrial Relations Systems

	Polarizing	Integrating
Society	hostile	acceptable
Bargaining	unequal struggle	bargaining as equals
Influence on decision-making	using their power in factory and street	sitting in the conference room
Strikes	often	seldom
Character of organization	movement	bureaucracy
Tendency	revolutionary	reformist
Degree of organization	low	high
Finance	poor	strong
Unity	fragmented	united

Source: W. Albeda, "Trade Union Attitudes and Management Responses" in *Workers' Participation* (Paris: Organisation for Economic Co-operation and Development, 1975), p. 17.

cisely because it favors union power and, in addition, costs more than work reform, without the latter's payoff potential in increased efficiency. The recession of the middle 1970s may have cooled the ardor for work environment, as it has for work reform schemes, in keeping with the higher priority accorded to employment.

Collective Bargaining and Work Humanization

Acceptance or rejection of work humanization seems to depend on whether the industrial relations of a country are polarized or integrated, or at some point in between.[17] Polarized systems, such as those in France and Italy, are likely to reject the kinds of collaboration represented by work reform and codetermination. Polarized systems find it difficult to sustain even the middle ground of collective bargaining, such as in the United States and United Kingdom, where the approach is both adverse and reciprocal; that is, the parties seek to redistribute price and power, but they are also aware that they share a minimum common ground in the viability of enterprise and economy. Ideal integration types are, of course, Norway and Sweden.

In Marxist terms, work reform is an attempt to reform capitalism from within through some diffusion of power at precisely the point that Marx thought capitalism was most vulnerable, namely, the labor process. The diffusion of power envisioned by work reform is largely on management's terms, designed to enhance individual or small-group power in task-oriented situations in the interests of efficiency. Collective bargaining is also a diffusion of power but, from management's viewpoint, rather less malleable and more institutionalized.

The collective bargaining response, especially in the United States, is "pro-capitalist" only in the sense that the environment of liberal capitalism appears to be the most conducive to bargaining effectiveness, which is what unions want more than anything else. Nonetheless, under liberal capitalism collective bargaining has undoubtedly achieved major penetrations into capitalist power on the shop floor and in the economy.

Codetermination and its variants begin with the socialist commitment of the European labor movement. The aim of codetermination is to alter capitalism so as to give the union and its auxiliaries, at the very least, an equal and positive voice in the management and ownership of enterprise. If codetermination has not altered capitalism's structure of power it has in some respects served as the vehicle for enlarging the scope of collective bargaining.

Work environment reform raises the prospect of deeper penetration into management rights than either collective bargaining or codetermination, even if its explicit ideology appears less challenging to capitalism. The new grounds for joint decision making granted under statute and collective agreements go to such classic management rights as shutting down operations for health and safety reasons and determining production processes, materials, and layout. The likelihood of real joint decision making is also much greater than in collective bargaining or codetermination where, in practice, the union is typically reacting to management initiatives. The immediacy of work environment to the rank and file and the union suggests a more initiating and aggressive union posture on these issues.

Notes

1. The analogies are Edgar Schein's in *Organizational Psychology* (Englewood Cliffs, N.J.: Prentice Hall, 1965).

2. Louis E. Davis, "The Design of Jobs" in Mary Weir, ed., *Job Satisfaction* (London: Fontana, 1976), p. 90.

3. Karl G. Gustafsson, "Implications for Trade Unions of the Trend Toward New Forms of Work Organisation. Norway" International Institute for Labour Studies, Geneva, December 1977 (mimeographed), p. 26.

4. Harry O. Hansen, "Implications for Trade Unions of the Trend Toward New Forms of Work Organisation. Norway," International Institute for Labour Studies, Geneva, December 1977 (mimeographed), pp. 23–24.

5. Gustafsson, "Implications for Trade Unions," p. 26.

6. Leo Teplow, "Impact of the Occupational Health and Safety Act on Collective Bargaining" in Richard Rowan, ed., *Collective Bargaining Survival in the 1970's* (Philadelphia: University of Pennsylvania Wharton School, 1973), p. 405.

7. See J. P. Windmuller and Richard D. Lambert, eds., *Industrial Democracy in International Perspective*, Annals of the American Academy of Political and Social Sciences reprint no. 431 (Philadelphia, May 1977), p. 24.

8. Hansen, "Implications for Trade Unions," p. 7.

9. Y. Delamotte, "The Attitudes of French and Italian Trade Unions to the 'Humanisation' of Work," *Labour and Society,* International Institute for Labour Studies, Geneva, January 1976.

10. Irving Bluestone, "Implementing Quality of Worklife Programs," paper, Work in America Institute, Chicago, April 28, 1977.

11. Letter from Irving Bluestone to Barbash, October 6, 1977.

12. *Ibid.*

13. See Jack Barbash, *Work in a Changing Industrial Society,* Organization for Economic Co-operation and Development, Paris, October 1974.

14. Bache Vognbjerg, Trade Union Advisory Committee president, introductory remarks at the Organization for Economic Co-operation and Development, international conference, Paris, October 1974.

15. W. Albeda, "Trade Union Attitudes and Management Responses," *Workers' Participation,* Organization for Economic Co-operation and Development, Paris, 1975, p. 22.

16. Engineering Employers Federation, *Codetermination in Germany,* London, 1977, p. 14.

17. See Albeda, "Trade Union Attitudes," pp. 16ff., and Jack Barbash, *Trade Unions and National Economic Policy* (Baltimore: Johns Hopkins Press, 1972).

The Development

Of Work Humanization Programs

Harold L. Sheppard

I N A DISCUSSION of the development of the work humanization movement, a few broad propositions or principles should be emphasized.

LEARNING FROM EACH OTHER

Although there is more commonality than there are differences among the Western industrialized societies and their institutions, there is a risk that the intercountry differences will appear by far to outweigh the commonalities. But that would be a mistake.

If we fail to recognize the primacy of the common features of our societies, we will tend to emphasize the reasons why we cannot learn from one another. There is no society in the group of countries I refer to that is so unique that it has nothing in common with the others, nor whose totality of efforts in the arena of work humanization is so idiosyncratic that no element can be adapted by one or more of the other societies.

For example, I do not believe that there is something unique and unreplicable about Sweden; I do not believe that its so-called homogeneity and size make it the only country in which the technology of assembling an automobile can be radically changed, or that other countries are so different from Sweden that their own auto industries cannot borrow or adapt that technology.

THE ROLE OF TECHNOLOGY

Work humanization as a concept should include attention to the role of technology, specifically the notion that it is possible, more than many of us have been taught to think, to adapt and modify technology to meet human needs and values. The key word here is *possible.* Possibility is quite distinct from feasibility or cost. Feasibility and cost must themselves be viewed within the context of human and social values.

NON-ECONOMIC VARIABLES

The role of non-market economists and of non-economic social scientists is to remind all of us, in dealing with the problems of work, that our species is more than *homo economicus,* that forces in addition to (not instead of) pecuniary gain motivate the species, and that life is more than the pursuit of bread alone. The failure to remember this has frequently led to poor decisions in the general sphere of economics, and in industrial relations, in particular.

FROM POLEMICS TO PRACTICE

Work humanization is no longer the controversial issue in the United States that it was only a brief four or five years ago. Few newspapers and periodicals, for example, publish articles about the topic with the same frequency, or in the same mood or style, as they tended to do in the early 1970s. The typical article today is about how this or that factory or office is doing something associated with work humanization, the improvement of the quality of work life, new forms of worker participation, etc. Sometimes the article answers the question, "Whatever happened to the humanization of work?"

The actors in the center of the stage have changed their scripts. For example, in the early 1970s, the vice president for industrial relations of one of the largest corporations in the United States was complaining about the publicity being given to the notion that workers were dissatisfied and were in need of improvements in the quality of their work life. Indeed, according to this executive, the publicity was nothing but a concoction of journalists seeking a headline or "pop sociologists" seeking publicity and/or projecting their own feelings onto truly *un*alienated workers.

For this executive—and I cite him only as an example—-there was no worker dissatisfaction problem. But only a few years later, in written testimony prepared for a congressional hearing, this same executive said, in effect, "No, there is no problem—but let me show you what we are planning to do about it in my company." A few years after that, executives of this same company boasted about the accomplishments of the company's enlightened and progressive policy of working with the union in a company-wide experimental program of improving the quality of work life, involving a company staff of at least 100 experts on the subject.

The same can be said about many unions. Particularly at the local level, there is less opposition and more receptivity than there was previously to the quality-of-work-life movement. Several private nonprofit and public organizations have held small group seminars designed to elicit the interest of unions and companies in trying out, within the framework of sheltered agreements, selected innovations in work organization, task arrangements, and worker participation. The attendance of unions and their subsequent agreement to continue discussions with third parties and frequently to try new approaches are becoming commonplace. It is no longer possible for one individual to keep up with the pace of activity and actual changes. The number of companies and unions, in both the private and public sectors, now engaged in quality-of-work-life activities is so great that clearinghouses are now organized to track their progress.

THE TYRANNY OF JARGON

Humanization of work should not, in my view, be confused with the old "human relations in industry" approach. It is unfortunate that it frequently is confused with that school of thought. Semantics often confuse the issue. Take the term "industrial democracy," for example. A few years ago, I was visiting a group of Swedish blue-collar trade unionists at their work place. They took me for an interview with members of the industrial democracy project team, whereupon I was immediately asked, in rather critical terms, why it was that, in the United States, workers and their unions were not interested in industrial democracy? I replied that I didn't know that American unions had *not* been interested in, and concerned about, industrial democracy. I had to remind my hosts, or tell them for the first time, that industrial democracy is a very old term in the United States; that it was the primary expression used in the early days of the labor movement in America, during the 1930s and 1940s, in its fight for recognition and in organizing drives; that many trade unionists had written books and articles and given speeches with industrial democracy as part of their titles; that we even had formed, years ago, a national organization called the League for Industrial Democracy, and that the organization also had campus chapters, the Student League for Industrial Democracy.

Industrial democracy can have many different manifestations, depending on the country, and within the country, depending on the historical period and on the specific unions involved. Furthermore, the related term, worker participation, has many different meanings and forms. In addition, our traditional usage of the term and its actual practice, here in the United States, may undergo still further changes. Also, much of what some observers would call worker participation takes place in American factories and offices under different labels.

Many American unions now involved in so-called experiments or innovations in the humanization of work, or improvements in the quality of work life, have been finding ways of integrating or accommodating the representative-democracy version of worker participation with other versions, especially those implied or made explicit in the recent literature on worker participation. While some attempts at worker participation simply fall apart after endless rounds of aimless meetings, greater direct involvement in decisions affecting one's work cannot be dismissed. Such involvement cannot be provided through formal collective bargaining or in grievance processes. The real challenge, of course, is to structure certain kinds of jobs to allow for increased decision-making, without reducing the positive role performed by the formal, even adversary, process.

And yet we cannot ignore findings that show, for example, that stress induced by certain jobs or work environments is less frequent in work situations where the level of participation is high. Nor can we ignore the effects of participation in the early period of the much publicized Bolivar project.* Before any real process of change began, about 300 workers were interviewed in great detail. They were asked questions about the level of decision-making they actually had and the level they felt they *should* have. Several weeks after the first experiment had begun, the level of decision-making the experimental group indicated they *should* have increased significantly over the level they had indicated in the first

---

* This was an effort involving a small car parts manufacturer and the United Auto Workers directed toward improvements in quality of work life, with Neal Herrick, Michael Maccoby, and myself as co-directors. For a recent third-party assessment of the project, see Barry A. Macy, "A Progress Report on the Bolivar Quality of Work Life Project" in *Personnel Journal*, August 1979.

interview before the experiment began. My interpretation is that the experience of making more decisions, which the experiment provided, generated a desire for, and a feeling of competence regarding, greater participation in decisions about work matters. In other words, the actual experience with greater workplace democracy, provided by the experiment, became the basis for wanting more democracy, if we include under the meaning of democracy having a say in work-related decisions.

THE RECIPROCITY OF MATERIAL AND PSYCHOLOGICAL DIMENSIONS OF WORK

The quest for humanization of work is much more complex than many of its most fervent advocates and practitioners might imagine. This is true especially from a perspective that defines the humanization of work as more than, for example, increasing worker autonomy in the performance of tasks, or fighting the temptation of managers and industrial engineers to simplify or fragmentize the structure of work. The humanization of work also includes attention to the physical and technological work environment, to the quality of life in general—the worker's health, general psychological well-being, mobility, and economic security.

In one sample of blue-collar male union members I studied in cooperation with the Pennsylvania AFL–CIO, a sizeable minority revealed a wide discrepancy between their life aspirations and expectations and their actual achievements, and simultaneously reported that their take-home pay was not enough to take care of their family expenses. This same group of men *also* were disproportionately in jobs whose tasks involved very little in the way of variety, autonomy, and a greater use of their full skill potentials. The lower the quality of their job tasks, i.e., the less humanized their jobs, the higher the proportion of workers with a discrepancy between aspirations and actual achievements and with inadequate incomes. Any effort aimed at humanizing the workers' tasks must therefore also recognize that without any improvement in take-home pay, general dissatisfaction or life discontent may not be changed at all. This *also* means, however, that raising the pay of workers does not make their work intrinsically more desirable.

THE QUALITY OF WORK IN DEMOCRATIC SOCIETIES

The focus on the quality of work life has emerged very often as a by-product, an unanticipated consequence, of an interest in other problems not at first associated with the notion of the humanization of work.

For example, Neal Herrick, a key Department of Labor official, was involved in the authorization of a national study of employment standards. The study, carried out in 1969 by the University of Michigan for the Department of Labor, was primarily designed to provide empirical background material on health and safety and other related working conditions. In the process of analyzing the results of that survey, Herrick became equally interested in the social–psychological dimension of working conditions. Today, eight years later, he is outside the federal government, working with more energy than before on the challenge of bringing both unions and management into the quality of work life movement.

In my own case, apart from the general interest I have had in the quality of work life for thirty years, my more recent interest in the subject was a result of a request in 1970 from Mike Johnson, the vice president for political activities of the Pennsylvania AFL–CIO. Johnson was primarily concerned about "hard-hattism" of his members as the Nixon–Agnew administration attempted to woo workers away from their traditional Democratic party loyalties. "What is causing the alienation among our members?" was the question that Johnson wanted to research. "Alienation" was Johnson's word, I want to emphasize, not that of some esoteric, academic, intellectual sociologist. The study I conducted for this purpose covered a wide range of topics, but the most intriguing findings had to do with the relationship of workers' tasks and their *non*-work life attitudes and behaviors, especially the political dimensions. It is possible that the quality of our work lives influences the level of participation in decision making in the realm of political democracy. I have found a relationship between the quality of tasks and the amount of political alienation and actual voting behavior—especially among anti-authoritarian blue-collar workers, who generally tend to be younger workers.

Bertil Gardell, in Sweden, has expressed the same theory, and has based it on his own empirical research. In British Columbia, Martin Meissner has conducted an exceedingly exact and precise study, showing the detailed relationship between the degree of activist effort associated with workers' tasks, on the one hand, and their level of activity in the community. Passive work is conducive to passive non-work life. Melvin Kohn and Leonard Pearlin, of the U.S. National Institutes of Mental Health, have shown empirically how, in Italy as well as in the United States, the "substance of work" impinges on nonwork behavior and self-concepts, including parent–child relations, etc. In Norway, Max Eldon, an American protegé of Einar Thorsrud, has written extensively on the same subject, especially with regard to democracy outside the world of work, insofar as it is influenced by the nature of the organization of work.

In my opinion, no labor movement in our democratic societies—unless it is merely an organization motivated exclusively toward gaining material benefits for employees—can afford to ignore the influence of the nature of a person's work on his or her general social and political values and orientation.

Labor unions need, naturally, to continue to enhance the economic well-being of their members. But much of that focus can be in vain if, at the same time, they do not extend their concern about humanizing work to a widened sensitivity to the role of work in achieving and sustaining greater democratic participation in the society at large.

References

Gardell, Bertil. "Psychological and Social Problems of Industrial Work in Affluent Societies." *Reports from Universtiy of Stockholm, Department of Psychology*, No. 474, September 1976.

_____. "Reactions at Work and Their Influence on Nonwork Activities." *Human Relations* 29, No. 9, 1976.

Kohn, Melvin L. *Class and Conformity: A Study in Values*. Homewood, Illinois: Dorsey Press, 1969.

Meissner, Martin. "The Long Arm of the Job." *Industrial Relations* 3 (1971): 239–260.

Sheppard, H. L. "An Integrated Approach to Manpower and Economic Development" in S.A. Levitan and I. H. Siegel, eds. *Dimensions of Manpower Policy: Programs and Research*. Baltimore: Johns Hopkins Press, 1966.

_____ and Neal Q. Herrick. *Where Have All The Robots Gone?* New York: Free Press–Macmillan, 1972.

University of Michigan Survey Research Center. *Survey of Working Conditions*. Washington, D.C.: U.S. Department of Labor, 1971.

Contributors

JACK BARBASH has had three careers. He has been a trade union economist, a government civil servant, and, since 1956, a university professor. He is currently John P. Bascom Professor of Economics and Industrial Relations at the University of Wisconsin–Madison and president of the Industrial Relations Research Association. He is the author of many books and articles about trade unions.

YVES DELAMOTTE teaches labor law at the Conservatoire National des Arts et Métiers. He was recently the director of the French National Agency for the Improvement of Working Conditions and has been an official of the Ministry of Labor. He has taught in France and other countries and has written several monographs and articles on industrial relations, including a study on the functioning of the grievance procedure in a large American firm.

EVERETT M. KASSALOW is currently the senior specialist in labor economics for the Library of Congress, Washington, D.C. He was professor of economics and industrial relations at the University of Wisconsin from 1964 to 1978. Previously he served as research director of the Industrial Union Department of the AFL–CIO and in research positions with the United Automobile Workers and the United Rubber Workers. He also served overseas as labor adviser to the U.S. Marshall Plan in Paris from 1954 to 1957. He is the author of numerous articles and books on international labor, including *Trade Unions and Industrial Relations: An International Comparison* (New York, 1969).

WALTER KORPI is professor of social policy at the Swedish Institute for Social Research and the University of Stockholm. His main areas of interest are social policy and political sociology; a recent publication is *The Working Class in Welfare Capitalism—Work, Unions and Politics in Sweden* (London, 1978). At present he is engaged in a comparative study of the consequences of working class mobilization on industrial conflict and distributive policies in eighteen Western nations.

DUANE KUJAWA is professor of international business at Florida International University and visiting professor and MBA program consultant at the University of San Francisco. He recently co-directed a major contract research effort for the Office of Foreign Investment in the United States, U.S. Department of Commerce, on management and employment practices of foreign multinationals in the United States. He has consulted for several public and private agencies and has published numerous books and articles on labor and multinationals.

GERHARD LEMINSKY is a member of the Institute for Economic and Social Research of the German Trade Union Federation. He has been editor-in-chief of *Gewerkshaftliche Monatshefte,* the theoretical and political monthly review of the Deutscher Gewerkschaftsbund (DGB) since 1971. He was a member of the Tripartite Commission of the German Federal Government on Economic and Social Change from 1971 to 1977.

SOLOMON B. LEVINE is professor of business and economics and chairman of the Department of International Business, University of Wisconsin–Madison. He taught for twenty years at the University of Illinois at Urbana–Champaign. He has traveled, studied, and taught extensively in Japan, and his publications focus on Japanese economic, social, and labor conditions.

RAYMOND MACDONALD is currently research director for the Allied Industrial Workers International Union, AFL–CIO. He has also served as research director for the International Molders Union and Lithographers & Photoengravers International Union and as economist for the AFL–CIO and the Asian–American Free Labor Institute. He is a member of the Executive Board of the Industrial Relations Research Association and the Labor Research Advisory Council. His publications include articles in the *AFL–CIO American Federationist.*

JOSE M. MARAVALL is assistant dean of the sociology department at the University of Madrid. He previously served as senior lecturer of the sociology department at Warwick University, Coventry, England. He has written widely on industrial and political sociology. His books include *Dictatorship and Political Dissent: Workers and Students in Franco's Spain* (New York, 1979). Maravall has contributed a chapter on "The Socialist Alternative" to the forthcoming book, *Spain at the Polls,* edited by H. Penniman.

BEN JAMIN MARTIN was recently director of the Spanish Labor Project of the Carnegie Endowment for International Peace. He has also held the position of Senior Labor Specialist for the Department of State and national staff representative with the United Steelworkers of America and the International Union of Electrical, Radio and Machine Workers. Martin has taught at American University and the Empire State Labor College and his articles and book reviews have appeared in many journals including *Relations Industrielles, Industrial and Labor Relations Review, Nation, Dissent, and Commonweal.* At present he is preparing a book on labor relations in post-Franco Spain.

RUDOLF MEIDNER has been senior economic adviser to the Landsorganisation i Sverige (LO) since 1971. Born and educated in Sweden, he was director of the Research Department of the LO from 1945 to 1966 and director of the Institute for Labor Studies at the University of Stockholm, 1966–71. He is the author of several books on Swedish wage policy.

RICHARD PROSTEN is director of research, Industrial Union Department, AFL–CIO. He was previously (1964–70) collective bargaining coordinator of the Industrial Union Department. He is currently president of the Washington, D.C., chapter of the Industrial Relations Research Association (IRRA). In 1978 and 1979 he served on the nominating committee of the national IRRA. Among his recent publications is "The Longest Season: Union Organizing in the Last Decade" which appeared in the *IRRA Proceedings, 1978.*

HAROLD L. SHEPPARD is a senior research fellow on the Washington staff of the American Institutes for Research. He is currently engaged in a study of the future of retirement age policy in five Western European countries. From 1963 to 1975, he was a staff social scientist with the W. E. Upjohn Institute for Employment Research. During that period he worked on projects dealing with the quality of working life, primarily among blue-collar workers, and was a primary contributor to the Health, Education, and Welfare report, *Work in America.*

KOJI TAIRA received his college education in the United States and taught at Ryukyu University, the University of Washington, and Stanford University. He was an official of the International Labour Office in Geneva, Switzerland, and is currently professor of economics in the Department of

Economics and in the Institute of Labor and Industrial Relations at the University of Illinois at Urbana–Champaign. He has written books and articles on economic development and labor in Japan.

DON J. TURKINGTON is a senior lecturer in the Industrial Relations Centre, Victoria University of Wellington, New Zealand. His research on industrial conflict has been published in several journals and a revised version of his doctoral thesis appeared as *Industrial Conflict: A Study of Three New Zealand Industries* (Wellington, New Zealand, 1976). He has been guest lecturer at numerous universities, including several in the United States.